Emotional
Intelligence
@ work

Published by Spa House Publishing
Cheltenham, Gloucestershire, UK
Copyright © 2014 JCA (Occupational Psycholigists) Ltd
The moral right of Jolyon Maddocks to be
identified as the author of this work has been
asserted in accordance with the
Copyright, Design and Patents Act, 1998

EIP™ is a trademark of
JCA (Occupational Psycholigists) Ltd
www.jcaglobal.com

A CIP catalogue reference for this book is available from
the British Library.
ISBN 978-0-9928089-0-7

Jacket and text design
Colin Robson
www.oxford-creative-design.com

Emotional Intelligence @ work

How to make change stick

Jolyon Maddocks

Acknowledgements

It was twenty years ago that John Cooper and I founded JCA with the purpose of helping organisations to get the best out of their people in a sustainable way. The key word here is sustainable; how to make change stick so people do not return to their old ways of behaving. This led us to the work of Will Schutz and The Human Element as a means of exploring the feelings and attitudes that underpin sustainable behaviour change and effective performance. Another key influence has been the work of Joe Griffin and Ivan Tyrrell from The Human Givens Institute, who have produced some of the most profound yet common sense explanations for the psychology of human behaviour. My gratitude goes to my primary influence Tim Sparrow, for sharing his wisdom and insight into the psychology of human emotions, and for developing with me the EIP theory and questionnaire. Also, to John Cooper, who has grown JCA into a business that has Emotional Intelligence and the EIP at the heart of what we do.

There are many others I would like to thank for their contributions to the development of the EIP and this book. To the founding members of the Centre for Applied Emotional Intelligence (CAEI) who provided the original test bed for the first version of the EIP (originally called the Individual Diagnostic Questionnaire). To my colleagues at JCA who have helped develop and enhance many of the EIP materials; Maria Clease, Rich Cook, John Cooper, Bill Davies, David Jenkins, Rob Jones, Steph Noble, Mia O'Gorman, Dean Pollard, Sophie Seex and Sarah Speers. To those editors and contributors who have helped make this a better book than it would otherwise have been; Jennifer Buttery, Jo Hennessy and Wendy Lord. In particular to Matt Evans for his thorough checking of the EI content, and Amanda Jenks for sharing her medical expertise, editing my several re-writes and supporting and encouraging me throughout this process. Finally, to my son William, who is a constant source of fun and learning, helping me to develop my own Emotional Intelligence.

About the author: *Jolyon (Jo) Maddocks is a founder of JCA and a Chartered Occupational Psychologist. He is the author of several highly influential and widely used products and programmes on Emotional Intelligence which have helped thousands of individuals develop their self-esteem, enhance their relationships and improve their performance at work. One of Jo's interests is competing in endurance sports, which has given him first-hand experience of the attitudes and behaviours necessary for sustaining high performance under pressure. Attributes which Jo believes all people can develop through Emotional Intelligence.*

Preface

Much has been written on the subject of Emotional Intelligence (EI) as a theory and as a way of explaining human behaviour. But what use is psychological theory if the user does not understand how to apply it in order to achieve long-term change and sustainable performance? Those who are reading this book may have already subscribed to the theory that EI is relevant to individual development. But how do they capitalise on this? This book enables the user, in particular the coach, to work with an individual and help them to become the very best they can be.

To help an individual develop his or her EI, the coach will need to know where the individual is starting from, which means they need some way of measuring the status quo. The Emotional Intelligence Profile (EIP™) measures current levels of EI and, subject to some level of self-awareness, assumes that development is possible. As such, the questionnaire provides a starting point for the development of a more emotionally intelligent approach to work and life. However, in order to use the results of the EIP to best effect, the user of the tool will not only have to understand the meaning of the scores obtained from the assessment. He or she will also need to grasp how to interpret the results for the individual in such a way that they can use the information to maximum advantage.

This book is designed to help the practitioner use the EIP to its best effect. It will help new users of the EIP convert their theoretical knowledge into good and effective practice with regard to both the measurement of EI and the development of it.

Running throughout this book is the principle that emotionally intelligent behaviour, thoughts and feelings are underpinned by emotionally intelligent attitudes. Therefore, in order to achieve lasting change and sustainable performance it is necessary to develop emotionally intelligent attitudes. This is implicit within all aspects of the EIP design and application, including the EIP scales, definition, theory and framework.

How to use this book

Psychometric tests must clearly define what they measure. There are many measures of EI and they vary in terms of the frameworks on which they are based. Therefore, Section One focuses on the definition of EI as measured by the EIP. A reader wishing to understand EI more broadly, its foundations, and how latest brain science underpins the EIP may find this section of interest.

Section Two explains the construction of the EIP, the different parts of EI as defined by the EIP framework, and describes the sixteen EIP scales. Readers looking for a thorough understanding of the EIP and how to measure EI should refer to this section.

Section Three considers issues of coaching with the EIP in the workplace and provides guidance on how to develop EI in others. This section is written for the practitioner coach, explaining step by step how to use the EIP, as well as more advanced coaching skills for creating change that sticks. The final chapter examines how EI and the EIP are applied in business in relation to leadership, teams and the organisation. At the end of each chapter is a summary section which will help the reader to gain a rapid overview of the chapter and to pull out some of the key points from it. For the reader seeking further information and discussion on the history of EI and deeper interpretation of the EIP scales, this may be found in the Appendix.

Contents

List of tables and figures:

Tables

Section One
Defining Emotional Intelligence (EI)

What is Emotional Intelligence (EI) and how is it defined by the EIP? How does EI fit into the structure of human personality and what is its relationship with the rapidly developing science of neuropsychology?

EI is concerned with how people manage themselves (their personality, potential and innate resources) to be both personally and interpersonally effective, how well they do this is largely determined by their attitudes. This approach to EI is strongly supported by neurological evidence which explains how attitudes influence feeling which fuel thinking and drive behaviour. Therefore, by changing attitudes it is possible to create lasting change in behaviours, thoughts and feelings.

Chapter One

What is Emotional Intelligence?

Introduction

The Emotional Intelligence Profile (EIP) measures the building blocks of an aspect of psychological functioning that is referred to as *Emotional Intelligence* (EI). In order to interpret the results of the EIP, individuals must first understand how EI has been defined and conceptualised by the developers of EIP as well as the theoretical rationale that underpins the development of the questionnaire.

1.1 Why the need for developing Emotional Intelligence?

The world and society have become ever more complex and demanding. Some of these changes in the working world include greater competition, increased technology and an exponential growth in information. Changes in the working world have been matched by demands and pressures in society with reduced social responsibility, financial insecurity, greater individuality and less community. Consequently many of the basic human emotional needs required for individual well-being are not being properly met.[1]

Some of these essential emotional needs include:

- *Achievement*
- *Attention*
- *Community and status*
- *Control*
- *Emotional connection*
- *Meaning and purpose to life*
- *Privacy*
- *Security*

The cumulative effect of these factors has put increased emotional pressure on individuals and their ability to cope. In the UK there are some 40 million working days lost every year due to stress with an estimated cost to the economy of well over £7 billion; up to 60% of employees are reported to suffer from stress at some point during their career;[2] and for generations born after 1945 there has been a tenfold increase in depression.[3] Human physiology and emotions evolved to deal with a more stable and less complex 'hunter gatherer' society, while the human brain and genetics have not kept up with the rate of change in society. However, humans are incredibly adaptive and have specific innate resources to cope, learn and respond to these challenges. Some of these innate human resources include:

- *Conscious self-choice*
- *Creativity and problem solving (such as IQ)*
- *Emotional management and relaxation*
- *Empathy, rapport building and awareness of others*
- *Habit formation*
- *Imagination*
- *Logical thinking and objectivity*
- *Reflecting and learning from the past*
- *Self-observation and emotional awareness*
- *Sleep and recovery*
- *Thinking about the future*

These resources are a part of being human, they represent a person's potential and manifest in their personality. Central to EI is learning how to harness and manage these innate capacities to meet a person's emotional needs so as to thrive and be happy (specific examples of how to do this are given in Chapter 7.4). When applied effectively, EI has proven to reap considerable benefits,[4] such as: reducing stress; building trust; enhancing resilience; raising engagement; improving leadership performance; developing team work; and increasing productivity. All of these benefits, and many more, can be aquired through applying the principles of Emotional Intelligence (EI) and in using the Emotional Intelligence Profile (EIP).

1.2 An historical perspective of Emotional Intelligence

Despite its recent popularity, EI has its roots in many other psychological theories and is not something newly discovered about human kind. EI integrates many of the different historical approaches from psychology: the importance of the unconscious mind, as highlighted by Sigmund Freud; the stimulus-response models of the Behaviourists; the power of experiential emotional encounter used by the Humanists, managing thinking as used in Cognitive Behavioural Therapy (CBT), and the most recent ground-breaking developments in brain science (brain tomography, scanning and imaging). In addition, EI also focuses on measurement (psychometrics) and effective behaviour (competencies), which have been dominant in business since the 1980s. EI is nothing new, having clear overlaps with everyday language, such as: wisdom; maturity; compassion; sincerity;

integrity; tolerance; and understanding. Therefore EI is an eclectic model that integrates the psychological domains of thinking (cognitive psychology), feeling (humanistic psychology) and behaviour (behaviourism).

The term 'Emotional Intelligence' was first used by Barbara Leuner in 1966[5] but came to prominence largely through the publications of Daniel Goleman.[6,7,8] The early historical influences before this time are numerous including the likes of philosopher Renee Descartes,[9] naturalist Charles Darwin[10] and psychologist David Wechsler.[11] Listed below are some of the more recent and significant publications that have contributed to the field of Emotional intelligence. Refer to Appendix 2 for a detailed overview on the history of EI.

Key milestones in EI

1983   Howard Gardner publishes *Frames of Mind* differentiating intrapersonal (emotional) intelligence from interpersonal (social) intelligence.[12]

1990   Peter Salovey and Jack Mayer describe an abilities based approach to EI. In 1997 they produce the MSCEIT™ measure of EI.[13]

1994   A growth in neurological evidence for emotional and social intelligence. Some notable researchers include Antonio Damasio,[14] Joseph LeDoux[15] and Lane & McRae.[16]

1996   Daniel Goleman[6] publishes his bestselling book; *Emotional Intelligence: why it can matter more than IQ,* followed by several other successful publications. This leads to the ECI 360,[17] a competency based measure of EI.

1997   Reuven Bar-On[18] publishes one of the first EI measures; the *Emotional Quotient Inventory (EQi).* He describes EI as an array of traits and abilities that are correlated with personality.

1998   Jo Maddocks and Tim Sparrow[19] define an attitude based model of EI, describing EI as a verb and as being *the practice of managing one's personality*.

The EIP originated as one of the first measures of EI in 1998. Since then there has been a proliferation of products for assessing EI, the majority of which are based on temperamental traits, intellectual traits and competencies (refer to Appendix 2). This contrasts with the EIP which is based on attitudes and how people manage their temperamental and intellectual traits (their personality). The EIP attitude based approach to EI is discussed below.

1.3 How EI can help people manage their personality

EI is about *how the individual manages their personality.*[19] This crucial aspect differentiates EI from other aspects of human personality. People cannot easily change their disposition or IQ but they can learn to manage them in order to maximise the effectiveness by which they apply the raw material they were born with. Personality traits, whether temperamental or intellectual are the *what* of a person's identity while EI explains the *how*; how an individual can be more effective through making the best use of their temperament and intellectual traits. The realisation of this crucial distinction was a defining moment for this author in his professional career. It was this distinction which made him understand how best to develop individuals' potential and make it sustainable (through changing attitudes, as will be discussed later), and which led to the development of the EIP.

The EIP is a psychometric test. There are literally thousands of psychometric tests available; together they measure a vast array of attributes relating to typical behaviour, values, motivation, abilities, aptitudes and more recently, competencies. All of these are aspects of what defines the human personality.

Psychometric tests have been developed out of an effort to discover and measure what makes one person different from another; they embrace the science of individual differences. But understanding the various characteristics that structure the human personality is only half of the story. It is also necessary to know how effectively the individual manages his or her attributes and that is where EI comes in.

Unlike the EIP, which is based on attitudes, most other EI theories and questionnaires define EI as either personality traits (temperaments), a cognitive capacity such as IQ or as a set of behavioural competencies. However, far from being synonymous with EI, these three aspects of personality are *dependent* on EI if they are to be applied effectively. The relationship between EI, personality temperament, IQ and competencies will now be discussed.

1.3.1 Emotional Intelligence and personality temperament

There are two main differences between EI and personality temperament.

1 *EI relates to an individual's effectiveness and perfomance, whereas personality temperament is concerned with predispositions or typical behaviour.*

2 *EI is changeable and can be developed, whereas personality temperament relates to typical behaviours that are relatively fixed.*

The first difference explains why measures of personality are not highly predictive of performance; most personality measures explain a maximum of 9% of variance in work performance.[20] In practice, people with different personality temperaments can achieve equally competent results but do so in different ways. What determines whether a person is effective is, to a large extent, down to how well they manage their personality; which is a function of their EI. For example, having an extraverted trait does not make a person effective at doing extraverted things such as communicating with people, just as having an introverted trait does not make someone *ineffective* at communicating with people. How effectively an individual behaves has a great deal more to do with their emotional state and underlying attitudes than their personality. For instance, feeling highly anxious before a meeting will interfere with an individual's capacity to communicate their thoughts effectively, or holding the attitude; *people don't want to hear what I have to say,* will inevitably interfere with them being an effective communicator.

The second difference is that EI is changeable and personality temperament is relatively fixed.[21] Personality theories typically focus on measuring enduring and stable characteristics such as traits and typology preferences in order to predict how a person will behave in the future. EI is not focused on a person's disposition but rather their attitudes and habits, both of which are changeable and can be developed; attitudes people may adopt and habits they can learn. Crucially, EI is about how people manage their behaviour by being self-aware in the current moment and making conscious choices about how to behave.

Another important distinction between personality temperament and EI is in how they are applied. Talking someone through their personality profile will usually increase a person's self-understanding and knowledge, which tends to happen in their thinking brain (the outer grey matter called the neocortex), but this does not necessarily result in behavioural change. Improving a person's EI occurs in a different part of the brain known as the limbic system (refer to Chapter 2 for a diagram of the brains structure). Here, people learn from emotional experience which is also where attitude and habit change takes place. Personality questionnaires are often useful for raising cognitive awareness, but this must be followed up by emotional awareness and experience if a person is to change their behaviour. This may also explain why many training and coaching programmes that focus largely on feedback and discussion, rather than taking action, do not create behaviour change in the workplace.[22]

Stand-alone personality questionnaires have far more developmental value for the individual when combined with EI. Personality describes *what* a person typically does and EI explains *how* they can do this more effectively. Together they provide a powerful combination for self-development.

This view of integrating EI with personality is supported by research. A number of extensive meta-analysis and predictive validity studies on EI and performance have found EI to add significant incremental validity over and above personality and cognitive intelligence measures.[23,24,25,26] One researcher, O'Boyle,[23] concludes: *moving forward, rather than seeing cognitive intelligence, the Five Factor Model* (personality)*, and EI as competing measures, researchers should focus on developing integrative models that include all three.*

1.3.2 Emotional Intelligence and cognitive abilities

Another area that may be differentiated from EI is cognitive intelligence (IQ). Research consistently shows that cognitive intelligence predicts no more than 25% of performance[27] begging the question, what does the other 75% relate to? Daniel Goleman, in his seminal book *Emotional Intelligence, Why it can matter more than IQ,*[6] suggests that much of it is related to EI. Indeed, most competencies or job advertisements are dominated by EI attributes, such as *good team player, copes well with pressure and is adaptable*. This does not suggest that EI alone accounts for 75% of people's job performance, nor indeed that a questionnaire could measure this; but how effectively people use both their IQ and personality temperament (their performance) is heavily influenced by their EI. (For a summary of performance-related studies on EI refer to Chapter 8.1).

EI is not just about how a person manages their personality temperament; it is also about how they manage their cognitive intelligence. How a person is feeling at a particular moment in time will dramatically affect their cognitive performance. This is highlighted by the example of a fear response activating the fight/flight/freeze mechanism that blocks a person from accessing their cognitive intellectual thinking. A person's ability to think clearly, make sound decisions, analyse information and all the other IQ related areas, can vary dramatically day to day and moment to moment. When a person feels anxious, stressed or hurried their cortical functioning can be severely impaired,[28] but when they are relaxed, alert and present in the moment they can think more clearly, learn more easily, have more creative insights and 'see the wood from the trees'. Therefore, enabling a person to become more aware of how their feelings affect their thinking and how to manage their emotional state will enable them to make better use of their cognitive intelligence.

One problem with the Intelligence Quotient (IQ) is that it is tested under standardised conditions to assess an individual's *maximum* performance rather than their *typical* performance. EI is more relevant to how a person will perform in their day to day life rather than in controlled conditions. Having a high IQ does not necessarily translate into higher performance unless it is backed up by high EI. A forty year follow-up study of eighty Ph.D. students at the University of California, Berkeley, found that social and emotional abilities were four times more important than IQ in predicting professional success and prestige.[29] If a person does not manage their emotions then it is far more difficult for them to maximise use of their thinking, and therefore their potential IQ. A study by Duckworth[30] found that children's exam results were correlated twice as strongly with their self-discipline (emotional control) than with their IQ scores. As with temperament, measuring IQ alone has limited developmental value for the individual, but when combined with EI, becomes a far more potent combination for enhancing clear and accurate thinking.

1.3.3 Emotional Intelligence and behavioural competencies

A third construct that is often confused with, but should be differentiated from, EI is competencies. Many EI measures describe EI as a set of competencies (behaviours and skills); in contrast, the EIP is underpinned by attitudes and feelings. Competencies do provide a useful reference point for benchmarking what behaviour is required in a specific context and whether this is being achieved. However, using competencies in isolation does not address *how* these behaviours may be achieved. Behavioural competencies are only achieved if backed up by the congruent attitudes and intentions, in that people are drawn to behave in ways that are consistent with their attitudes.

Changing behaviour is often short-lived if it is not supported by a parallel change in attitude. For example, an organisation introducing customer service competencies is unlikely to succeed if its employees do not want to be of service to others (their attitude). On the other hand people who do want to be of service to others will quickly acquire their own set of appropriate behaviours that are congruent with their attitudes. In practice, behavioural competence is an inevitable outcome of someone who has complementary attitudes, but is a futile endeavour for those whose attitudes are different. EI enables people to understand their own attitudes and align them with their behaviours. When people behave in ways that are inconsistent with their attitudes this will create anxiety and stress (a state known as cognitive dissonance) until they change their behaviour or their attitude. A study (using the EIP) on the EI of prison officers found that those officers who had low regard for prison inmates (their attitude), but who were required to treat inmates with respect (their behaviour) suffered considerably more stress and burnout than officers who had regard for prison inmates (their behaviour matched their attitudes).[31] Therefore, the key to developing behavioural competence is to adopt appropriate attitudes through the process of being emotionally intelligent. (Refer to Chapter 8.2.3 for further links between EI and competencies).

1.3.4 The relationship between personality, EI and competencies

There is a clear relationship between personality, EI and competencies:

- *Personality represents who a person is and includes their temperament and innate resources (such as IQ).*
- *EI is how well a person learns to manage their temperament and harness their innate resources (their potential).*
- *Competencies are how this manifests in terms of a person's work performance and behaviours.*

EI is therefore the 'glue' or the 'missing link' that turns individual personality (potential) into effective performance and may be summarised as:

Personality + EI = Performance

Consider the analogy of a car (*personality*) and its driver (*EI*); the skilled driver will listen to the engine, develop a feel for the car, keep it well maintained and continually improve their handling skills in order to get the best from the car in terms of economy, sustainability and *performance*.

The psychological process of turning personality into performance outcomes through EI is described below in the definition of EI, and is fully explained by the neuroscience of EI in Chapter 2.

1.4 The definition of Emotional Intelligence

The term EI is not unique and there are several alternative labels that may be used for this concept including:

- **Emotional Quotient[32] (EQ):** *refers to the measurement of EI. The EIP does not include a single EQ score of EI as the construct is multifaceted and its different components do not necessarily correlate positively.*
- **Emotional Literacy[33] (EL):** *used mostly in counselling and education, EL refers to developing emotional awareness and vocabulary.*
- **Emotional Competence[34] (EC):** *used mainly in business, EC refers to the development of emotional skills and behaviours.*

- **Emotional Creativity**[35] **(ECr):** *a less commonly used term, ECr is the ability to experience and express original, appropriate and authentic combinations of emotions.*
- **Social Intelligence**[36] **(SI):** *refers mainly to the interpersonal aspects of EI and was the precursor to the term Emotional Intelligence.*

Alongside these are many other descriptors often used to define EI, such as common sense, empathy, emotional maturity and wisdom. The term Emotional Intelligence (EI) which is about the intelligent use of the emotions (or *thinking about feelings*) fits closely with the JCA definition of EI given below.

Part 1 *Emotional Intelligence is the practice of managing one's personality, to be both personally and interpersonally effective.*

Part 2 *This is achieved through the habitual practice of thinking about feeling and feeling about thinking to guide one's behaviour.*

Part 3 *The extent and effectiveness by which an individual does this is determined largely by their attitudes.*

The first part of the definition describes *what* it is to be emotionally intelligent and incorporates the link between personality (which includes IQ and other innate resources) and EI, as discussed previously. It also refers to the two main parts of EI being both *personal* and *interpersonal*, which form the two strands of the EIP framework (described in Chapter 1.6 below).

The second part of the definition describes *how* to be emotionally intelligent. It defines EI as a *habit*, that is, something an individual can become better at doing with practice and which will become easier and more automatic over time. The definition also describes EI as a *practice*; that is, something a person *does* (a verb) rather than something they *have* (a noun). This requires being aware of oneself and others in the present by noticing, thinking about, labeling and interpreting emotions in the body which involves *thinking about feelings*. This in turn helps a person form their Self Knowledge (an understanding of themselves) and Knowledge of Others, which can be drawn upon when deciding how to behave (as described in Chapter 4.2). The definition also includes *feeling about thinking,* which involves recognising intuitive bodily responses alongside a thought, such as; *feeling uneasy about a decision*. Not every feeling and thought will be consciously analysed in this way since people quickly form automatic, unconscious and habitual responses. However, to make sure these habitual responses are effective and remain appropriate it is necessary to engage in this process, or in other words; to *manage one's personality* (*Part 1* of the EI definition).

The third part to the definition describes *when* people are emotionally intelligent (when they hold EI attitudes); *the extent and effectiveness of their EI being determined largely by their attitudes*. Thoughts and feelings do not occur randomly, they are the response to a stimulus which has been perceived, interpreted and filtered through their underlying attitudes. It is a person's attitudes that largely influence their thoughts and feelings which in turn drive their behaviours.

The close relationship between attitudes, thoughts, feelings and behaviours is explained in the next chapter which looks at EI from a psychological and neurological perspective. The attitudes that underpin emotionally intelligent behaviour (as defined by the EIP scales) are described below.

1.5 The attitudes that underpin Emotional Intelligence

Most approaches to examining EI have tended to start at the top, focusing on the outcomes of being emotionally intelligent in terms of behaviours, skills and competencies and linking these to the importance of feelings. The EIP, however, was developed from the bottom up, starting with the underlying attitudes of EI.

Fig.1.1 A metaphor for EI

Consider the metaphor of a tree, with attitudes being the *roots* of EI that deter-

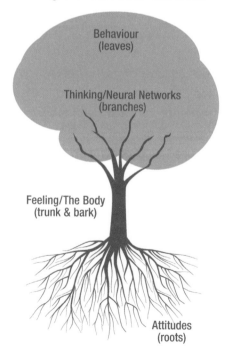

mine feelings (represented by the *trunk,* or body, which is where feelings are experienced), that then influence thinking (the *branches*; like neural networks of the brain), which then translate into behaviours (the *leaves* in their different shapes, sizes and colours). Therefore, in order to understand the essence of EI it is necessary to look deeper into the underlying attitudes.

This metaphor may be extended to include the earlier description of EI, of the individual harnessing their innate resources to meet their emotional needs (such as using their imagination to think positively, reasoning to solve problems and empathy to connect). Similarly a plant has the innate resources (roots to absorb water, leaves to absorb sunlight and bark for protection) to meet its basic needs.

How well an individual manages to get their emotional needs met throughout their life will largely determine what attitudes they hold towards themselves, others and the world in general. A person's attitudes will greatly influence how they feel, think and behave, as described in Chapter 2. It is only therefore through developing emotionally intelligent attitudes that people will develop and sustain emotionally intelligent behaviours as reflected by the EIP definition of an attitude.

The EIP definition of an attitude:
An evaluative position (based largely on feelings) towards oneself, others, a situation, an idea, etc. that predispose the individual towards certain behaviours or responses.
This fits closely with the workplace definition of the term as defined in www.businessdictionary.com: *A predisposition or a tendency to respond positively or negatively towards (or away from) a certain idea, object, person, or situation. Attitude influences an individual's choice of action, and responses to challenges, incentives, and rewards (together called stimuli).*

Drawn from humanistic psychology, such as Transactional Analysis (TA) theory, and underlying beliefs and assumptions about human nature, eight attitudes or mindsets have been defined which help explain the essence of EI. The eight EI attitudes and their relationship to the EIP scales are described below (also refer to Table 3.2). The EIP scales are described fully in Chapter 5.

Attitude 1: *However you are and others are, is OK.*
This attitude forms the bedrock to the framework of the EIP, which underpins all of the EIP scales as explained in Chapter 4.[3] The attitude is related to the OK Corral model of Transactional Analysis which includes the first two scales of the EIP; Self Regard (I am OK) and Regard for Others (You are OK). Regard in this sense is focused on accepting and valuing a person for their *being*, not necessarily liking or approving of their *doing* (behaviour). In practice this attitude may be severely tested; to still have regard for and value someone regardless of their behaviour. An example of having Regard for Others may be a parent who, despite their child's misbehaviour, will still retain deep feelings of love and compassion towards them (this does not mean they will be accepting of the child's misbehaviour). Note that this attitude applies as much to oneself (however you are, is OK) as it does to others.

Attitude 2: *Everyone is in control of and responsible for their actions.*

This is a tough one as it implies that the buck stops here, with oneself. When this attitude is adopted it will facilitate more empowering and responsible behaviour, but if not adopted a person is more likely to feel helpless and be blaming of others. Comments like; *you made me do it* or *it's not my fault,* imply that people do not have choice or control over their own behaviour. The most relevant scales to this attitude are Personal Power (scale 6; being in charge of and responsible for one's outcomes in life) and Authenticity (scale 10; inviting the trust of others by being reliable, principled, consistent and knowable).

Attitude 3: *No one else can control our feelings.*

This may sound obvious, yet everyday comments like; *you made me angry* or, *you upset me,* suggest that someone else has control over the other person's feelings. However, what a person feels is determined by their internal interpretation of the event, otherwise all people would feel the same about the same situation, when in fact *people are different* (EI attitude No. 4) and have different emotional responses to the same situation. In confrontation, one person may feel scared and another feel anger. Or, on losing a job, one person may feel upset and another feel joy, and so on. This has significant implications on EI, as individuals who believe that others control their feelings are likely to be Emotionally Under Controlled (scale 13), Aggressive (scale 14) and Over Dependent on others (scale 15). This attitude does not discount the reality that people will trigger emotions in others. But the trigger (usually an unconscious attitude) and the resulting feelings belong to the individual and are something they may choose to change through the practice of EI.

Attitude 4: *People are different; they experience the world differently, feel different things and want different things.*

People often nod sagely at this in agreement yet, in practice, they are surprised, mystified or annoyed when people do not act the way they expect them to. It is very easy to slip into generalisations about people and to assume that other people have the same perceptions as we do. Oscar Wilde had some good advice on this*; do not do unto others as you would have them do unto you as their tastes may not be the same.* Recognising that people are different by raising Awareness of Others (scale 4), rather than forming assumptions about them, will help develop an appreciation of others and their unique value (Regard for Others; scale 2), and increase Flexibility (scale 8) to adapt to people's differences.

14

Attitude 5: *Feelings and behaviour are separate.*

EI is literally *the intelligent use of emotions*, or as previously defined; *the practice of using thinking about feeling (or feeling about thinking) to guide behaviour.* When people have an *emotional hijack*, such as when feelings of anger get the better of them, they may go straight from feelings to behaviour without thinking. Comments like, *I couldn't help it,* suggest that the person has not learnt to separate their feelings from their behaviour, which in turn can result in emotionally unintelligent behaviour such as poor Emotional Resilience (scale 5), low impulse control (scale 7; Goal Directedness), Emotional Under Control (scale 13), and aggressive Conflict Handling (scale 14).

Also note that EI is defined as a verb (*the practice of...*) which involves managing the relationship between thoughts, feeling and behaviour in the present.

Attitude 6: *All feelings are justified, acceptable and important.*

Feelings tell people what they want, like, dislike, need and fear. Judging feelings as unacceptable or unimportant may lead a person to deny those feelings that are unpleasant or less acceptable to them. If an individual is unaware of their feelings (scale 3; Self Awareness) they will be less able to manage them appropriately or respond to their emotional needs. This may result in bottled up feelings, resentment, hostility, stress, ill-health, inflexibility, defensiveness, and generally less emotionally intelligent behaviour.

There are several steps or hurdles to becoming aware of and acting upon feelings.

- *The individual must initially notice their feelings, for example, my tummy tingles;*
- *then pay attention to them, this matters;*
- *then give them significance, maybe I feel nervous;*
- *then think about their feelings, I want to relax;*
- *and take them into account when deciding how to act, I will take some deep breaths.*

This applies both to the individuals own feelings and the feelings of others; if they disregard other's feelings as unimportant then they are less likely to understand or relate effectively with people (scale 4; Awareness of Others).

Attitude 7: *Change is possible.*

EI is based upon attitudes, habits and skills, all of which are learned or acquired and therefore changeable.[37] If something is learnt it can be unlearnt. It is this attitude which has become the foundation to those working in the field of people development, and of particular relevance to EI. Unfortunately many EI metrics attempt to justify their scales by correlating them with personality traits. But personality traits differ from EI in two distinct ways; personality traits are more constitutional (inborn) and therefore less changeable than EI, and personality traits are not about being effective, which EI clearly is.

Personal development does not require changing personality traits, but rather learning how to *manage* them (which is our definition of EI), for example, by moving outside of one's comfort zones, changing a long running habit or adopting new attitudes. For this reason personality traits and EI go hand in hand, as EI is the practice of making best use of 'who' we are, our resources and potential. This attitude, that *change is possible,* is particularly relevant to scale 8; Flexibility, and will also support Balanced Outlook (scale 12) and Reflective Learning (scale 16). Refer to Chapter 7 for methods on how to develop EI.

Attitude 8: *People have a natural tendency towards growth and health.*
Everyone can develop their EI, which is not a fixed or limited capacity. However, much innate human potential is left undeveloped because of people's internal interferences and defences. Aristotle illustrated this concept (which he called *Physis*, the Greek for 'inherent nature') with a cabbage seed which, if given the right environment in which to flourish, is predisposed for growth and health but will also wither in the wrong environment. It is helpful here to apply the formula by Timothy Gallwey;[38] *Performance = Potential – Interference*. In practical terms this means first helping people to recognise their *Potential* and resources and then to identify and dismantle their *Interferences* such as limiting beliefs and restrictive habits, and replace them with emotionally intelligent attitudes, habits and skills. Once the Interferences are removed then people, as with all living things, will naturally develop their potential and improve their *Performance*. Personal growth and development is facilitated by scale 16; Reflective Learning.

As well as their theoretical relevance, the eight EI attitudes also have strong practical implications. It is not intended that people should adopt these eight attitudes as 'truths' but, in practice, when people behave in ways that are not emotionally intelligent they will tend to have breached one or more of the these attitudes. Therefore if individuals can adopt the EI attitudes, they will find it easier to behave with greater EI. For this reason the scales of the EIP were constructed around the eight attitudes and help to explain why someone may find it either easier or more difficult developing any of the EIP scales. For example, a person who has difficulty developing their Flexibility (scale 8) may not endorse Attitude 7; that *Change is possible*, or someone who scores low on Personal

16

Power (scale 7) may not accept Attitude 2; that *Everyone is in control of and respon-sible for their actions*.

When considering the above set of attitudes the reader is encouraged to distinguish between what they think is true and agree with (reflecting their belief) and what they actually do in practice (reflecting their attitude), since what a person does in practice is often a better indicator of their attitudes, than what they may sometimes claim. Someone may say they believe in *being honest* (their belief) but in practice they with-hold or tell lies. A person may not be consciously aware of their underlying attitudes that drive their feelings and behaviours, because attitudes live in the deeper and usually less conscious emotional centres of the brain (the limbic system). Beliefs on the other hand, live in the higher, usually more conscious thinking centres of the brain (the neocortex). These different parts of the brain and their roles are explained in the next chapter.

1.6 An organising framework for Emotional Intelligence

The EI attitudes and definition underpin the development of the EIP and have led to the EIP framework, an organising structure to describe the different parts of EI. A brief description of the EIP framework is given below (Table 1.1), and Chapter 4 is dedicated to explaining this framework as it forms the basis to using and interpreting the EI reports.

EI is divided into two streams that were derived from the work of Howard Gardner[12] who defined several types of intelligence including *Intra*personal Intelligence (or Personal Intelligence) and *Inter*personal Intelligence. These two streams relate to part 1 of the EI definition; *to be both personally and interpersonally effective.*

The two streams are then divided into three levels, which are related to the three parts of the EI definition; *what, how* and *when*:

What is EI? Definition (part one); *Emotional Intelligence is the practice of managing one's personality to be both personally and interpersonally effective.* This relates to the Behaviour scales (top level) of the EIP framework that are grouped under the themes of Self Management (*personally effective*) and Relationship Management (*interpersonally effective*).

How are people emotionally intelligent? Definition (part two); *This is achieved through the habitual practice of thinking about feeling and feeling about thinking to guide one's behaviour.* This relates to the Feeling scales (middle level) of the EIP framework; Self Awareness and Awareness of Others. The complete EIP framework, (explained in Chapter 4.2.1) also includes Reflective Learning (*thinking about feeling*) in this middle level.

When are people emotionally intelligent? Definition (part three); *The extent and effectiveness of an individual's EI is determined largely by their attitudes.* This relates to the Attitude scales of Self Regard and Regard for Others (bottom level), which are derived from the first and primary EI attitude; *However you are and others are, is OK.*

Table 1.1 The EIP framework

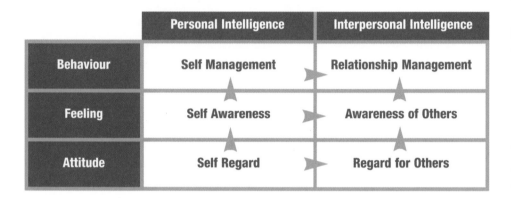

	Personal Intelligence	Interpersonal Intelligence
Behaviour	Self Management	Relationship Management
Feeling	Self Awareness	Awareness of Others
Attitude	Self Regard	Regard for Others

It should be noted that the framework has arrows of influence which go from left to right and from the bottom up, such that Attitude (bottom level) influences Feeling (and thinking) (middle level), which in turn influences Behaviour (top level). It is therefore a person's Attitude that will lead to them achieving congruent, consistent, enduring and desirable Behaviour. The rationale for this sequence is drawn from the neurological evidence for EI described in the next chapter. The close link between these psychological factors, the EIP definition and the EIP framework is summarised in Chapter 2.3 and Table 2.4.

1.7 Some misunderstandings of Emotional Intelligence

Before concluding this chapter on *What is Emotional Intelligence?* it is worth saying something about what EI is not. There are a number of specific misunderstandings which either undervalue or overestimate the potential value of EI, some of which include:

EI is something people are born with:

Emotional Intelligence is based on attitudes, habits and skills, none of which people are born with. The great benefit therefore is that EI can be developed by anyone who chooses to develop it. Research on the EIP has shown that EI, rather like wisdom, increases with age.

EI is a single score:

Representing EI as a single scale (such as EQ) can be misleading. EI is not a single construct, but is multifaceted. People can be strong in some areas and weaker in others. Reducing EI to a single score is unhelpful for understanding individual differences, strengths and development opportunities.

Women are more emotionally intelligent:

Research on EI has shown that females on average score higher on some aspects of Relationship Management and Regard for Others (scale 2). However, males on average score higher on the Self Management scales such as Self Regard (scale 1), Personal Power (scale 6) and Goal Directedness (scale 7).

EI is new (a fad):

Although EI was popularised in 1996,[6] it has been used widely within education since 1980 and different terms have been around for similar concepts since the 1920's (refer to Appendix 2 for an historical overview of EI). EI is not a 'fad'; its popularity has continued to grow in business for personal, team and organisational development, it is well supported by neuroscience (refer to Chapter 2) and there is continued research demonstrating its benefit to individual performance and productivity (refer to Chapter 8 for details).

EI is just naval gazing (self-reflection):

Developing EI requires emotional Self Awareness (scale 3) and Reflective Learning (scale 16) but this is only one element of EI. The EIP framework is made up of six parts (as described in Chapter 4.1) which includes, turning Self Awareness (Feeling) into effective Self Management and Relationship Management (Behaviour).

EI is just another term for soft skills:

Soft or interpersonal skills such as being tactful, showing appreciation and asking for help are important in developing and maintaining relationships. However, they are unlikely to be sustained if they are not backed up by underlying EI attitudes (as described earlier in this chapter). For instance, someone who learns assertiveness skills like saying *No* to requests, will soon return to their old behaviours if underneath they do not hold a correspondingly emotionally intelligent attitude such as; *However you are and others are is OK* (EI attitude No. 1).

EI is just about being nice to people:

Although EI is about having Regard for Others (scale 2), this does not necessarily mean agreeing with their behaviour. The challenge with Regard for Others is still valuing a person despite disapproving of what they may do. EI also involves being assertive (scale 14) and being willing to have difficult conversations with people which requires high Self Regard (scale 1). Giving difficult feedback to a colleague; seeking critical feedback from others; standing up to a line manager; being prepared to be in the minority; and risking disapproval from others, are all examples of EI behaviour that go beyond 'just being nice to people'. The scales of Self Regard and Regard for Others are described in Chapter 5.1 and form the foundation to the other fourteen EIP scales.

EI is about letting out all of your feelings:
People who bottle up emotions until they explode may benefit from learning how to notice and express their feelings sooner while they are more manageable. On the other hand, people who allow their emotions to control them would benefit from learning how to manage their feelings so as not to express them indiscriminately. Many of the EIP scales are about getting the right balance between too much emotional expression (uncontrolled expression of feelings) and too little (bottling feelings inside). These are called *multi-scales* and are described in Chapter 5.1.

EI is a panacea:
EI has become increasingly popular and is a label often attributed to a wide range of personal development courses, products and approaches without any clear definition or rationale. Over-stating the benefits of EI will only devalue it in the long run. Also, some of the existing models of EI are simply repackaging existing personality questionnaires or competency frameworks. Users of the term *Emotional Intelligence* should be clear as to its definition, understand how it differs from other psychological constructs and recognise the boundaries of where and how it may be applied.

This first chapter has provided a definition and overview of EI. The next chapter discusses the different psychological and neurological aspects that underpin EI and the EIP theory.

Summary points from Chapter One

- The term Emotional Intelligence was popularised in the 1990s but as a concept has been around much longer with labels such as emotional literacy, maturity and wisdom.

- Traditional psychometric tests focus on what are thought to be stable aspects of psychological functioning, such as personality traits and cognitive abilities. Such tests aim to predict future behaviour and/or raise self-knowledge in the individual. However, the durability of traits and cognitive abilities has led to a pessimistic view of IQ and personality as *destiny,* and does not allow for the possibility that people can manage their personalities and become more effective, even in situations in which they are naturally less compatible or comfortable.

- Humans possess a set of unique resources that enable them to cope with the ever increasing demands and changes of modern society. It is the individual's ability to harness their innate attributes, (such as using their imagination, thinking through problems and learning from experience) that will enable them to meet their emotional needs (such as the need for security, emotional connection and meaning) which is what constitutes being emotionally intelligent. Suggestions on how to do this are given in Chapter 7.

- A person's *innate resources* represent their *potential* and manifest in their *personality*. There is a close relationship between EI and personality. EI is the 'missing link' that turns personality (potential, temperament and innate resources such as IQ) into effective performance (behavioural competence).

- EI is reflected by what a person *does* in the present moment, rather than what a person *is*. EI is therefore described as a verb (*the practice of*) not a noun, and is about *being* emotionally intelligent rather than *having* Emotional Intelligence.

- EI is defined in three parts;

    What **it is to be emotionally intelligent:** *Emotional Intelligence is the practice of managing one's personality* (which includes their innate resources such as IQ) *to be both personally and interpersonally effective.*

How to be emotionally intelligent: *This is achieved through the habitual practice of thinking about feeling and feeling about thinking, to guide one's behaviour.*

When are people emotionally intelligent: *The extent and effectiveness by which an individual does this is determined largely by their attitudes.*

- This chapter has described eight underlying attitudes which are the foundation of EI upon which the EIP is based. In so far as people adopt these attitudes, they will potentially behave with greater EI.

- The definition and attitudes that underpin the EIP have led to the development of the EIP framework and scales (described in Chapter 4.1). The EIP framework shows the arrows of influence that start from the bottom up; where Attitude (the *When* of EI) influences Feeling (the *How* of EI), and Feeling leads to Behaviour (the *What* of EI). It is therefore a person's attitudes that will enable them to achieve and sustain desirable behaviours. This psychological sequence, which is supported by neuroscience, is explored in detail in the next chapter.

● ● ●

Chapter Two
The neuroscience of Emotional Intelligence

Introduction

The phrase *Emotional Intelligence* (EI) incorporates feeling (*Emotional*) and thinking (*Intelligence*), both of which are created and experienced within the brain and the body. The purpose of this chapter is to examine the neurological basis for EI to confirm the definition and theoretical foundation given to the EIP.

The model of EI on which the EIP is based emphasises attitudes as the key determinant influencing feeling, thinking and behaviour. Other models of EI are based on skills, competencies, personality traits and cognitive capacities, rather than attitudes. As will be explained below, when judged against the neurological evidence it is the attitudinal component that gets to the core of what Emotional Intelligence actually is.

2.1 The evolution of the brain

Looking at how the human brain evolved starts to explain, if only crudely, the relationship between the elements of EI (thinking, feeling, behaviour and attitude) at a neurological level. The triune brain model by Paul MacLean[1] divides the brain into three broad evolutionary stages from the reptilian, to the mammalian to the primate.

According to MacLean, the earliest reptilian parts of the brain (the central nervous system) enable the primary survival functions; fight, flight, freeze and reproduction. As reptiles evolved into mammals they developed more advanced neurological functions, such as the visceral limbic system in the brain where emotions are created to reinforce learned behaviour through stimulus-response conditioning, that is, reward (positive feelings) encourages and pain (unpleasant feelings) discourages any given behaviour. This emotional learning mechanism allowed mammals to learn and adapt rapidly to their environment, and much automatic and habitual behaviour is largely the result of such conditioning. As mammals evolved into primates the growth of the neocortex enabled their capacity for conscious choice. The neocortex (Latin for 'new bark') is the outer part of the brain which is involved in higher level processing such as the interpretation of and deciding how to act upon feelings.

Unlike computer technology, human beings are unable to dispose of and replace outdated software; evolution means that much of the earlier primitive neurological programmes have been retained. For example, much of what is required in people's day to day activities, from routine habits to in-depth thinking is greatly influenced by the reptilian brain for instincts and survival, and the mammalian limbic brain for emotions, well-being and motivation.

It is worth noting that MacLean's model is a simplification of the brain's evolution, as natural selection has reprogrammed all parts of the brain to work in combination and the processing of feelings is not exclusive to the limbic region.[2] In addition, different parts of the brain may have existed long before they developed their functionality, such as conscious awareness in the prefrontal cortex, as explained below. In principle, however, different parts of the brain that evolved to focus largely on instincts, feelings and conscious thinking is still a relevant and useful separation of its functions.

2.1.1 The evolution of the conscious brain

It is worth examining the brain's evolution in a little more detail to consider not only *how* the brain evolved but *why* it did so. This helps explain why Emotional Intelligence is necessary to becoming an emotionally healthy and well-adjusted human being.

Table 2.1 A chronology of the brain's evolution

Years ago	Stage in the brain's evolution
3.5 billion	The first forms of life emerge with single cell organisms.
500 million	The first primitive *reptilian brainstem* appears. A basic system of nerves for movement.
220 million	The late Triassic period saw the start of *mammalian* life forms.
60 million	Earliest *primates* recorded.
6 million	Early members of the human lineage, Primate hominids (bipedal: upright and walking).
200,000	Earliest recordings of Homo sapiens genetic DNA.
60-40,000	The brain's '*big bang*'. Human primates develop the capacity for consciousness, creative thinking and cultural development.

As can be seen from the table above, it is only a fraction of the brain's evolutionary timescale that separates today's human brain from the reptilian brain. It is fascinating to note how rapidly the brain's evolution has accelerated and a wonder as to how soon and in what form the brain's next evolutionary leap forward will be.

The first significant leap forward in the brain's evolution coincided with the beginning of warm blooded mammalian life. Being warm blooded meant mammals could regulate their body temperature and hence had the ability to move around whatever the external temperature,[3] (unlike reptiles and fish which are cold blooded and cannot regulate their own body temperature and are therefore dependent on the external temperature to determine their mobility). However, the advantages that warm bloodedness gave mammals, came at the cost of needing to conserve their energy, as around 80% of mammals energy is spent maintaining their internal body temperature. If a mammal responded to every emotional impulse, such as chasing a moving leaf, they would soon exhaust their energy supplies necessary for survival. Nature's answer to this was to evolve the brain (the limbic region in particular) so that it could learn from past experiences and make energy-efficient choices. Rather than simply responding instinctively to every stimulus, the mammalian brain was able to draw upon past emotional learning (positive and negative reinforcement) to determine its responses accordingly (albeit at a purely unconscious emotional level).

However, repressing and not acting upon every emotional impulse (such as to chase a moving leaf) would in time cause an unhealthy build-up of un-discharged emotion (stress) on the autonomic nervous system and eventually cause these instincts (such as to respond to danger or opportunities of food) to be dulled or even switched off, which would be catastrophic to their survival. Nature's remedy was to allow the unfulfilled emotional expectations to be acted out and expressed metaphorically through the process of dreaming (REM sleep).[4] Discharging these emotions through dreaming allowed these instincts to be preserved (this is explained further in Chapter 2.5).

The functionality of the mammalian brain is still inherent in today's human brain but over time has developed some powerful upgrades! The second significant step forward in the brain's evolution was the development of the brain's frontal lobes (the prefrontal cortex) and the emergence of consciousness, a mere 40,000 years ago. This is known as the brain's 'big bang' and gave rise to many of the innate human resources described in Chapter 1.1. It allowed humans to develop an awareness of 'self' – a self-concept, to make considered decisions and to think about how to respond to their feelings (from the mammalian limbic brain). It also gave conscious access to the higher brain functions of the left and right hemispheres in the neocortex, which for the previous 160,000 years had been relatively underused. The left hemisphere is the 'analytical' side of the brain which processes language, rational thinking and analysis. The right hemisphere is the 'creative' side that applies imagination, abstract thinking and inference. This conscious access to 'thinking' allowed humans to be creative, consider ideas, reflect on the past, and think about the future. It also led to the development of complex language and so allowed generations to pass on their learning, wisdom and experience. In essence having consciousness is what makes us human, the results of which are all mankind's achievements.*

Giving access to conscious awareness also opened the doorway to human psychological frailties and the need for humans to learn how to manage their conscious thoughts and feelings. Without this, the right hemisphere, with its capacity for imagination could easily anticipate all the possible problems that *might* happen, thus creating excessive anxiety and worry. Poor management of the right hemisphere may also result in irrational, distorted and exaggerated thinking if it wasn't balanced by the reasoning and reality checking of the left hemisphere. Taken to a more extreme level, being locked into the right hemisphere can result in being out of touch with reality and hence vulnerable to anxiety disorders, depression and schizophrenia.**

The analytical left hemisphere also needs to be properly balanced with the wider perspective and context setting of the right hemisphere. Without this a person could become obsessively analytical, over rational and fixated on specific thoughts making their behavior rigid, inflexible, and unable to connect properly with people, all of which are necessary to maintain satisfactory human relationships. At a clinical level, excessive left brain thinking is related to conditions such as obsessive-compulsive disorders, Asperger's and autism.***

As well as managing their left and right hemispheres, a person needs to learn how to manage their mammalian limbic brain which has evolved the capacity to learn and create new patterns on how to respond to the environment (a 'pattern' is the neurological equivalent of an attitude). This process, called 'pattern matching', is explained in Chapter 2.4. Without some degree of conscious monitoring and updating, a person's emotional response to events would become outdated and inappropriate. For example, childhood patterns such as depending on others, responding impulsively and being rebellious are not as acceptable in adulthood.

Learning how best to use and develop the innate gifts of the human brain is a large part of being emotionally intelligent. Using the *right brain* for imagination and positive thinking, the *left brain* to think through problems rationally and keep perspective, the *frontal lobes* to understand and choose how to respond to feelings, the emotional *limbic brain* to create constructive attitudes (patterns) and habits, and the 'dreaming brain' for REM sleep to enable the body and brain to recover and process unresolved emotions. These, along with many other approaches to developing EI, are explained in Chapter 7. The remainder of this chapter describes in more detail how the brain processes feelings, thoughts and attitudes and why this is integral to being emotionally intelligent.

26

* According to the *social brain hypothesis*,[5] evolution of the prefrontal cortex was also necessary to support human social interaction which, being complex and unpredictable, requires greater brain processing capacity. One such structure is the ventromedial prefrontal cortex (VMPFC) which has the capacity for making fast decisions based on emotional (somatic) feedback, or gut feelings.[6] This is described in the next section on 'How feelings influence thinking'. The ventromedial cortices are also involved in the anticipation and prediction of future outcomes, particularly those impacting personal relationships.[7]

** Aside from the drawbacks of emotional disorders these conditions are also associated with periods of great creativity and genius. Many of the historical pioneers, scientists, inventors and writers were diagnosed with mental disorders. People with bipolar disorder (an oscillation between the left and right hemispheres) often experience moments of profound insight and creativity in-between phases. Another such group are those who are high performing on the autistic spectrum. These individuals often show extraordinary intellectual abilities of analysis, concentration and memory, but lack many of the attributes associated with EI, such as balanced judgment, flexibility, empathy, communication and social skills.

*** One theory of autism[8] proposes that the mammalian templates for reading context (such as in social situations) have been detuned or switched off, (from an evolutionary standpoint this may have been to allow greater conscious access to the neocortex). Without the mammalian limbic system having the capacity to interpret and predict context, the individual is left feeling bewildered and confused. In order to minimise their anxiety, the individual attempts to control their environment and create predictability, usually through excessive left brain activity such as repetitive actions, avoiding or controlling social interaction, categorical thinking and rigid behaviours. This kind of emotionally unintelligent behavior is not confined to autism, and can be seen in many people under stress as they fall back on their more primitive survival templates.

Human well-being falls across a broad spectrum from being emotionally unhealthy to being highly emotionally intelligent. The focus of this book is on the top end of this spectrum, although, it is as well to recognise that a person can move and inhabit the full breadth of this spectrum during their lifetime. However, by developing their EI, a person can learn how to become and remain emotionally healthy and productive throughout their life.

2.2 How feelings influence thinking

Understanding the brain's evolution provides a useful explanation for how feelings influence thinking. Because the brain evolved outwardly there are more connections from the deeper limbic system (feeling brain) to the neocortex (thinking brain) than there are from thinking to feeling.[9] Therefore, the more primitive, instinctive and emotional parts of the brain often exert greater influence over a person's thinking than their thinking does over their feeling. As a result, instinctive drives (from the reptilian brain) such as breathing, being startled and the fight or flight response are almost irrepressible. This also explains why strong emotional urges (from the limbic brain) such as phobias are difficult to overcome through rational thinking. A person with a phobia of spiders or flying may consciously understand (in their neocortex) that the spider will not hurt them or that the aeroplane is unlikely to crash but will still hold the emotional and debilitating fear. Even less extreme emotional states will influence a person's thinking, such as creating positive thoughts when they feel happy and negative thoughts when they feel sad.[10] Rather than being dominant, a person's thinking is often subservient to and largely influenced by their feeling.

Research has also shown that information is sent to and perceived by the feeling (limbic) brain momentarily before it reaches the higher thinking brain.[11] This is consistent with other research showing that the decision to act precedes consciousness, in that people prepare to take an action 0.3 seconds before they are aware of choosing to do so.[12] This notion challenges the Cartesian philosophy of thinking being the essence of humanity (*I think therefore I am*) which has pervaded Western society in general, and can be seen particularly in education (IQ), business (rational decision making) and therapy (cognitive-behavioural).

Feelings not only influence thinking, but are instrumental in our decision making. Making decisions would be near impossible if people had no emotional attachment to them. Emotions tell a person what they want, like and desire, without emotional impulse there would be no conviction or confidence in any decision. This has been demonstrated by Antonio Damasio,[13] a neurosurgeon who studied patients who had damage to their ventromedial prefrontal cortex, a part of the brain involved in emotional processing. In these cases the patients retained their ability to think and to feel normally, but could not combine the two (to think about their feeling and feel about their thinking). As a result, without laborious analysis, they were unable to make even the most basic decisions, and were almost entirely lacking in sound wisdom or judgment. Feelings help guide thinking, they provide a sense of conviction to decisions as well as a wealth of deeper intuitive knowing about what is best, right or wrong (what may be referred to as gut instinct or hunches). Far from being random, inconvenient distractions, feelings provide 'intelligent' feedback on how to act (a closer examination of Damasio's research may be found in Appendix 2; *The neuroscience of emotion*).

The interdependent relationship between thinking and feeling is included in part two of the EI definition (Chapter 1.4): *the habitual practice of thinking about feeling and feeling about thinking to guide one's behaviour* which involves noticing, thinking about, labelling and interpreting feelings in the body. Conscious awareness of feelings helps an individual to develop their self-knowledge and draw upon this when experiencing similar feelings in the future. For example; *I notice myself becoming tired and irritable, and based on past experience I know this is a good time for me to take a break.* This process applies as much to others as it does to oneself, by noticing the feelings of others and forming knowledge of others. The definition also includes; *feeling about thinking,* wich involves having feelings about one's thoughts, such as feeling confident about a decision, or feeling excited about a new idea. In summary, there is a co-dependent relationship between thinking and feeling with each influencing the other and both holding equal status and value.

2.3 How the brain processes attitudes, thoughts and feelings

Feeling and thinking are the midpoint in the EI process, but what happens before and what happens after the midpoint? The first part of this process occurs when stimuli are initially received by the brain through the sensory thalamus and instantly scanned by the reptilian and mammalian parts of the brain for any potential danger. The reptilian brain contains the instinctive reflexes for danger, such as to flinch at sudden movements or jump at a loud bang, whereas the mammalian brain contains learnt responses to danger in a region called the amygdala (Greek for and the shape of an almond).

If the amygdala identifies the stimuli as a serious threat, it will send a powerful emotional response to act upon the perceived danger (the 'fight or flight' mechanism) and bypass the higher thinking brain. The primary function of the amygdala is to keep the individual alive and safe; in evolutionary terms, if the individual stopped to think through their options while under attack they may be too slow to react and survive. Thus, when a person has a fear response (also termed an 'emotional hijack')[14] the thinking brain is literally incapacitated and the reactive amygdala takes charge. The amygdala may be likened to a 'security guard' with the power to press the alarm and evacuate the building (flight), lock the doors (freeze) or call the emergency services (fight). Such a life-saving response is fine if a person is in real danger, but not so useful if the danger is just perceived rather than real. For example, if while making a presentation an individual has an emotional hijack then, due to the effects of adrenalin, they may start to sweat, their body shake (preparing for flight), their voice tremble and their ability to think clearly will be severely impaired. From the day a person is born they will encounter numerous frightening experiences that become etched onto the amygdala as a permanent implicit memory, thus resulting in the same fear response being triggered if ever a similar stimulus is presented again. This can be seen from observing people's phobias, irrational fears, post-traumatic memories and excessive emotional reactions.

Although potentially embarrassing, people do not die from fear. The purpose of the brain's fear response is to keep the person alive, which is why it exists as one of our primary emotions. The amygdala is also involved in processing other primary emotions, such as joy, disgust, anxiety and anger[15] which all have their roots in human evolution and survival. Caruso[16] describes the survival purpose of fear as *let's get out of here*, sadness as *help me*, disgust as *don't eat that*, and anger to give the person energy to fight. Further explanation on the evolutionary basis for emotions is given in Appendix 2. There does not need to be a full-on amygdala reaction for thinking to be impaired. Too much emotion will interfere with clear rational thinking as 'emotional thinking' is more blunt and categorical (good/bad, right/wrong), thus leading to less refined decision making. Stress has been shown to amplify implicit emotional memories in the amygdala (causing fear) but impair access to explicit 'event' memories in the hippocampus, thus preventing the individual from placing the stressful event into context which would otherwise help them to calm down emotionally and cognitively.[17,18] EI involves getting the right balance between thinking and feeling; enough feeling to guide and inform thinking, but not so much as to be overpowering. More details on how to do this may be found in Chapter 7.1.4.

Fig. 2.1 Regions of the brain most relevant to EI

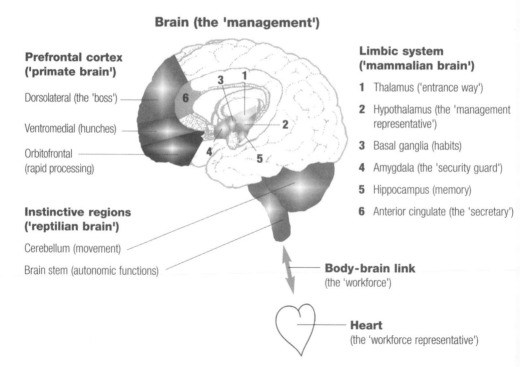

Brain (the 'management')

Prefrontal cortex ('primate brain')

Dorsolateral (the 'boss')

Ventromedial (hunches)

Orbitofrontal (rapid processing)

Instinctive regions ('reptilian brain')

Cerebellum (movement)

Brain stem (autonomic functions)

Limbic system ('mammalian brain')

1 Thalamus ('entrance way')

2 Hypothalamus (the 'management representative')

3 Basal ganglia (habits)

4 Amygdala (the 'security guard')

5 Hippocampus (memory)

6 Anterior cingulate (the 'secretary')

Body-brain link (the 'workforce')

Heart (the 'workforce representative')

Having gone through 'security checks' by the amygdala for any danger, stimuli are instantly 'pattern matched' with innate templates and past experiences (the pattern matching process might be likened to an internet search engine seeking a match to the stimulus). Past experiences are stored in many deeper regions of the brain (such as the amygdala and the contextual memory stores of the hippocampus)[19] not as literal memories but as metaphorical representations (patterns) that are attached to emotional tendencies. The connection between any particular stimuli, the pattern match and its corresponding emotional 'tag', is referred to in EIP theory as an *attitude*, defined earlier as; *the habitual and evaluative position a person holds towards any given stimuli* (further explanation of pattern matching is given in Chapter 2.4, also refer to Table 2.2. for an example).

Once the percept (what has been perceived) has been tagged with emotional significance, it is sent to the higher thinking brain (neocortex) and the hypothalamus, which trigger an emotional experience (feelings) within the body. The hypothalamus may be seen as the 'management representative' that communicates between 'the management' (the brain) and 'the workforce' (the body) through the release of hormones (feelings). The relationship between the brain and body is explained in Chapter 2.6.

The percept, with its emotional tag, is also received by the anterior cingulate which communicates with the memory stores of the hippocampus. The anterior cingulate may be likened to the boss's 'secretary' dealing with routine responses, without having to alert the conscious mind (the dorsolateral prefrontal cortex) referred to as the 'boss'. As long as the required action is familiar (a habit), the 'secretary' will fire off the necessary neural network that initiates the appropriate behavioural habit without disturbing the 'boss'. The neural networks for habits live mainly within a deeper part of the limbic system called the basal ganglia which frees up the higher parts of the brain for conscious thinking.

Thus, much automatic habitual behaviour is the consequence of an initial attitude or pattern match. Even the most mundane behaviours have their roots in emotion and attitude which will usually pass them by unaware, as long as the individual acts upon them and fulfills the emotional expectation. If they do not follow their impulse then the feeling will steadily increase, often becoming overpowering. This may happen, for example, when a person tries to change a habit which can be tremendously difficult (such as changing a routine, going on a diet or starting an exercise schedule) as the brain and body continue to send emotional messages to repeat the existing habit of behaviour. However, through continued repetition the old patterns will reduce as new neural pathways are formed.

Not all behaviour is habitual and automatic. Humans have the capacity to be self-aware and make conscious choices. The 'boss' (the conscious thinking brain) can choose to become involved and self-observing, such as when a person decides to change an automatic habit, become aware of their feelings or think about their behaviour. The 'boss' is also alerted to pay conscious attention when the individual learns something new, is involved in more complex decisions or is faced with a challenging situation.

To summarise the entire psychological process from stimulus to response, stimuli are initially connected with their emotional significance through a pattern matching process in the emotional based region of the brain (the limbic system) and checked for possible danger in the amygdala (the 'security guard'). A pattern match will attach an emotional tag to the percept and send this direct to the hypothalamus, triggering an emotional experience in the body, and send a message to the anterior cingulate (the 'secretary') to initiate a response. From here it is either processed unconsciously by the basal ganglia as an automatic habit, or consciously through the prefrontal cortex (the 'boss') where the individual chooses how to respond/behave. Their behaviour will deliver a certain outcome (positive or negative) either reinforcing or discouraging their behaviour, as illustrated by the two example tables below.

Table 2.2 The six psychological stages of EI

Stages	Example process
Stimulus	A colleague criticises their work.
Attitude/ Pattern match	Which triggers their underlying attitude of; *I am incompetent.*
Feeling/Emotion	This is experienced in their body as feeling deflated.
Thought	Their conscious self-talk is; *Why should I bother?* *(note that this stage may be bypassed by an automatic habit)*
Behaviour/Habit	Their automatic response is to withdraw.
Outcome	Their performance gets worse and they communicate less.

Understanding the six 'stages' of the psychological process helps explain the different ways in which EI can be developed. For example, if a person has difficulty in handling conflict they could address it at each stage in the process as follows:

Table 2.3 **Examples of EI development**

Stages	Example application: handling confrontation
Stimulus	They avoid the cause or change the situation.
Attitude/ Pattern match	They can replace negative attitudes such as; *people won't like me if I disagree,* with helpful ones such as; *people's differences are valuable.*
Feeling/ Emotion	They can practice breathing techniques to stay calm before, during and after confrontation.
Thought	They can challenge their negative or passive self-talk, such as; *what I think does matter.*
Behaviour/ Habit	They can repeat useful habits or phrases, such as; *please give me a moment to think about that,* before agreeing to do something.
Outcome	They can visualise or role-play acting assertively with a person who is behaving aggressively towards them.

(How to develop EI in all of these 'stages' is discussed in Chapter 7)

Although the explanation of the brain in this chapter may seem sequential and reductionist, in practice many of these processes are happening almost simultaneously, instantaneously, interdependently and continuously, with the different parts of the brain being interlinked and multifunctional. The brain has been likened to a quivering web with millions of synaptic connections firing at every moment. The three levels of the brain (mammalian, primate and reptilian) are inter-connected by the orbitofrontal cortex, which contains super-fast neuronal transmitters called spindle cells, which instantly link instinct, emotion and thought. This explains why, for example, people can make snap decisions on whether they trust someone from first impressions. In addition, the relationship between thinking and feeling is more cyclical than sequential. Feelings trigger thinking as much as thinking fuels feeling. However, it is useful to separate out these psychological functions as they offer different doorways into personal development (refer to Chapter 7).

The six stages may be more accurately represented as a cycle with a connection between each of the psychological facets. Each facet has a primary link in the order of the cycle (such as Behaviour leads to an Outcome), but also has a secondary influence on each of the other four facets (such as Behaviour influences Feeling). For example, by standing upright and talking assertively (Behaviour) a person may start to feel more confident (Feeling), or making a positive facial expression can elicit positive feelings.[20] The relationship between the six psychological facets may be abbreviated by the acronym SAFE-TBO. A helpful reminder for this acronym is *SAFE To Be Oneself*, which fits with the premise of EI being about Self Regard and unconditional self-acceptance.

Fig. 2.2 **The SAFE-TBO model**

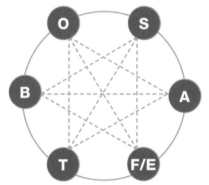

S	*Stimulus*
A	*Attitude/Pattern match*
F/E	*Feeling/Emotion*
T	*Thinking*
B	*Behaviour/Habit*
O	*Outcome/Performance*

The SAFE-TBO model had direct influence on the construction of the EIP. It highlights the importance of attitudes in influencing feelings, thoughts and behaviour, which supports the rationale for constructing the eight underpinning EI attitudes described in Chapter 1.5. The SAFE-TBO model is also represented in the three part definition of EI; *When, How* and *What* (refer to Chapter 1.4), and by the EIP framework (refer to Chapter 1.6) which consists of four levels; Attitude, Feeling, Thinking* and Behaviour. The relationship between these EIP models is shown in Table 2.4.

Table 2.4
Links between the EIP definition, EIP framework and SAFE-TBO model

EIP definition of EI	EIP framework	SAFE-TBO model
		Outcome/Performance
What: ... *to be both personally and interpersonally effective*	Behaviour	Behaviour/Habit
How: ...*EI is the habitual practice of thinking about feeling...*	Thinking*	Thinking
	Feeling	Feeling/Emotion
When: ... *EI is determined largely by a person's attitudes...*	Attitude	Attitude/Pattern match
		Stimulus

(*Refer to Chapter 4.2.1 for a description of the complete EIP framework).

At the heart of the psychological model and EIP is a pattern matching process reflecting a person's attitudes. Attitudes are one of the key features that differentiate the EIP from other personality (temperament/trait), cognitive and competency based models of EI. The next section looks in more detail at how patterns and attitudes are formed.

2.4 How attitudes form in the brain

The term 'pattern matching' was used by Joe Griffin,[21] a dream researcher, to explain his theory of how the brain perceives, interprets and gives meaning to stimuli. A pattern match occurs when stimuli are recognised by the brain as belonging to a previously identified class of stimuli. A 'pattern' is effectively an internal representation of external stimuli. Patterns can be both innate (instinctive templates) and developed through experience, and are stored as metaphorical representations (which is just as well as it would require an enormous brain to store every event and experience in full detail).

Each pattern is tagged with an emotional significance that is released once a pattern has been matched. The emotional tag takes the form of a neurochemical messenger which stimulates a response in the higher parts of the brain, thus forming a connection between the feeling (limbic) brain and the thinking (neocortex) brain. The emotional tag may also bypass the thinking brain, such as in a perceived emergency where it may activate an immediate physiological and emotional reaction (fight/flight/freeze).

The emotional tag attached to a pattern may be seen as the neurological equivalent of an attitude. As defined earlier, an attitude is: *an evaluative position (based largely on feelings) towards oneself, others, a situation, an idea, etc. that predisposes an individual towards (or away from) certain behaviours or responses.* A pattern is certainly this; patterns are *evaluative* in that they have an emotional response (such as like, want, dislike, fear) and they are *towards/away from* (or in response to the perception of) any given stimuli. In this sense the emotional tag *predisposes an individual,* directing them to think and behave in a certain way. In effect, through pattern matching the individual has both the stimulus and the response within them. Using the previous example (Table. 2.3) the individual has a pre-existing pattern (and therefore expectation) for the stimulus of 'being criticised', which connects with their attitudinal response of *I am incompetent*, and their emotional response of feeling deflated. Having an automated process for responding to previously experienced stimuli enables the individual to free up and focus their conscious attention elsewhere, for taking in additional information and learning new things. However, as in this example, it may be necessary to first become aware of and then to check if the underlying attitude (*I am incompetent*) is constructive or needs to be revised (refer to Chapter 7.3 and how to develop constructive attitudes).

Griffin[22] proposed that people form and adapt their patterns (attitudes) in the dreaming phase of sleep (indicated by rapid eye movement; hence being known as REM sleep). He termed this the *expectation fulfilment theory* of dreaming, whereby any unfulfilled expectations from the previous day are metaphorically acted out in their dreams. He concluded that this both preserves the integrity of their existing patterns and allows new patterns to be formed or reconfigured. Preserving existing patterns is, of course, essential, as it is not always appropriate or possible to act upon all emotional states, such as lust, anger and excitement. Over time this may result in these patterns being evolved out or switched off, which in the case of sexual desire could be catastrophic for the human race. Griffin's theory states that people act out their emotional expectations metaphorically through dreams in order to preserve their instinctive patterns and adapt their learnt patterns. Patterns (attitudes) are formed throughout a person's life; new-born babies for example have to form many new patterns as they make sense of the world, so spend some 80% of their sleeping time in the REM state[22] compared with 25% for adults. It is also worth noting that people drift in and out of the REM state to varying degrees constantly during the day as they form and adapt new patterns, such as when daydreaming, using their imagination, or whenever their attention is focused. In this way patterns are formed and adapted throughout life, influencing how people respond to events in terms of their feelings, thoughts and behaviours, and are therefore an integral part of Emotional Intelligence.

2.5 How the brain helps regulate feelings

Apart from pattern formation, REM sleep has another essential purpose which is to deactivate unresolved emotions and anxiety from the previous day. This is vital to Emotional Intelligence as sleep cycles are part of emotional management enabling the individual to recover emotionally and physically from the previous day. Leaving emotions unresolved would interfere with the individual's capacity to think clearly, resolve problems and generally cope with day to day life.

By metaphorically acting out emotional expectations through dreams the individual discharges their unfulfilled wishes and emotions. Dreaming may be seen as nature's therapist and a natural coping mechanism… up to a point. REM sleep can only manage so much excess emotion before a person suffers negative consequences. A person who experiences a lot of anxiety or stress will need to spend more time in the REM sleep state to work through their built-up emotions. The REM state is initiated by a firing of the orientation response, which has the purpose of focusing a person's attention and activating their imagination, which enables the individual to dream. Because of this alerting 'orientation response', dreaming sleep is not restful and can leave a person feeling tired if they do not get sufficient recuperative non REM sleep (stages 3 & 4 delta wave sleep which restore glucose and builds the immune system). This is why, for example, a person who is anxious or depressed and sleeps for a long time (engaged mostly in REM sleep in order to process unresolved emotion) still feels tired when they wake up. Also, because their orientation response is exhausted (from continuous firing) they find it difficult to focus their attention while awake and to engage in daily life. This becomes a downward spiral; if a person feels tired in the morning they will be less able to cope with the following day's stressors, which will build-up more unresolved anxiety and so the individual will require more REM sleep the following night, so perpetuating the cycle. This will eventually lead to extreme tiredness with high levels of unresolved anxiety, sleep problems, general exhaustion and depression.

If the person's anxiety continues then they will require so much REM sleep that they may wake up still in the REM trance. In this 'waking sleep' the person is still sleeping but with their eyes open, that is, having to perceive the external stimuli of the world through their dreaming brain. They may be unable to distinguish dreaming from waking reality and suffer psychotic symptoms such as; hallucinations (dreaming whilst awake) hearing voices (the left brain's language system linking with the right brain's imagination) and catatonia (a natural occurrence during REM sleep of numbing the senses and paralysis to avoid physically acting out one's dreams).

The key to recovery and avoiding stress related problems is for the individual to manage their level of arousal during waking hours, thus allowing their innate coping mechanism (REM sleep) to pick up the slack and support them while they sleep. Some ways to manage arousal levels include; noticing early signs of anxiety, taking time out for rest and recovery, learning relaxation exercises and allowing sufficient time for sleep (specific information on managing and reducing stress are given in Chapter 7.4). The importance of this is not just for an individual's mental health but for maximising day to day performance in work and life in general. People who are more able to manage their daily emotions through EI will recover quicker from stress, feel more energised in their life and be more productive in what they do.

2.6 The body - brain interaction

This chapter has so far explored the neurological foundations of Emotional Intelligence. However, it would be naïve and remiss not to consider the brain as part of a single system within the body. Extending the organisational metaphor for parts of the brain (the security guard, the boss and the boss's secretary), the whole brain may be seen as 'the management' and the body as 'the workforce,' and both must work together in harmony. This is highlighted by the strong influence thoughts and feelings have over a person's physical health (a field of research known as psychoneuroimmunology – PNI). Certain emotions such as prolonged stress, anxiety, grief, hostility, suspicion and pessimism, and the hormones these release in the body can double the risk of many diseases including: heart disease, asthma, arthritis, skin diseases, ulcers and headaches.[23] Chronic stress in particular is known to weaken the immune system, accelerate the onset and development of ill-health, and slow down recovery from illnesses such as viruses, diabetes, bowel disease and cancer.[24]

Communication between the brain and the body is a two-way process, or a continuous 'loop'. The body responds to messages sent from the brain (through the activation of neural pathways and the release of hormones), and the brain responds to feedback from the body (such as changes in heart rate, blood pressure, muscle tension, facial expression and so forth). Feedback from the body is also delivered through emotions which, as described earlier (*How feelings influence thinking,* Chapter 2.2), have been shown to provide 'intelligent' information to inform thinking and decision making. Such findings are also supported at a biochemical level, as demonstrated by the communication between the heart and brain (discussed below in Chapter 2.8).

Communication from the brain to the body is done largely through the hypothalamus (the 'management representative') which co-ordinates actions of the endocrine and nervous systems, releasing hormones which can then act as either inhibitory or releasing factors for hormones secreted by the anterior pituitary, which are then experienced as feelings within the body. Communication between the body and the brain is highly complex, involving many bodily systems – in particular the heart (the 'workforce representative'), as discussed in section 2.8.

2.7 The importance of feelings

Feelings and emotions are the main form of communication between the body and the brain. The words 'emotion' and 'feeling' are often used interchangeably, but feeling (or affect) may be seen as a person's subjective experience (conscious awareness) and labelling of their emotional or physiological state. Feelings that are experienced for a prolonged period of time are termed as 'moods'. There are three main sources of feelings:

Physiological: *hunger, thirst, nausea, pain, heart rate, etc.*

Emotional: *anger, fear, happiness, guilt, pride, envy, desire, etc.*

Intuitive: *gut feeling, instant judgements and inner-knowing.*

(More detail on the sources of feelings can be found in Appendix 1, scale 3; Self Awareness).

Primary or basic feelings are universal and common to all people (such as anger, joy, fear, sadness, disgust and anxiety), which form multiple combinations and degrees of intensity[25] (such as envy, embarrassment, jealousy and guilt), rather like a colour palette which has infinite variations on the primary colours. Some emotions are present from the moment a child is born and most emotions will be present after the first few years of life:

0-3 months: *babies show the emotions of happiness, interest, sadness and disgust.*

4-6 months: *emotions of anger and surprise develop.*

18-24 months: *emotions related to conscious awareness of oneself appear, such as embarrassment, empathy and envy.*

30-36 months: *emotions related to self-awareness in a social context appear, such as pride, shame and guilt.*

Feelings have their origins in survival and keeping people safe, such as anger to fight, anxiety to pre-empt risk and disgust to avoid dangerous food. They tell a person when their emotional needs are not being met such as jealousy/envy to meet the need for status, and guilt to meet the need for connection. Feelings also reward people when their emotional needs are being met such as feeling pride in a meaningful achievement. However, a person's *actual* needs may be different from what they *feel* they need. The perception of whether or not a person feels their needs are being met will be dependent upon their attitudes which filter their interpretation and experience of life. Feelings can be divorced from actual reality, but for an individual their feelings *are* their reality. People will often substitute their real needs (such as for status) with a superficial 'need' such as for material goods, typically promoted through society and advertising (*buy this car and you will be important and feel significant*). Unfortunately such rewards are only short term emotional 'fixes' requiring constant feeding, and do not address the real under-lying core human need. (Refer to Chapter 4.3.2 for further explanation of 'fixes'/defensive behaviours. Refer to Chapter 7.4 on how to meet emotional needs and Appendix 2 for more information on the origin of emotions).

Feelings are neither good nor bad in themselves, what matters in EI is how the individual learns to interpret, respond to and manage their feelings. If they do not manage their feelings effectively they can:

- *Cause prolonged distress*
- *Interfere with their thinking*
- *Distract their attention*
- *Cause them to behave inappropriately*
- *Stop them from sleeping*
- *Cause them to become weak and ill*
- *Deplete their energy*
- *Cause them to feel unhappy and depressed.*

On the other hand, if the individual learns to manage their feelings effectively they can:

- *Help them to empathise with others*
- *Guide their decision making as to whether something is right or wrong*
- *Provide them with intuitive awareness*
- *Alert them to danger*
- *Focus their attention*
- *Cause them to feel joy and motivation.*

By focusing attention on their feelings, an individual will gain valuable feedback about their attitudes. Feelings are the emotional response to a pattern match with their attitude templates; for example, if a person feels angry when people ignore them this may indicate that they have a strong need for attention. People sometimes choose to deny their feelings particularly when they are painful, such as when feeling humiliated, ashamed or upset. Feelings do not just disappear but will manifest in other ways such as becoming stressed and unwell, rigidly defensive or in sudden emotional outbursts (refer to Chapter 4.3.2 for examples of defensive behaviour). It is important therefore to accept all feelings as messages from the body and try to understand their origins (as described in EI attitude No. 6; *All feelings are justified, acceptable and important*). In an organisational context it is rather like the board of directors (the brain) ignoring the concerns of the workforce (the body) which will sooner or later lead to strike action (becoming ill). If a person's feelings are unpalatable then they need to look at the internal cause of their feelings (their attitudes) and not ignore the feeling messages. Advice on how to pay attention to and manage feeling states is given in Chapter 7.4.

It is worth considering some of the key hormonal neurochemicals that create feeling states. There are two primary chemical motivators in life, one is dopamine which gives a feeling of desire or the need for something and the other is serotonin which gives a feeling of reward or pleasure from doing or getting it (serving as a feedback mechanism). By nature, a person receives less reward each time they repeat an action. Therefore, a person needs to increase the level of what they do in order to get the same level of satisfaction. If this wasn't the case then humans would be perfectly content repeating the same action over and over again (rather like most other species on the planet) and would not have developed the desire for learning, creativity and setting new challenges. The catch to this however, is that people can just as easily become motivated towards or addicted to negative rewards as they can to positive rewards, such as unhelpful habits, defensive behaviours and physical addictions.

There are many other chemicals relevant to Emotional Intelligence that form part of the dynamic endocrine (hormonal) system; such as oxytocin and vasopressin, which are involved in relationships and feelings of caring, bonding, empathy, trust and love. Another important chemical that influences Emotional Intelligence is the steroid cortisol. This, along with noradrenaline is released during times of stress and anxiety, it stimulates the amygdala (fight and flight response) and prepares the body for action, which can be useful in small doses, but in the long run will deplete the immune system and makes a person more susceptible to ill-health. Learning how to manage the body's emotional system so as to minimise prolonged stress, maximise positive motivation and reinforce useful habits is discussed further in Chapter 7.

Löveheim[26] provides a useful model that summarises the relationships between three of the main neurotransmitters and Silvan Tomkins'[27] eight basic emotions. According to the model, fear is produced by the combination of low serotonin, high dopamine and low noradrenaline.

Table. 2.5 **Relationship between neurotransmitters and emotions**

Basic emotion	Serotonin	Dopamine	Noradrenaline
Shame/humiliation	Low	Low	Low
Distress/anguish	Low	Low	High
Fear/terror	Low	High	Low
Anger/rage	Low	High	High
Contempt/disgust	High	Low	Low
Surprise	High	Low	High
Enjoyment/joy	High	High	Low
Interest/excitement	High	High	High

Neurotransmitters, neurochemicals and hormones are made up of peptides which are in themselves made up of amino acids. These peptides (e.g. hormones) act as information messenger molecules and are able to reach all tissues within the body and brain via the bloodstream and cerebrospinal fluid by locking onto their matching receptors, therefore acting as a type of remote communication between the organs of the body. Candace Pert[28] describes peptides as the 'molecules of emotion'. Peptides bind with their specific receptors and start off a long chain of physiological and/or neurological reactions, which can then result in emotions that influence behaviour. One can say that emotions whether conscious or unconscious are created at a chemical level within the body and brain.

An important feature of peptide receptors is that they have the potential for change in terms of their quality, quantity and biochemical composition.[28] This is determined by all of a person's experiences, such as what they eat, their physical activity and emotional experience. The emotion-carrying peptides and their receptors, contained throughout the body, have far reaching effects; in filtering a person's perception, directing their attention, informing actions and influencing decisions. In this regard, the body has an 'innate intelligence' that learns, develops and has an emotional memory.

One group of peptides relevant to emotional experience are neuropeptides, which along with their receptors, have a particularly high concentration in the limbic (emotional) region of the brain (about 85% of them)[28] and most of these are contained within the hippocampus (the main memory centre). Neuropeptides (the information carriers) and their receptors extend outside of the limbic region to other parts of the body joining the brain, glands and immune system in a network of remote communication. The complex interaction between the body's organs is coordinated into a single web by peptides and neuropeptides. Candace Pert uses a helpful metaphor of the body being like an orchestra that follows the information on the musical script (peptides) to produce music (emotions). The orchestra includes many leading roles such as the conductor (the brain) and the lead violinist (the heart), and it is the relationship between these two organs that will now be discussed.

2.8 The heart in relation to EI

Before closing on this section it is worth looking at the close relationship between the heart and the brain. Communication between the heart and brain is a two way process with as much information being sent from the heart telling the brain what to do as there is the reverse. This is done neurologically (through the nervous system), biochemically (through hormones and neurochemicals produced in the heart and brain), mechanically (through the blood vessels) and intrinsically through its own conduction system (through electrical signals which coordinate contraction of the heart muscles). The heart communicates with different parts of the brain including; the amygdala, triggering positive and negative memory patterns; the thalamus, a pathway to decision making and mental clarity; and the medulla, influencing the autonomic nervous system (such as blood pressure). Clearly too, the brain influences the heart. Dramatic alterations in cardiac rate rhythm and contractility have been induced experimentally by stimulation of various regions of the brain. For example, variations in heart rate can be triggered by stimulating the posterior hypothalamus which is involved in the cardiac response to changes in environmental temperatures.[30] An organisation called HeartMath has developed techniques to enable the individual to self-regulate heart rate rhythm and by doing so influence the range of brain functions,[31] in other words, using feelings to influence their thinking. Key findings from this research have shown that getting the heart and brain synchronised (through creating a regular heart rate rhythm) is beneficial to body and brain functioning. This balances the parasympathetic nervous system (which slows down heart rate) with the sympathetic nervous system (which increases heart rate); rather like getting the right balance between the break and the accelerator in a car.

Research in this area has gone further to show that the heart's influence is not only internal but external or social.[32] The heart releases an electromagnetic field that can be detected by a Magnetometer three feet from the body, such that emotions are broadcast from the body and may be detectable by other people. This may be one of the mediums by which people can empathise with others or sense the emotional climate in a group. Incidentally, the brain also emits an electromagnetic field, but only about one inch from the body. Far from being a purely mechanical pump responding to the brain's requests, the heart is to some extent self-determining and there is on-going research into how the heart influences both emotions and thinking.* These are all vital aspects of EI and continued research into the neuroscience of the heart and brain will provide an even fuller picture for understanding the neuroscience of Emotional Intelligence.

This chapter has described the psychological and neurological aspects of EI, which strongly influenced the construction of the EIP, described in the next chapter.

---

* Regulation of the heart's functions is a result of the interplay between its intrinsic conduction system, the autonomic and peripheral nervous systems, and hormonal controls. The heart's own intrinsic conduction network allows the heart to beat independently of the autonomic, peripheral nervous systems and hormonal control. For example, the rhythmic contractions of atria and ventricles do not depend on autonomic nerve stim-

ulation, but result from impulses generated within the heart itself. (Without this intrinsic conduction system, cardiac transplantation would be impossible, as all nerve connections are severed during surgery).

The heart's complex intrinsic nervous system contains around 40,000 neurons called sensory neurites, which detect circulatory hormones and neurochemicals and senses heart rate and pressure information. The hormonal, chemical, heart rate and pressure information is then translated into neurological impulses and sent from the heart to the brain through several afferent (flowing to the brain) pathways. For these reasons the concept of the 'heart brain' was first introduced by Dr J. Andrew Armour in 1991.[29]

Afferent nerve pathways from the heart enter the brain through the medulla located in the brain stem through two main pathways. One afferent pathway is the vagus nerve which carries parasympathetic information from the heart to the medulla after passing through the nodose ganglian (a processing centre). The second afferent pathway travels from the heart to the extrinsic cardiac ganglia (located in the thoracic cavity; also a processing centre) which has direct connections to organs such as the lungs and oesophagus, and is also indirectly connected via the spinal cord to many other organs including the skin and arteries.

Afferent signals from the heart to the brain have a regulatory role over many autonomic system signals that flow out of the brain then back to the heart, blood vessels, other glands and organs. In addition, once these signals reach the medulla in the brain, they can then travel to the sub-cortical areas (such as the thalamus and amygdala) and then cascade up into the higher centres of the brain, where they may influence perception, decision making and other cognitive processes.

Summary points from Chapter Two

- The triune brain theory explains how the brain evolved the capacity for 'reptilian' instincts, 'mammalian' feelings and 'primate' conscious thinking. All three levels play an important role in EI.

- Evolution into warm blooded mammals coincided with the development of the limbic system in the brain. This allowed mammals to make emotionally driven (but still unconscious) choices based on previous learning rather than purely instinctive reptilian responses.

- The major evolution in the brain came about relatively recently (40,000 years ago) with what is known as the brain's 'big bang'. This gave humans greater 'access' to their prefrontal cortex and with this the capacity for self-*awareness, self-choice* and the *conscious* use of the left and right hemispheres of the brain.

- Consciousness in the right hemisphere enabled humans to use their imagination to reflect and learn from the past, to think about the future, to be creative, invent things and to develop culturally. Consciousness in the left hemisphere gave humans the capacity for reasoning, problem solving and to develop complex language, which in turn allowed humans to pass on their learning to future generations. (Many of the innate human resources are described in Chapter 1.1).

- However, consciousness and self-awareness also gave rise to human emotional vulnerability and the need to learn how to manage the different faculties of the brain (that is, to be emotionally intelligent). For example, learning to use the imagination for positive thinking rather than for excessive worrying, and self-awareness for self-development rather than creating self-doubt.

- It is a person's innate resources and vulnerabilities that make them human and reflect their personality. How well a person learns to manage these aspects of their personality is largely determined by their attitudes, which are what influence a person's feeling, thinking and behaviour.

- The perception of whether or not a person *feels* their needs are being met will be dependent upon their *attitudes* which filter their interpretation and experience of life. Feelings can therefore be divorced from actual reality, but for an individual their feelings *are* their reality.

- An attitude is the neurological equivalent to a 'pattern match'. A pattern is a metaphorical representation of past experience and innate knowledge. When stimuli are perceived and matched to a pattern in the deeper limbic brain, they trigger an emotional response (experienced as feelings in the body) which feeds up to the higher thinking structures of the brain. Therefore feelings provide important feedback on a person's attitudes and strongly influence their thinking.

- The psychological processing of stimuli may be summarised by the acronym SAFE-TBO; Stimuli are pattern matched with Attitudes that initiate Feelings (Emotions), that fuel Thinking and drive Behaviour, which in turn lead to Outcomes. These psychological stages are integral to the EIP and are mapped onto the EIP definition, framework and attitudes (refer to Table 2.4).

- Understanding the various psychological and neurological processes that influence behaviour (SAFE-TBO) has helped identify the different aspects of EI and how each of these can be developed, as presented in Chapter 7.

- An important aspect of EI is achieving the right balance between thinking and feeling, as any excess in emotion can interfere with a person's capacity for clear thinking (their IQ). For example, a perceived threat may trigger the survival response (fight, flight or freeze) in the amygdala, which can disengage a person from their higher level thinking.

- One of the brain's innate resources is the capacity to deactivate unresolved emotion during the dreaming (REM) stages of sleep. This works effectively as long as a person is not over-burdened with excessive amounts of emotional arousal, which would then not leave enough time for other forms of recovery sleep. It is therefore important that a person learns how to manage their emotions and levels of arousal during the waking day, through becoming aware of their feelings and developing their EI.

- The brain is one part of a single system; the body. For the whole system to work in harmony it is vital that the brain listens to feedback (feelings) from the rest of the body. Feelings not only tell a person what they need and want, they also provide *intelligent feedback* to inform decision making. Developing emotional self-awareness enables an individual to respond, think and act appropriately and is the cornerstone to Emotional Intelligence (as shown by the EIP framework).

● ● ●

Section Two
Interpreting the Emotional Intelligence Profile

Having read Section One the reader will be familiar with the definition, theory, psychology and neuroscience of EI, and how this underpins the EIP product. Section Two describes the construction, structure and interpretation of the EIP scales.

However much the construct of Emotional Intelligence might appeal and make sense, the issue of how to measure it is a separate one. Before going on to use the EIP product, the user must be satisfied with the psychometric properties of the instrument, the construction of the items and scales, and evidence for its validity and reliability, which are to be found in Chapter 3. Having done this they will need to understand the core meaning of the scales and how to interpret these. Chapter 4 describes the EIP framework that provides an organising structure for the sixteen EIP scales. Chapter 5 gives an interpretation of each scale and the relationship between scales. Having gained the necessary knowledge and understanding of the EIP through Section Two the user will be ready to progress on to Section Three, which explains how to apply the EIP product in a coaching and business context.

Chapter Three

How the EIP was constructed

Introduction

Before using any psychometric instrument, it is important to become familiar with the theory and rationale behind its development and the statistical properties that qualify it to be a psychometric product. Only by doing this is it possible to understand where it may be appropriately applied and to evaluate the validity (accuracy) and reliability (consistency) of the tool. In this chapter the rationale for the EIP, its technical construction, psychometric properties and the EIP scale definitions are explained. A separate EIP technical manual is available from JCA Occupational Psychologists Ltd. for anyone wishing to examine statistical data behind the EIP construction.

3.1 Rationale for developing the EIP

The EIP reflects the different backgrounds of its creators; Jolyon Maddocks is an Occupational Psychologist with expertise in behavioural measurement and Tim Sparrow a Psychotherapist with expertise in emotions. The EIP combines the elements of hard objective empirical assessment with a humanistic, people-centred understanding; an essential balance for any measure of EI. The humanistic side of the product emphasises that people can change, gives respondents their item responses to explore and addresses deeper areas such as Self Regard. On the assessment side the EIP provides standardised scale scores, normative comparison results and predictive scale interpretations. This unique aspect of the EIP means it appeals to a wide spectrum of users; to the left brain, analytical thinker who takes a more 'scientific' approach and to the right brain, holistic thinker who takes a more 'artistic' approach.

An objective in producing the EIP was to fill the diagnostic gap between personality and competencies. Personality questionnaires help individuals understand their behavioural characteristics and potential but not necessarily how to change their behaviour. Competencies shine a light on what behaviours a person may aim for, but not how to make this happen. EI is the 'how to' part that explains how a person can manage their personality to become personally and interpersonally competent. Placed together, personality, competencies and EI provide a very powerful triad for personal development.

This realisation, that there was a missing link between personality and competencies, came about from the author's experience of using personality questionnaires in coaching. This often resulted in what may be called the 'so what' factor; having identified the individual's characteristics, the question still remained as to what the individual could do to change or develop their behavioural competence. Inevitably the coach would find themselves drawn down the path of discussing the client's attitudes and feelings as the route to changing their behaviour.

The attitudinal basis for the EIP has its origins in earlier work conducted by the author whilst working with teenagers who were perceived as being hard to help, demotivated and as having low self-esteem. Having spent some years developing behavioural change programmes for this client group, it was observed that all too frequently they would return to their old negative and unhelpful behaviours. This was demonstrated by the high percentage of individuals who began apprenticeships but did not complete them. After interviewing the young people, parents, training providers and employers it became apparent that beneath the behavioural challenges were a clear set of attitudinal blocks. These attitudes included; a lack of enthusiasm towards opportunities (motivation), a resistance to forego short-term gratification for longer-term gains (ambition), an inflexibility to change their behaviour (adaptability), an unwillingness to persevere when things went wrong (perseverance) and negative expectations and aspirations (low self-esteem). The remedy for this was to create a set of activities to assess the client's attitudinal blocks and their readiness for completing an apprenticeship. Alongside the assessment were programmes to encourage the client to shift their attitudes to a more constructive position, which resulted in a marked improvement in retention and ultimately employability. This became known as MAPS[1] which stands for Motivation, Ambition, Adaptability, Perseverance and Self-esteem; the key attitudinal blocks that initiated the development of the EIP scales.

The success of these programmes led to the author's conviction that attitude change was important for subsequent and sustainable behavioural change, which is supported by a long history of psychological research: LaPierre,[2] Festinger,[3] Eagly,[4] Huczynski[5] and Makin.[6] At around this time, there was also a growth in neurological research highlighting the importance of feelings,[7,8,9] providing a clear rationale for how attitudes influence feelings which impact on decision making and behaviour. As described in Chapter 2, this research has strongly influenced the theory and design of the EIP.

The creators of the EIP also drew upon their experience and expertise in three psychological models of human development; FIRO® theory,[10] Transactional Analysis (TA)[11] and The Human Givens.[12] FIRO® theory is described in Appendix 4 and provides a proven method and model for developing behaviour and relationships, through understanding feelings and attitudes. In the author's view, the work of Will Schutz was well ahead of its time and closely resembles what has since become known as Emotional Intelligence. Many of the techniques JCA recommend for creating an emotionally intelligent organisation in Chapter 8 are adapted from FIRO® applications. Another key influence on the EIP was TA theory which is represented in the EIP framework, the underlying attitudes of EI and the Attitude Matrix that links together all of the EIP scales (refer to Chapter 4.1). The third key influence on the EIP is the work by Griffin and Tyrell from the Human Givens Institute. Their clear explanation of human emotional needs and innate resources provides a strong foundation for EI. Also, their description of the brain's processes helped inform the development of the SAFE-TBO model (see Fig.2.2). This model explains how attitudes influence feeling, thinking and behaviour, and is represented in the EI definition and the EIP framework (refer to Chapter 2.3 and Table 2.4).

3.2 Features of the EIP

There are several unique features of the EIP that differentiate it from other approaches. Perhaps the most salient feature is that the EIP is an attitude based model focused on sustainable change, which runs through all aspects of the EIP, including the rationale and definition of EI, the theoretical basis for the EIP and the EIP report itself. These features are listed below:

3.2.1 The theory of EI

- EI is based on attitudes. Other approaches view EI as personality traits, a set of competencies or an aspect of cognitive intelligence.
- EI is about being in the moment. It is a verb or a 'doing' word. Other models of EI see it as being relatively fixed, or more constitutional.
- EI is multi-faceted in that most people will have strengths and weaknesses. Other approaches describe EI as being reduced to a single construct or 'EQ' score that people have more or less of.
- EI is described as the practice of managing one's personality (which includes IQ). Other definitions of EI describe it as an aspect of personality and intelligence.

3.2.2 The theoretical basis

- The EIP framework (see Chapter 3.3 below) provides an organising structure for different aspects of EI, this includes:

  - A six part framework which is unique to the EIP
  - Personal and Interpersonal forms of Intelligence
  - Three levels of EI; Behaviour, Feeling and Attitude

- The Attitude Matrix (described in Chapter 4.1) which combines Self Regard and Regard for Others gives a theoretical structure and underlying rationale for each of the sixteen EIP scales. The Attitude Matrix is unique to the EIP.
- The sixteen EIP scales are underpinned by a philosophical approach in the form of eight EI attitudes (described in Chapter 1.5). In essence when people behave in ways that are not emotionally intelligent (as defined by the sixteen EIP scales) they will be breaching one or more of these attitudes. Few other EI products have a theoretical foundation that underpins the scale construction.
- The EIP is based upon scientific evidence from current neuroscience (described in Chapter 2). There are direct parallels between the neuropsychological stages of processing attitudes (SAFE-TBO), the EI definition and the EIP framework (refer to Table 2.4). Other approaches to EI focus mainly on behaviours without consideration to the biological roots.

3.2.3 The EI Profile
- Particular to the EIP report is a list of all item responses and their scores. This provides the reader with ownership of, and the information to understand, their scores. Ultimately, only the respondent knows why they gave the answers they did. Very few psychometric measures do this as the items are purely statistically derived rather than meaningful in themselves.
- The EIP was designed specifically for personal development; whereas most other EI measures are used for selection and assessment purposes. This allows for greater relevance in that the items, scales, theory and reports are all constructed for personal development.
- The EIP multi-scales (explained in Chapter 6.1.4) show variations in and patterns of behaviour. For example, a person who is Over Trusting (Scale 11) may also become Mistrusting if they are constantly let down by people. Identifying behavioural and emotional patterns in this way is essential to EI yet unique to the EIP.

3.3 Technical construction of the EIP
The EIP was initially produced in 1998 by Jolyon Maddocks and Tim Sparrow[13] as one of the earliest measures of EI.

The first phase of development involved a comprehensive review of the existing theories of EI and assessment products. At this time there were relatively few other EI models and an absence of any team measures of EI so it was decided to develop two products, one for team EI and a second for individual EI. Both products share the same EI principles, and the links between the individual (the EIP) and the team

(Team EIP) measures are described in Chapter 8.3.1. The description below refers to the Individual EIP, although both products were developed concurrently using similar methodology.

Following this review the authors defined the constructs and theoretical rationale for both instruments. This was drawn from their experience across several, mostly humanistic, theories of development, including:

- *FIRO® theory*[10]
- *Gestalt*[14]
- *The Human Givens approach*[12]
- *Neurolinguistic programming*[15]
- *The neuroscience of emotions*[8]
- *Personality trait theory*[16]
- *Psychometric theory*[17]
- *Psychological type theory*[18]
- *Transactional Analysis*[11]

These theories helped the creators devise the foundations for their model of EI and the EIP which included:

- *A premise for EI based on emotional needs and innate resources*
- *A three part definition of EI*
- *Eight humanistic attitudes that underpin EI*
- *A six part neuropsychological process for EI*
- *A framework model of EI*
- *A set of matrices for exploring attitude, feeling and behaviour*
- *Sixteen constructs of EI*

Item production and trialling was carried out over a two to three year period, producing three versions of the items, norms and product. The individual tool was originally called the Individual Diagnostic Questionnaire (IDQ), then changed to Individual Effectiveness (ie) and more recently to the Emotional Intelligence Profile (EIP). The Team tool was originally called the Team Diagnostic Questionnaire, then Team Effectiveness (te) and updated in 2013 to the Team EIP. Each iteration of the EIP has included enhancements to the report narrative and design but the founding models, scale structure and items have remained unchanged.

Items were designed to be 'diagnostic' rather than just a means of generating scores. This meant they needed to be relevant, meaningful and provocative so they could be shared with the client when exploring their EIP scale scores. Item test development included 'empirical keying' of items by experts (a process by which items are defined and agreed by experts in the field). The experts were individuals who had attended a nine month part-time programme in EI and were all qualified EI practitioners with the CAEI (Centre for Applied EI). At that time, the centre was the only UK organisation that gave formal training in EI that met a standard to gain expertise in EI.

The first two editions of the questionnaire were trialled by thirty EI practitioners as part of their own applied diploma projects. These projects were conducted on specific population groups. Qualitative feedback was also collated on items and relevance of the scale-constructs, which led to the third version of the individual measure.

Subsequent statistical analysis was conducted on version 3.0 of the items and scales. These are detailed more fully in the technical manual[19] available from JCA and confirm evidence for acceptable levels of validity and reliability.

3.3.1 Structure and scoring of the EIP scales

The sixteen scales of the EIP are structured within a six part framework. This separates the scales into either Personal or Interpersonal aspects of EI. It also splits them into three levels:

- *Behaviour (Self Management and Relationship Management scales)*
- *Feeling (Self Awareness and Awareness of Others scales)*
- *Attitude (Self Regard and Regard for Others scales)*

This is presented as the EIP framework shown below and described in detail in Chapter 4.1.

Table 3.1 The EIP framework

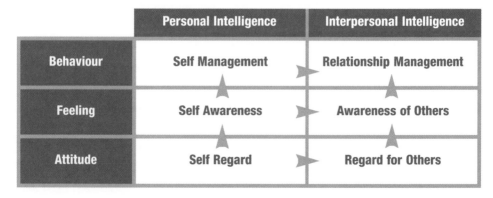

	Personal Intelligence	Interpersonal Intelligence
Behaviour	Self Management	Relationship Management
Feeling	Self Awareness	Awareness of Others
Attitude	Self Regard	Regard for Others

The only scale not included in the EIP framework is scale 16 (Reflective Learning), which is not so much an aspect of EI but rather an important part for its development.

All the EIP scales are compared against a selected normative group and are scored from 1-10 representing decile bands. A decile score of 1 would represent being in the lowest 10% of that particular norm group. Within the narrative report, the scores are presented in five bands; very low (decile 1), low (deciles 2-3), average (deciles 4-6), high (deciles 7-8) and very high (decile 9-10).

There are two types of scale; *linear scales* (scales 1-10 & 16) and *multi-scales* (scales 11-15). The linear scales (see Fig. 3.1) are scored so that higher scores represent higher levels of Emotional Intelligence, such that higher Self Awareness (scale 3) is preferable to lower Self Awareness. For multi-scales (see Fig. 3.2) the most emotionally intelligent score is represented by the middle green bar and the least emotionally intelligent scores are at the extremes (the two enclosing red bars). Therefore multi-scales are made up of three separate sub-scales. For example, with Trust (scale 11), it is better to score high on Carefully Trusting (the middle scale) and low on Mistrusting and Over Trusting. An explanation on how to interpret linear and multi-scales is given in Chapter 6.1.3.

Fig. 3.1 **Example linear scale**

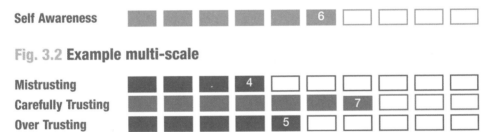

Fig. 3.2 **Example multi-scale**

Response options for the EIP range from 1-5 [Strongly Disagree;1, Disagree; 2, Neither Agree nor Disagree; 3, Agree; 4, Strongly Agree; 5]. There are 136 items in total with 6-8 items per linear scale, 12 items (4 items for each of the three sub-scales) for the multi-scales, and items are presented in scale order from scale 1-16. For the linear scales, approximately half are negatively phrased (where high scores represent low EI) and half are phrased positively. Varying between positive and negative items helps to minimise 'response set', such as a respondent always giving the same answer to questions or not thinking about the answer they will give. Of the multi-scales, the two red sub-scales are phrased negatively, such as for Mistrusting and Over Trusting, and the green sub-scale, Carefully Trusting, is phrased positively.

There is a slight negative skew on several of the scales, meaning that respondents tend to rate themselves slightly higher on average than the middle score of 3. The downside of this is that it reduces the range of differentiation in scores between people. However, since the emphasis of the EIP is on people having potential for growth (see EI attitude No. 8, chapter 1.5) the question is not how far a person deviates from the midpoint (as with classical test theory) but how far a person deviates from the highest point of 5.

3.4 Psychometric properties of the EIP

The EIP is a *psychometric test** meaning it conforms to principles of measurement that quantify the precision and accuracy of its scales in differentiating between people. It also provides a facility for predicting how the individual's responses to the questionnaire relate to how they are likely to behave in real life situations. However, accurate interpretation not only depends on the robustness of the measuring tool, it also depends on the respondent's accuracy of self-reporting and the assessor's understanding of the psychometric test. Understanding the psychometric properties of a test will tell the assessor how much confidence to place on a scale score, the likely margin of error and how closely it correlates with other scales.

There are five key properties that distinguish a psychometric test:

1 **Reliability**　　　*How consistent the test is*
2 **Validity**　　　　*How accurate the test is*
3 **Objectivity**　　　*To what extent personal subjectivity is minimised*
4 **Standardisation**　*To what extent any influences on test conditions are kept constant*
5 **Discriminating**　*How well the test discriminates*

The main indicators of a test's quality are its reliability and validity:

● *Reliability asks how consistent a test is in measuring the same aspect. There would be little use in developing a measure of EI if it measured something different every time it was used.*
● *Validity asks whether the test measures the construct it claims to measure. Again, there is little point in a test that measures something if the user does not know what it is measuring or if it is not measuring what the user intended.*

---

* 'Test' is the conventional term for a questionnaire developed from psychometric principles.[17] Users of the EIP are advised to use the terms 'questionnaire' as opposed to 'test' which may infer that it is being used for selection or as a 'pass/fail'.

A simple analogy to this is throwing several darts at a dart board. Reliability is how bunched together the darts are and validity is how close the darts are to their intended target. A darts player whose throwing is unreliable will never have high validity!

Reliability and validity are usually measured using correlation. Correlation shows the degree to which variables co-vary. For example, do people who perform well in their job score higher in a test than people who do less well in their job? The degree of correlation is scored from 0 (no correlation) to 1 (perfect correlation) and may be positive (when both variables increase together) or negative (when one variable increases and the other decreases). A correlation coefficient is also shown by the letter 'r' (for regression), such as $r=0.75$. It is important to remember that correlation doesn't mean causation, as many things co-vary but do not cause the other, like height and shoe size.

A correlation should also be checked for its level of significance which assesses how likely is it that the correlation is due to chance. A usual acceptable level of significance for a psychometric test is a 5% probability of chance (or a 95% level of confidence) expressed as $p \leq 0.05$. The level of significance is likely to be higher if the correlation (r) is higher and the number of people in the sample (n) is higher. Correlation coefficients and levels of significance for reliability and validity studies may be found in the EIP technical manual.[19]

3.4.1 Reliability

The three main ways of assessing a test's reliability, based on correlation, are:

Test-retest: Does the test get the same results on a repeat application with the same group? This is less relevant to the EIP which, by its nature as a development tool, is designed to get different (hopefully improved) results over time.

Alternate or parallel form: Do different versions of the same test get consistent results? This is more relevant to ability tests where there may be different forms of the same test to prevent candidates becoming familiar with the items over repeated completions. The EIP has been correlated between a set of respondents who completed the EIP online and then completed it again with paper and pencil. This study was done to check there were no significant differences due to the method of administration.

Internal consistency: Do items within the same scale get higher correlations (converge) and items from different scales get lower correlations (diverge)? This is one of the most robust checks for reliability, and has been repeated several times on the EIP.

Confidence in scores

There is some controversy as to what constitutes an acceptable level of internal reliability. The purpose of high reliability is that the test will produce consistent results and that the items are measuring a common construct. However, if a test scale has very high reliability (r >0.84) it may be because what is being measured is very discrete and narrow in meaning. This issue is of particular concern when the scales of the questionnaire are supposed to be overlapping in meaning, as narrower (high reliability) scales are less likely to overlap. A common error made by test users is to assume that high reliability implies high validity, as very high reliability can indicate that the scale does not reflect the full breadth of the scale definition. The recognised minimum standard for internal reliability is r=0.70. The mean internal reliability of the EIP is r=0.75.

The reliability of a test determines the margin of error (standard error of measurement; SEM) probable when interpreting a score. As a rule of thumb, based on the EIP scaling, it is recommended to apply a 1.5 decile band either side of the score. Therefore, a decile of 5 would have a confidence range from decile 3.5 to 6.5. More specifically a test user may have 68% confidence that an individual would score +/- 1.5 deciles if they were to repeat the EIP.

The SEM is also relevant when comparing between scales and is known as the standard error of difference (SED). This is the difference required between two scores to be confident the difference is repeatable rather than due to error or chance. For the EIP, a difference of 2 deciles is recommended to be reasonably (68%) confident that the difference between any two scales is genuine and not due to measurement error.

3.4.2 Validity

Whilst reliability of a test identifies whether the test is a consistent measure and is hitting the *same* part of the target each time (the dart analogy), it does not tell the user whether they are hitting the *right* part of the target consistently. Therefore validity examines whether the test measures what it purports to measure. In test construction there are several forms of validity to be considered:

Face validity: This refers to whether a test *appears* to measure what it is claiming to measure. Just because a test has a lot of 'gloss' does not mean it has much technical strength in terms of validity and reliability. The EIP has high face validity having been regularly updated with bespoke branded reports used by multinational and blue-chip organisations.

Faith validity: Faith validity can be a useful guide when choosing a test. If a test has stood the test of time and is recommended by experienced test users then it has a pedigree and may give a person faith in its validity. However, the test user should be careful not to assume a test is appropriate and valid because of the 'sales patter'. The EIP was one of the earliest EI products on the market (since 1998) and has become the EI product of choice for many consultants, Occupational Psychologists and organisations, having established a positive reputation.

Content validity: Content validity questions to what extent the test covers the ground it is supposed to be measuring. The EIP constructs are all defined within the book, the items are designed to cover the domain of the constructs and each scale includes between 8-12 items. Content validity is also indicated by the internal reliability (described previously) of the items within each scale.

Construct validity: Theoretically, construct validity is the most important measure of validity and asks if the test measures the construct it purports to measure. The other measures of validity are useful in as much as they may demonstrate construct validity. The EIP has been correlated with several other well established tests. The aim here was to check that scales correlate positively with other scales that are similar (convergent validity) and negatively with other scales that are opposite or different (divergent validity).

Some of the construct validity studies that have been undertaken between the EIP and other products include:

- *FIRO® Element B*
- *GMA abstract reasoning*
- *Identity*
- *JTI (Type)*
- *MBTI®*
- *NEO-PI-R (the big 5)*
- *Quintax (the big 5)*
- *Scenarios*
- *Systems thinking*
- *Thinking styles*

(Refer to the EIP technical manual for details and further updates)[19]

Criterion related validity: Criterion related validity is the most common method of demonstrating the relationship between test scores and job performance. The EIP however is used for personal development rather than job selection. Several studies have been carried out to determine how job performance has improved over time for individuals who have received EI coaching and support. The EIP has also been correlated with various job performance and development criteria as listed below:

- *Reduced burnout and increased job satisfaction in prison officers*
- *Increased commitment and civic virtue*
- *Increased job satisfaction*
- *Increased leadership development at a large multinational organisation*
- *Improved leadership emergence*
- *Raised leader-member exchange quality*
- *Increased organisational commitment*
- *Reduced stress in the work place*
- *Improved worker relations*

(Refer to the EIP technical manual for details and further updates)[19]

3.4.3 Standardisation, objectivity and norm selection

'Standardisation' and 'Objectivity' are about minimising personal or subjective input. Administered online, the EIP questionnaire is a standardised process. Every user has the same instructions and completes the same questions in the same order on screen. There is minimal room for deviation, however, as with any self-report questionnaire, there is room for error. Standardisation may be reduced if the respondent makes errors in their responses, lacks self-awareness, is inaccurate, feels tired, is unwell or takes long breaks between questions.

Standardisation is important when comparing the individual's responses to a comparison or norm group. This comparison shows how much higher or lower a person scores when compared to a specific norm group. To make an equal comparison, it is important that both the individual and the comparison group complete the same questions in the same way.

Objectivity is concerned with the interpretion of an individual's scores from their profile and is about minimising personal subjectivity. The narrative interpretation and scores on the EIP are generated mechanically, based on a preset formula. However, objectivity has its limitations and skilled users of the EIP will want to add their own experience and subjective skills when interpreting profiles. They will need to balance the EIP results with other information gathered through the exploration process, and they should look carefully at the relative balance between the different scale scores. These subjective skills of interpretation are detailed in Chapter 6.2.

Interpretation of EIP scores should also take account of the chosen comparison norm group. For example, research on the EIP has shown senior managers to score higher on most scales than middle managers. Therefore any given individual will score relatively lower compared to senior managers than when compared to middle managers. Data on the relative differences between each of the norm groups is available in the EIP technical manual. The EIP offers the following comparison norm groups:

- *General working population*   *one option*

The modal description of the General working population (the entire norm group) is: employed, equal gender split, age range of 35-45, middle to senior management occupational level, both private and public sector, blue-chip organisations and predominantly white UK based workers.

- *Age*   *five options*
- *Gender*   *two options*
- *Occupational level*   *six options*
- *Occupational sector*   *ten options*
- *Country of origin*   *twenty eight options*

Unless the user has a specific preference, it is advised that they select the largest sized norm group (General working population) as larger norm groups contain less sample error and are more representative across the working population. Choosing specific norm groups for comparison is useful when this is the specific context in which the product will be used, such as, nominating senior managers for executive level coaching. Bespoke internal organisational norms can also be created for specific groups.

3.4.4 Discriminating

Discrimination is not a dirty word. The main purpose of any test is to discriminate between who has more or less of a particular attribute, or the relative strengths and development areas for an individual. The important point is that the user knows what they are measuring and that the test is valid and reliable in this context. In the UK, it is unlawful for employers to discriminate on the grounds of ethnic origin, gender, age and disability. Evidence of group differences in these areas are an indicator of potential adverse impact (either direct or indirect discrimination). The EIP is used for personal development rather than job selection. However, it is still valuable and highly recommended for the test user and employer to monitor for these differences. The purpose of the EIP is to help the individual differentiate between their strengths and areas for development. JCA have conducted an extensive review on the data for over 12,000 completions of the EIP, to look at differences between population groups in gender, age, ethnicity, occupational sector and job level. These may be found in the EIP technical manual.[19]

3.5 The core meaning of the EIP constructs

Understanding a profile of test scores in the context of an individual requires a meeting with the test-taker to explore their results (the exploration process is discussed in Chapter 6.2). Before meeting the test-taker, the test user or coach needs to form some hypotheses (interpretations) on the basis of the test scores. At this stage it is important to clearly understand the core meaning at the heart of each of the scales and not to go beyond the meaning of the data. The core meaning of a test scale may be defined as; *the essential aspect of what is being measured by a scale and what differentiates it from all the other scales in the test.* In the EIP, each of the scales is measuring an attribute that has a *unique influence* on an individual's overall Emotional Intelligence. Test users can understand the nature of that unique influence by initially learning the core definitions of the sixteen EIP scales presented in the table below. Table 3.2 shows the EIP scales in relation to the EIP framework (described in Chapter 4.1) and the EI attitudes (described in Chapter 1.5).

Table 3.2 The EIP scale definitions

EIP framework	EIP scales	Core meaning of the EIP scales	Related EI attitudes*
Attitude	Scale 1 Self Regard	*The degree to which an individual accepts and values themselves.*	However you are and others are, is OK.
	Scale 2 Regard for Others	*How much a person accepts and values others (as distinct from liking or approving of what they may do).*	However you are and others are, is OK. People are different: they experience the world differently, feel different things and want different things.
Feeling	Scale 3 Self Awareness	*The degree to which a person is in touch with their physiology, feelings and intuitions.*	All feelings are justified, acceptable and important.
	Scale 4 Awareness of Others	*The degree to which a person is in touch with the feelings of others.*	People are different: they experience the world differently, feel different things and want different things. All feelings are justified, acceptable and important.

EIP framework	EIP scales	Core meaning of the EIP scales	Related EI attitudes*
Behaviour: Self Management	Scale 5 Emotional Resilience	*The degree to which an individual is able to pick themselves up and bounce back when things go badly for them.*	Feelings and behaviour are separate. However you are and others are, is OK.
	Scale 6 Personal Power	*The degree to which a person believes that they are in charge of and take sole responsibility for their outcomes.*	Everyone is in control of and responsible for their actions. No one else can control our feelings.
	Scale 7 Goal Directedness	*The degree to which a person's behaviour is aligned with their long-term goals.*	Feelings and behaviour are separate.
	Scale 8 Flexibility	*The degree to which a person feels free to adapt their thinking and behaviour to changing situations.*	Change is possible. People are different: they experience the world differently, feel different things and want different things.
	Scale 9 Connecting with Others	*The extent and ease with which an individual makes significant connections with other people.*	However you are and others are, is OK. People have a natural tendency towards growth and health.
	Scale 10 Authenticity	*The degree to which an individual invites the trust of others by being principled, reliable, consistent and known.*	Everyone is in control of and responsible for their actions.
Behaviour: Relationship Management	Scale 11 Trust	*The tendency for a person to trust others.*	However you are and others are, is OK. People have a natural tendency towards growth and health.
	Scale 12 Balanced Outlook	*How effectively an individual balances optimism with realism.*	Change is possible.
	Scale 13 Emotional Expression and Control	*The degree to which an individual achieves appropriate balance in the expression and control of their emotions.*	No one else can control our feelings. All feelings are justified, acceptable and important. Feelings and behaviour are separate.
	Scale 14 Conflict Handling	*How well conflict is handled; how assertive a person is.*	Feelings and behaviour are separate. However you are and others are, is OK.
	Scale 15 Interdependence	*How well an individual manages to balance taking themselves and others into account.*	No one else can control our feelings. Everyone is in control of and responsible for their actions.

EIP framework	EIP scales	Core meaning of the EIP scales	Related EI attitudes*
Developing EI	Scale 16 Reflective Learning	*The degree to which Emotional Intelligence is enhanced by the individual reflecting on what they and others feel, think and do, noticing the outcomes these produce, and altering their patterns accordingly.*	People have a natural tendency towards growth and health. Change is possible.

* Note that all of the EI attitudes have some influence on all of the scales, in particular EI attitude No. 1; *However you are and others are, is OK*. The EI attitudes listed for each scale are those with the most specific relevance.

Having learnt the core definition of the sixteen EIP scales the user may go on to enrich their understanding by reading Chapter 5, which explains the meaning of the scales and their relationship to one another. For those seeking further insight and wider knowledge of the scales, they may refer to the descriptions given in Appendix 1.

Summary points from Chapter 3

- The key reason for developing the EIP was to produce a product that would facilitate change in attitudes leading to a sustainable change in behaviour. This was brought about by the author's experience of working with young people to raise their motivation and self-esteem. He found that by shifting their attitudes towards a more positive mindset they were far less likely to revert back to their old negative behaviours.

- A second key influence was the author's experience of coaching with personality questionnaires and 360 behaviour measures. He perceived there to be a 'missing link' between the two; how to transfer personality and potential into behaviour change and performance. This he defined as Emotional Intelligence; the capacity of an individual to manage their personality to be both personally and interpersonally effective.

- There were a number of other key influences in developing the EIP theory, including; the application of FIRO® theory for improving self-awareness and relationships, the practical relevance of TA theory for personal development, and the application of neuroscience for self-development explained by The Human Givens Institute. All of these approaches have their foundations in the application of attitudes and feelings for personal development.

- The EIP has several unique features that distinguish it from other models of Emotional Intelligence. These include:
  - *The definition of EI as a process (a verb).*
  - *The theory of EI; to manage one's personality (their innate resources and potential).*
  - *A strong underpinning rationale for the EIP, which includes a set of eight EI attitudes and a grounding in neuroscience.*
  - *The six part EIP framework that explains the relationship between the different parts of EI.*
  - *A set of multi-scales that measure emotional and behavioural patterns.*
  - *The EIP being a dedicated developmental (rather than selection) assessment tool.*

- The EIP was constructed using psychometric principles ensuring that the test has robust levels of reliability and validity for its purpose. Those wishing to examine the statistical properties of the EIP, normative data and other research, can refer to the technical manual,[19] which is frequently updated and available to download from www.jcaglobal.com.

- The EIP scales are standardised and scored as deciles from 1-10 and can be compared to various norm groups. A score of 7, for example, represents scoring higher than or equal to 70% and lower than 30% of the comparison group.

- Before using the EIP it is important that the coach is well grounded in the psychological theory of EI and has a clear grasp of the core meaning for each of the sixteen EIP scales.

● ● ●

Chapter Four
Interpreting the EIP framework

Introduction

The EIP consists of sixteen scales of Emotional Intelligence. These were derived from the EI attitudes and theory described in Chapters 1 and 2. The EIP scales are organised and structured within a framework that represents the theory of EI in a way that is easy to understand and practical to apply in coaching. The framework consists of six parts separated into three paired matrices; Attitude, Feeling and Behaviour. This chapter explains how to interpret the framework and the EIP matrices.

4.1 The EIP framework

Emotional Intelligence is a combination of skills, attitudes and habits that distinguish superior from run-of-the-mill performance both in life as a whole and at work. The different parts of EI are brought together and organised by the EIP framework described below. This consists of two streams:

Personal Intelligence: the individual being intelligent in picking up what is going on inside themselves (Self Awareness) and acting on these feelings and notions (Self Management).

This includes aspects such as; the individual knowing what they want, motivating themselves to achieve their goals, dealing with challenges and setbacks, maintaining their physical and emotional well-being, improving their work-life balance, being confident in their decisions and actions, having clarity of thinking and adapting to new situations.

Interpersonal Intelligence: the individual being intelligent in picking up what is going on for other people and between people (Awareness of Others) and doing what they need to do to manage this (Relationship Management).

This includes aspects such as; knowing what others want, building trusting relationships, leading and managing others, helping motivate others, team working, coaching people and managing confrontation constructively.

There are three levels to the EIP framework; at the deepest level Emotional Intelligence is influenced by the individual's attitudes, in particular their attitude towards themselves (Self Regard) and their attitude towards other people (Regard for Others). This in turn influences (and may distort) their Self Awareness and Awareness of Others

(Feeling), which manifests in their Behaviour (Self and Relationship Management). In summary, an individual's *Attitude* (the deepest level) creates their *Feeling* (the middle level) that manifests in their *Behaviour* (the top level).

The relationship between the six parts of Emotional Intelligence is shown in the EIP framework below:

Table 4.1 **The EIP framework**

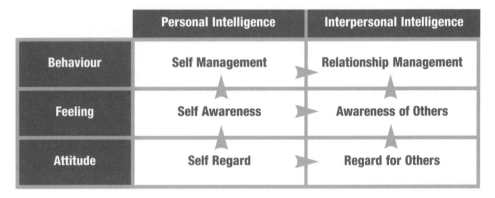

	Personal Intelligence	Interpersonal Intelligence
Behaviour	**Self Management**	**Relationship Management**
Feeling	**Self Awareness**	**Awareness of Others**
Attitude	**Self Regard**	**Regard for Others**

4.2 How the six parts of the EIP framework relate to each other

The arrows on the framework indicate the predominant direction of influence between the six parts of the framework. These move from left to right and from the bottom upwards, although there is also an influence, to a lesser extent, in the opposite direction.

The left to right arrows indicate that Personal Intelligence impacts on a person's Interpersonal Intelligence. People who are low on Personal but high on Interpersonal Intelligence may focus so much attention on the welfare of others that they fail to take care of their own needs and eventually become too unwell or exhausted to be of any help to others. It is difficult for a person to look after others if they do not look after themselves; on an aeroplane passengers are instructed to place their own oxygen masks on first, before aiding others, including their children.

The left to right arrows of influence also apply to each of the three levels. At the Attitude level if an individual feels bad about themselves (low Self Regard) they are more likely to become critical towards others (low Regard for Others). At the Feeling level if an individual is unaware of their own feelings (low Self Awareness) they will be less able to empathise with the feelings of others (low Awareness of Others). At the Behaviour level if an individual does not manage their own feelings; such as feeling angry (low Self Management), this is likely to impact upon how they handle conflict and their relationships (Relationship Management).

The arrows also move from the bottom upwards. On the left side of the framework (Personal Intelligence); if an individual has high Self Regard (Attitude) they will be more open to all of their feelings (both positive and negative), rather than ignoring or distorting them (high Self Awareness), which will help them to manage their behaviour appropriately (high Self Management). On the right side of the framework (Interpersonal Intelligence); if an individual has low Regard for Others (Attitude) they may negatively distort their perceptions of others (low Awareness of Others), which may cause them to be more guarded or hostile towards people (low Relationship Management). consider some further examples:

Example 1: It is possible to have high Self Awareness and Awareness of Others (the middle layer) but fail to put this into action, and therefore be low on Self Management and Relationship Management (the top layer). For example, the 'navel gazer' who is full of self-understanding but fails to put this into action, or those who engage in a lot of personal development but don't change, and people who 'talk the talk' but don't 'walk the walk'. Awareness is an important basis for development but is only as useful as what a person does with it.

Example 2: An individual can be high on Self Management but have low Self Awareness. This may suggest a tendency to follow learned patterns of behaviour, rather than being in touch with what they want for themselves and what makes them happy. For example, living out one's parents' dream, doing what is expected by others, or cruising through life waiting for something to happen. This is a common issue often dealt with in coaching sessions, where an apparently successful and capable individual is feeling unfulfilled and dissatisfied with their life. From time to time it is necessary for the individual to 'check in' with themselves to find out if what they are doing is still satisfying or whether their needs and wants have changed. If an individual leaves it too long then they may lose touch with their essence and their sense of purpose, living their lives on 'autopilot'. It may take a significant life event such as retirement, divorce, ill-health, redundancy or bereavement to give them a 'wake-up call' and prompt them to re-engage with what they want through developing their Self Awareness.

Example 3: A person with strong Relationship Management and low Awareness of Others may appear to others as being rehearsed and artificial. If an individual does not show Awareness of Others they may be seen as inauthentic despite having good communication and interpersonal skills (Relationship Management). For example, a leader may deliver a well prepared and slick presentation but this may fail to engage or motivate people if the leader does not identify with, empathise or understand their audience.

There is also a strong link between the top and bottom levels of the framework; Attitude and Behaviour, people's behaviour tends to be consistent with, and is a good indicator of, their attitudes. This is illustrated below with an example for each of the EIP scales.

Table 4.2 Example attitudes and behaviours for each EIP scale

EIP scale	Example attitude	Example behaviour
1 Self Regard	I am OK	Accepting positive feedback
2 Regard for Others	Others are OK	Praising people
3 Self Awareness	Feelings are important	Noticing early signs of stress
4 Awareness of Others	People's opinions matter	Listening to others
5 Emotional Resilience	Problems are only temporary	Persevering after a setback
6 Personal Power	I am capable and competent	Taking responsibility
7 Goal Directedness	I have a clear sense of purpose	Not being easily distracted
8 Flexibility	Failure is useful feedback	Trying out new experiences
9 Connecting with Others	People are mostly decent when you get to know them	Initiating conversation with others
10 Authenticity	It is important to follow your principles	Being consistent
11 Trust	Everyone has potential	Delegating work to others
12 Balanced Outlook	There are many things to look forward to	Being motivated and enthusiastic about the future
13 Emotional Expression and Control	People are interested in what I think and feel	Communicating openly about oneself
14 Conflict Handling	My thoughts and opinions are valuable	Speaking up for oneself
15 Interdependence	Teamwork is useful	Collaborating with colleagues
16 Reflective Learning	Past experiences provide valuable learning	Keeping a self-development journal

On the EIP framework, Attitude and Behaviour are connected by Feeling (the middle level of the framework). Feelings are feedback that help the individual to understand their underlying attitudes. Feelings are also what drive people to behave as they do, and awareness of feelings helps an individual to manage their behaviour, just as awareness of how others are feeling helps them to manage their relationships.

4.2.1 Reflective Learning and Self Knowledge

The EIP framework above (Table 4.1) shows that Self Awareness links to and enables Self Management, and Awareness of Others links to and enables Relationship Management. However, this is a simplification; between Awareness and Management lies Self Knowledge and Knowledge of Others. A person may be acutely aware of their own and others feelings (Awareness) yet not know what to do about it (Knowledge). For that they also need to draw upon experience about themselves (Self Knowledge) and about others (Knowledge of Others). Knowledge of self and others is developed through the process of Reflective Learning, or *thinking about feeling* which is one part of the EI definition.

For example:

- *An individual notices themselves becoming very excited by a new idea (Self Awareness).*
- *They reflect on past experiences in similar situations (Reflection/Thinking).*
- *Which has taught them that they can be over-optimistic (Self Knowledge).*
- *They therefore decide not to rush into making a decision (Self Management).*

This process, which includes Thinking (Reflection) and Knowledge, completes the EIP framework as shown below. (More detail on the process of Reflective Learning scale 16, may be found in Appendix 1).

Table 4.3 The complete EIP framework

	Personal Intelligence	Interpersonal Intelligence
Behaviour	Self Management	Relationship Management
Knowledge	Self Knowledge	Knowledge of Others
Thinking	Self Reflection	Reflecting on Others
Feeling	Self Awareness	Awareness of Others
Attitude	Self Regard	Regard of Others

The reader may recall from Chapter 2 that the EIP framework is derived from and maps onto the definition of EI and the psychological stages of EI (SAFE-TBO) as shown below.

Table 4.4
Links between the EIP definition, EIP framework and SAFE-TBO model

EIP definition of EI	EIP framework	SAFE-TBO model
		Outcome/Performance
What: ...to be both personally and interpersonally effective	Behaviour	Behaviour/Habit
How:...EI is the habitual practice of thinking about feeling...	Thinking	Thinking
	Feeling	Feeling/Emotion
When: ...EI is determined largely by a person's attitudes...	Attitude	Attitude/Pattern match
		Stimulus

Each pair of scales on the three levels of the EIP framework is combined to form a series of 2x2 matrices. The next section describes the relative balance between each pair of scales from the framework and how these are interpreted.

4.3 The Attitude Matrix

The first matrix below shows the balance between the Attitude scales of Self Regard and Regard for Others. These scales form the bottom layer of the EIP framework. Taken together they constitute a person's Core Attitude or 'Life Position'[1] which is extremely powerful in determining not only their Emotional Intelligence but their perception of themselves, others and of life in general.

The concept of 'Life Positions' (Core Attitudes) comes from TA (Transactional Analysis), and is based on the idea that when babies arrive into the world (uninvited) they are confronted with two life questions: *who am I and am I OK?* and; *who are all these other people and are they OK?* As babies, this conscious thinking is largely undeveloped, so their response is at an unconscious emotional and evaluative level, that is, *I am and people are either OK* (good, valuable, trustworthy, to be respected and safe) *or Not OK* (bad, worthless, unreliable, unworthy of respect and dangerous). These form the individual's initial Core Attitudes on life, which may be consolidated or modified depending on the individual's experience through life.

Originally described in TA as the 'OK Corral', the Attitude Matrix provides a simple shortcut for the Core Attitudes. In brief, the top right of the matrix is the; *I am OK* (Self Regard) and *You are OK* (Regard for Others) position, often shortened to I+ U+ or the 'Ideal' box. This is the emotionally intelligent, 'get on with' and mentally healthy attitude.

The bottom left refers to the *I am Not OK* and *You are Not OK* (I- U-), the Blocked or 'get nowhere with' attitude. The bottom right refers to the *I am OK* and *You are Not OK* (I+ U-), Critical or 'get rid of' position, and the top left is the *I am Not OK* and *You are OK* (I-U+), Submissive or 'get away from' position.

Because attitudes underpin feelings and behaviour the other EIP scales can be mapped onto the Attitude Matrix. Someone whose attitude is Critical (I+U-) is more likely to display low Flexibility, low Awareness of Others, be Mistrusting, Over Independent and Aggressive, compared to someone from the Submissive position (I-U+) who is likely to be low on Self Awareness, Personal Power and Goal Directedness, and be Over Trusting, Passive and Over Dependent. (Detailed scale combinations can be found in Chapter 5).

Table 4.5 Links between the Attitude Matrix and the EIP scales

	Low Self Regard	High Self Regard
High Regard for Others	**Submissive position** *I'm Not OK, You're OK (I- U+)* *Get away from ('flight')* EIP scales: *Low Self Awareness* *Low Personal Power* *Low Goal Directedness* *Over Trusting* *Pessimistic* *Emotionally Over Controlled* *Passive* *Dependent*	**Emotionally Intelligent / Ideal position** *I'm OK, You're OK (I+ U+)* *Get on with ('healthy')* EIP scales: *High on all EIP scales*
Low Regard for Others	**Blocked Potential position** *I'm Not OK, You're Not OK (I- U-)* *Get nowhere with ('freeze')* EIP scales: *Low on all EIP scales*	**Critical position** *I'm OK, You're Not OK (I+ U-)* *Get rid of ('fight')* EIP scales: *Low Awareness of Others* *Low Flexibility* *Low Connecting with Others* *Mistrusting* *Over Optimistic* *Emotionally Under Controlled* *Aggressive* *Over Independent*

Note: a description of how the Core Attitudes are linked to each of the scales is given in Chapter 5.1 and Appendix 1.

4.3.1 How to interpret and explore the Attitude Matrix

Self Regard and Regard for Others are in some ways the most difficult scales to measure accurately as they are representing deeper, underlying, often unconscious, attitudes rather than specific observable behaviours. The scores on the EIP may be influenced by how an individual was feeling about themselves at the time of completing the questionnaire, not that they are necessarily in that position permanently. In fact, people can move between positions quite readily in response to their current circumstances and specific environmental factors, such as their current work situation, the state of their personal relationships, how their day has been and how they are feeling at any particular moment. The EIP coach should therefore look to distinguish, through discussion with their client:

- *What is their pervading Core Attitude/Life Position*
- *Where they are on the matrix at that time in their life*
- *How they feel about themselves at that specific current moment in time*

When using the Attitude Matrix during exploration of the EIP, it is important to emphasise that holding a Core Attitude does not mean an individual will always behave in this way. Core Attitudes explain where a person tends to return to and feel most familiar. During a stressful period a person is likely to fall out of the Ideal position and into a more defensive position. How easily this happens will depend on how strong their Self Regard and Regard for Others are. Where these are both strong an individual is likely to spend more time in the Ideal position.

There is an interesting pattern in how a person may move between the Attitude positions from Blocked Potential to Critical to Submissive to Ideal. The least effective position is Blocked Potential (I- U-). One way to help people progress from this position is for them to become slightly more selfish and self-focused; to look after themselves even if this is at the cost of others, so moving them into the Critical position (I+U-). The Critical position can help people feel more energised and able to take control over their circumstances than when being in the Blocked position. The Critical position, by definition is masking a low Self Regard, so a natural development from here is to become aware of this low Self Regard and therefore move into the Submissive position (I- U+). Often when people have finished blaming and criticising others they recognise the futility of this and how their complaining had more to do with their own mood and feelings than about those they were criticising. From the Submissive position an individual is ready to progress to the Ideal position (I+ U+) and accept themselves more fully despite their imperfections.

4.3.2 The defensive positions

Any time a person falls out of the Ideal position, they are falling into a defensive position. A defence is a temporary measure to protect a person from more negative and uncomfortable feelings they may have about their self-concept (reflecting a low Self Regard). Defences or coping mechanisms work by distorting a person's perception of reality to fit with the kind of self-concept that allows them to feel better about themselves, such as pretending that everything is fine when it is not (denial). Because defensive behaviours provide temporary relief to negative feelings (a 'pay-off') they can become insatiable and addictive. The problem is that by distorting reality a person is reducing their Self Awareness which means they are less able to identify and resolve the underlying causes of their defensive behaviour.

Defensiveness is characterised by rigid and inflexible behaviour, for example, a person may feel the need to Be Perfect in everything they do in order to feel OK about themselves, known in TA as a *condition of self-worth*. However, high Self Regard is about having *unconditional* self-acceptance meaning that a person still feels OK about themselves despite not being perfect in what they do. Some of the classic defence mechanisms and conditions of self-worth within each of the Attitude Matrix positions are described below. Note that defences are formed as attitudes, experienced as feelings and expressed as rigid behaviours. Defensive attitudes are usually unconscious attitudes, that a person has formed about themselves and about how to get on in the world. The relationship between defensive attitudes and the EIP scales is shown below.

Table 4.6 Defences linked to the Critical position

(High Self Regard and low Regard for Others)*

Defence	Description (attitude/pay-off)	Most related EIP scales
Blaming	*By blaming others I avoid having to look at what I do not like about myself.*	Defensive blaming reflects low Regard for Others masking low Self Regard.
Anger	*By being angry with others I can dominate them. Being right makes me better than the other person.*	Being angry reflects Aggressive Conflict Handling and low Emotional Control.
Helping/Rescuer	*If I focus on helping others with their problems then I can avoid looking at my own problems. The Helper defence is also described as 'Identification' where the individual transfers 'I don't like me' into 'You don't like you.'*	The Rescuer views others as unable to cope (low Regard for Others). Others may therefore become Over Dependent on them.

Defence	Description (attitude/pay-off)	Most related EIP scales
Be Perfect	*Through experience I have learnt that I am Not OK if I am ever wrong or make a mistake, however small.*	A 'Be Perfect' defence indicates a lack of self-confidence (low Personal Power) being overly self-critical (low Self Regard) and having negative expectations (Pessimistic).
Be Strong	*My upbringing has taught me that I am only OK if I do not have, or at least express, feelings, needs or signs of weakness.*	A 'Be Strong' defence leads to low Self Awareness (of one's feelings), being Emotionally Over Controlled and Over Independent.
Railroad (I win, you lose)	*By bullying, shouting and being aggressive I can railroad others so that I get what I want, at least for now.*	Bullying indicates a low Regard for Others masking low Self Regard. Likely to be Aggressive (Conflict Handling), have low Awareness of Others and low Flexibility.
Get rid of/move against	*If I move against others and get them out of my way they will no longer be a threat to me.*	Feeling threatened by others may lead to being Mistrusting, low Flexibility, Aggressive and Over Independent.
Displacement	*The Critical position is also a form of 'displacement' where the individual transfers 'I don't like me' into 'I don't like you'.*	Displacement reflects low Regard for Others, and will undermine Connecting with Others, Trust and Interdependence.

* Note that the Critical position is masking low Self Regard

Table 4.7 Defences linked to the Submissive position
(Low Self Regard and High Regard for Others)

Defence	Description (attitude/pay-off)	Most related EIP scales
Self-blaming	*The pay-off from criticising myself is that I avoid having others criticise me first. It also gets others to reassure me that I am OK and people will expect less of me.*	Self-blaming indicates low Personal Power and may result in low Goal Directedness and low Emotional Resilience.
Guilt/shame	*I know what I have done is wrong, but horrible people wouldn't feel remorse as I do, so I must be an OK person.*	Guilt occurs when a person behaves in a way that contradicts their values, so is related to Authenticity.
Worrying	*Because I worry about other people and situations I am not selfish and must be a caring person.*	People who worry about but do nothing to change the situation are likely to be low on Personal Power.
Demander	*By repeatedly requesting that others tell me that I am competent, likeable and significant I get others to do for me what I do not do for myself, that is; to like myself.*	Demanding reassurance from others indicates low Self Regard, low Emotional Resilience, low Personal Power, low Goal Directedness and being Over Dependent on others.

Defence	Description (attitude/pay-off)	Most related EIP scales
Please Others	*My experience has taught me that I can only feel OK about myself if I always put others first and keep them happy.*	'Please Others' suggests having low Self Regard with high Regard for Others. This may result in low Self Awareness, low Goal Directedness, low Authenticity, being Over Trusting and Over Dependent.
Hurry Up	*I have learnt through experience that I must not relax or take my time over things if I am to be OK.*	The 'Hurry Up' driver may lead to exhaustion (low Emotional Resilience), unrealistic expectations (poor Balanced Outlook) and a lack of Reflective Learning.
Get away from others	*One way I cope with feelings of inferiority is to move away from others and avoid the risk of being humiliated.*	Avoiding others will reduce Awareness of Others, Connecting with Others, Trust and Interdependence.
Seek harmony (I lose, you win)	*If I am willing to forgo my own interests I will avoid conflict and being criticised by others.*	Seeking Harmony in this way reflects low Self Regard and high Regard for Others which can result in low Goal Directedness, low Authenticity, and poor Conflict Handling (Passive).

Table 4.8 Defences linked to the Blocked Potential position

(Low Self Regard and low Regard for Others)

Defence	Description (attitude/pay-off)	Most related EIP scales
Victim	*Whatever I do is not good enough for others, people have got it in for me and it is therefore not my fault and I am not responsible for my problems.*	The Victim attitude represents low Personal Power and will result in low Emotional Resilience and low Goal Directedness.
Disappointment	*I am a good person (better than other people) and despite trying my best for others, people let me down which is also why I don't succeed.*	Disappointment in others may be caused by Over Trusting people and being Over Optimistic.
Denier	*There are no problems and everything is OK. By ignoring any problems and pretending that everything is OK the Denier does not have to face the painful reality of their own negative feelings.*	The Denier will be distorting reality by being low on Self Awareness, Over Optimistic, Mistrusting, and less inclined to learn from experience (Reflective Learning).
Try Hard (but don't succeed)	*The message I have received during my upbringing was that suffering is good and that I am OK so long as I try hard. It's the trying that counts not the achievement.*	This defence may mean ignoring feelings of discomfort (low Self Awareness) and possible burnout (low Emotional Resilience).

Defence	Description (attitude/pay-off)	Most related EIP scales
Withdrawal or Passive Aggressive (I lose, you lose)	By withdrawing from situations I can avoid conflict without giving in to the other person. There is nothing I or anyone else can do to help me or to change my situation so I will give up trying and stop making any effort.	Passive-aggressive behaviour reflects poor Conflict Handling and will sabotage effective collaboration (Connecting with Others and Interdependence).
Get nowhere with /projection	The Submissive position is also a form of 'Projection', where 'I don't like me' is transferred into 'You don't like me'.	Giving up reflects low Personal Power, low Emotional Resilience, low Goal Directedness, and a Pessimistic attitude. Assuming that others do not like them may reflect a distorted Awareness of Others.

There are several messages a child may receive that tell them what not to do but do not tell them what *to do*. These are termed counter injunctions in TA and can become significant blockers to a person's psychological development, emotional maturity and Emotional Intelligence. Some of these include:

Table 4.9 **Defensive blockers**

('Do not' messages leading to low Self Regard)

Defence	Description (attitude/pay-off)	Most related EIP scales
Don't feel	It is Not OK for me to have or express feelings. For example, a child may be told don't cry, or that they don't feel the way they do.	This will reduce Self Awareness and Emotional Expression.
Don't think	It is Not OK for me to think for myself or make my own decisions. (For example, a child whose ideas are ridiculed, is not given choice or responsibility, is constantly told to be quiet and discouraged from ever daydreaming).	This can reduce a person's Personal Power, Goal Directedness (being too impulsive) and Reflective Learning.
Don't be close	It is Not OK or safe for me to get close to people.	Will reduce Connecting with Others and increase Mistrusting, Emotional Over Control and Over Independence.
Don't be a child	It is Not OK for me to be a child and I am only OK if I behave as an adult.	Reduces spontaneity, fun, and openness (Emotional Expression and Authenticity) and Connecting with Others.
Don't grow up	It is Not OK for me to be an adult and I am only OK if I stay as a child.	Reduces Personal Power and increases Over Dependence.
Don't belong	I do not truly belong or fit in here or anywhere else.	This will undermine relationships (Connecting with Others) and teamwork (Interdependence).

Defence	Description (attitude/pay-off)	Most related EIP scales
Just don't...	*Constantly being told no, not to do anything and to stop. Also being overprotected or stifled as a child.*	May reduce initiative (Personal Power), curiosity (Goal Directedness), creativity (Flexibility) and Emotional Expression.

It should be noted that all defensive behaviours are the manifestation of defensive attitudes and their associated feelings. However, it is not easy to know whether any given behaviour is defensive or not. A person may be critical of others because they feel bad about themselves (defensive) or because they are giving justifiable feedback to someone to help them improve (non-defensive). The key indicators of defensive behaviour are:

- *The behaviour is inappropriate to the situation.*
- *The behaviour is overused.*
- *The person would feel particularly uncomfortable if they did not use this behaviour.*
- *The feelings associated with the behaviour are excessively prolonged (e.g. feeling guilty long after the event).*

For example, a person may like to take charge of events and be in control, but if they find it extremely difficult and uncomfortable not being in charge or to follow others, then this is likely to be a defensive behaviour. The challenge for the individual however, is to become aware of their defensive behaviours, feelings and attitudes. This is often diffi-cult because the purpose of defences is to reduce a person's awareness of their painful feelings and is accompanied by a distorted perception of their behaviour. One way to identify defences is to develop one's Self Awareness and notice their unpleasant feelings and what situations elicit these feelings. Also, to review the other fourteen EIP scale scores that are derived from Self Regard and Regard for Others, which will help the individual to learn how to manage these.

4.3.3 The Attitude Matrix descriptions

The Attitude Matrix is simplified and summarised in the table below and is shown in the EIP reports. The top right hand corner of the matrix is called the Ideal position (I+ U+). The least desirable position, Blocked Potential (I- U-), is towards the bottom left hand corner. People will inevitably spend time in each of the four positions and under sufficient stress will fall out of the Ideal position into one of the other three positions. How easily they do this will depend on how far they are normally from the top right hand corner. The four Core Attitudes are summarised below.

Fig. 4.1 The Attitude Matrix

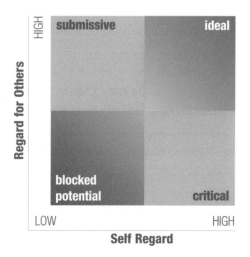

Ideal

The top right quadrant is labelled 'Ideal' and is the most positive position. Scoring high on both Attitude scales is a strong basis for developing personal and interpersonal effectiveness. It indicates a generally positive perception of self and of others which will help in coping effectively with life's demands, being open to self-development and behaving with Emotional Intelligence as measured by the other fourteen EIP scales.

Blocked Potential

The bottom left quadrant is labeled 'Blocked Potential' and is the least emotionally intelligent position. If both Attitude scale scores are low in relation to the comparison group, it indicates that currently, or during times of stress, an individual may have a more negative perception of themselves and of others. They may therefore find it more difficult to cope with life's demands and possibly become critical of themselves and of others. They may currently be feeling stuck and unsure of how to change their feelings, behaviour and circumstances, tending to see more problems than solutions. This is an uncomfortable position to be in, if neither they nor anyone else is of value then they may feel there is little that can be done to improve or change their situation.

Critical

The bottom right quadrant is labelled 'Critical'. If the Self Regard score is higher than the Regard for Others score it suggests that under stress they may tend to become critical and blaming of others. The Critical position links to several aspects of Emotional Intelligence such as being less Aware of Others, less Flexible towards others, Mistrusting,

Aggressive and Over Independent. Note that the Critical position is also a mask for low Self Regard, as blaming others can be a coping strategy to distract a person from considering the negative feelings they have about themselves.

Submissive

The top left quadrant is labelled 'Submissive'. If the Regard for Others score is higher than the Self Regard score, it suggests that under stress an individual may tend to become self-blaming and negative towards themselves. This may manifest in aspects of Emotional Intelligence such as being less confident (low Personal Power), less focused on what they want (low Goal Directedness), Over Dependent, Over Trusting of others and backing down under conflict (Passive).

4.4 The Feeling Matrix descriptions

The second matrix, below, explores the balance between the Feeling scales of Self Awareness and Awareness of Others, and may also be referred to as the 'Engagement' Matrix. These dimensions form the middle layer of the EIP framework. The emotionally intelligent position is to be fully aware and Present, towards the top right hand corner. The least effective position is to be Less Aware, towards the bottom left hand corner.

Fig. 4.2 The Feeling Matrix

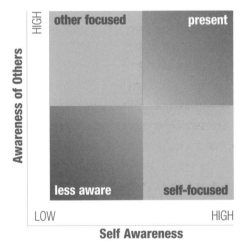

Present

The top right quadrant of the Feeling Matrix is labelled 'Present' and is the most positive combination. When an individual is Present they are in touch with their feelings and the feelings of others. They are aware of their surroundings and the people around them. High Self Awareness and Awareness of Others (when combined with high Self Regard) may reflect a sense of feeling alive and energised by life, so may result in being active and experiencing life to its fullest, such as through learning, self-development and connecting with people.

Less Aware

The bottom left quadrant is labelled 'Less Aware' and is the area requiring most development. People who score low on both Self Awareness and Awareness of Others may not be closely in touch with their own feelings or the feelings of others. If a person does not notice their own feelings, then they have little internal feed-back on what they personally want and about how to manage their own behaviour. Equally, if they do not notice others, then they may have difficulty understanding people, building friendships and socialising. In the long run, they may feel their lives are not fulfilling and feel out of touch with themselves and people around them.

Self Focused

The bottom right quadrant; high Self Awareness and low Awareness of Others is labelled 'Self Focused'. This is essentially when a person focuses more on them-selves than on others and becomes self-absorbed. One of the best ways to improve self-esteem is to connect with people, attend to others needs and not to ruminate on one's own feelings. 'Self Focused' can indicate being more self-contained and not being drawn to or interested in other people. This may be fine if a person chooses to live a solitary existence, but not so good if, like most people, they operate in a social context both in and out of work.

Other Focused

The top left quadrant; low Self Awareness and high Awareness of Others is labelled 'Other Focused'. There can be a tendency for some people to be more attentive to the feelings of others than to what matters to them. In the short term this may be positive for others, however, if people do not look after their own needs and become exhausted or unwell, it can become increasingly difficult for them to help other people. Furthermore, Self Awareness is an important element for developing Awareness of Others, as empathy towards others is experienced as a feeling the individual has within their own body.

4.5 The Behaviour Matrix descriptions

The third matrix shows the balance between the Behaviour scales of Self Management and Relationship Management and may also be referred to as the 'Performance' Matrix. These two parts form the top layer of the EIP framework and are about how people apply themselves to be both personally and interpersonally effective. The emotionally intelligent position is to be Effective; the least desirable position is to be Self Limiting (low on both scales).

Unlike the Attitude and Feeling matrices, which represent specific EIP scales, the Behaviour Matrix represents clusters of the EIP scales. This is because the Behaviour Matrix reflects EI behaviours which include eleven of the EIP scales. The Attitude Matrix on the other hand represents the Core Attitudes (Self Regard and Regard for Others) and the Feeling Matrix represents awareness of feelings (Self Awareness and Awareness of Others).

Self Management relates to most of the EIP linear scales, including Emotional Resilience, Personal Power, Goal Directedness, Flexibility, Authenticity, and to the multi-scale of Balanced Outlook. Relationship Management relates to most of the EIP multi-scales, including Trust, Emotional Expression and Control, Conflict Handling, Interdependence, and to the linear scale of Connecting with Others. In practice all scales will have some relevance to both Self Management and Relationship Management, such as Flexibility (a Self Management scale) may impact on Relationship Management in terms of how willing a person is to adapt to others. (Note that in the EIP reports the linear and multi-scales are shown on separate pages).

Fig. 4.3 The Behaviour Matrix

Effective

The top right quadrant of the Behaviour Matrix, labelled 'Effective', is the most posi-tive combination, where both Behaviour scale scores (Self Management and Relationship Management) are high in relation to the comparison group. It suggests that a person is operating effectively and is capable of balanced leadership, building strong relationships and achieving their goals, whether that is on their own or through working with others. They are likely to be self-motivated, productive, make things happen and remain focused. They are also probably good at understanding others, building rapport, getting the best from others and as a result may do well in roles requiring cooperation and group interaction.

Self Limiting

The lower left quadrant is labelled 'Self Limiting' and is the area requiring most develop-ment. Scoring low on both dimensions presents a fairly negative picture of how a person's Emotional Intelligence manifests in practice. With a Self Limiting profile, an indi-vidual may still hold positive attitudes and be aware of feelings but fail to put this into action in their life. If so, they may need to find ways of being more proactive or learn some key life skills to start employing their hidden potential.

Self Driven

The bottom left quadrant is labelled 'Self Driven'. If Self Management is higher than Relationship Management a person may be more productive and effective at managing their own behaviour and achieving their own goals than doing this through others. Perhaps they like to do things to their own inner high standards and may find building relationships, influencing and working with others more difficult and less motivating. They could improve this by becoming more proactive in their Relationship Management, such as making time for others, acting assertively, being spontaneous, building trust and sharing their feelings with others.

Facilitative

The top left quadrant is labelled 'Facilitative'. When Relationship Management is higher than Self Management this suggests that an individual may enjoy group interaction and joint endeavours, and be effective at engaging others and at building cooperative rela-tionships. However, they may find it more difficult managing their own behaviour to moti-vate themselves and achieve their personal goals. Spending time alone, reflecting on their personal goals, how they are operating and how these align, might prove useful to someone with a Facilitative profile.

86

Although the EIP matrices may seem quite categorical in their interpretation, there are two important considerations users should take into account. Firstly, which of the four quadrants a person's score resides in indicates their typical default position, particularly when under stress. This does not mean they are permanently in this position, as people will spend some of their time in each of the four quadrants. It is the role of the coach to explore how much time they spend in each position, what causes them to fall out of the ideal top right hand quadrant and how they manage to get themselves back there. Secondly, where an individual scores within a quadrant is also relevant. A person who scores in the top right hand corner of the 'Blocked Potential' quadrant is also bordering on the 'Ideal' quadrant. This is therefore reflected by the more precise narrative description in the EIP report.

This chapter has provided an organising structure (in the form of the EIP framework) for understanding the different parts of EI, which include the sixteen EIP scales that are described in the next chapter.

Summary points from Chapter 4

- The different elements of Emotional Intelligence (the theory and the sixteen EIP scales) are integrated and organised by the EIP framework.

- The cornerstone to EI and the EIP framework is Self Regard. Ultimately, all the other EIP scales are there to develop Self Regard; unconditional self-acceptance (or 'usa' for short!).

- The EIP framework separates EI into two elements; Personal Intelligence and Interpersonal Intelligence. Both elements are made up of three levels;
  - *Attitude (Self Regard and Regard for Others)*
  - *Feeling (Self Awareness and Awareness of Others)*
  - *Behaviour (Self Management and Relationship Management)*

- Each level of the EIP framework (Attitude, Feeling and Behaviour) is paired into a 2x2 matrix resulting in four positions or quadrants. The quadrants provide an ideal platform for coaching, by asking the client the following questions:
  - *What percentage of time do they spend in each of the four positions?*
  - *What causes them to fall out of the green position?*
  - *How do they get back into the green position?*

- The Attitude Matrix is the deepest level of the EIP framework which describes the relationship between the Core Attitudes of Self Regard and Regard for Others (the first two EIP scales). Based on TA theory this determines four Life Positions:
  - *Ideal*
  - *Blocked Potential*
  - *Critical*
  - *Submissive*

- Any time a person falls out of the Ideal position they are falling into a defensive position which may be reflected by low scores on any of the other fourteen EIP scales. Defences are formed as attitudes, experienced as feelings and expressed as rigid and inappropriate behaviours.

- The Feeling Matrix combines the middle level of the EIP framework, which describes the relationship between the next two EIP scales of Self Awareness and Awareness of Others. The four positions of the Feeling Matrix are:
  - *Present*
  - *Less Aware*
  - *Self Focused*
  - *Other Focused*

- The Behaviour Matrix combines the top level of the EIP framework, which describes the relationship between the Self Management and Relationship Management scales. The four positions of the Behaviour Matrix are:
  - *Effective*
  - *Self Limiting*
  - *Self Driven*
  - *Facilitative*

- The EIP framework and the three matrices help the user to understand the relationship between Personal and Interpersonal aspects of EI, see higher level patterns between scales, and to connect the three psychological levels of the EIP. This has considerable benefit to the coach in helping them interpret profiles and explore this with the individual (as discussed in Chapter 6).

●　●　●

Chapter Five

Interpreting the EIP Scales

Introduction

This chapter looks at the meaning of each EIP scale and the relationship between them. Interpreting the complete EI Profile of sixteen scales is a skill that can be continually improved upon, for which there are a number of levels. To help the user acquire the knowledge and subjective skills of interpretation, the following eight levels of interpretation are recommended.

Eight levels of interpretation for the EIP scales

1 *Understand the sixteen EIP scale definitions given in Chapter 3.*

2 *Understand the meaning of low, average and high scores for each scale (described below).*

3 *Examine the relationship between pairs of scales (described below).*

4 *Consider the relationship between groups of scales (presented as scenarios in Chapter 5.5).*

5 *Look for overall scale patterns and relationships using the EIP framework and matrices described in Chapter 4.*

6 *For the inquisitive user, they may be interested in the statistical relationship between scales (found in the EIP technical manual).* [1]

7 *For more advanced interpretation of the scales the user may refer to Appendix 1.*

8 *Over time the user will gain much of their deeper understanding of scales through using the EIP with different clients. (A detailed explanation of how to explore the EIP with clients is given in Chapter 6).*

Described below is an interpretation of the EIP scales for low (Decile 1-3), average (Decile 4-7) and high (Decile 8-10) scores. There is also a description of scale combinations. These are listed separately for each scale with an explanation of how the scale may influence and support development for each of the other related scales. Looking at the relationship between pairs of scales in this way is a useful starting point for interpreting scale profiles.

The first set of scales to be examined are the linear scales (scales 1-10 & 16) where high scores represent higher EI. There is no negative interpretation given to high scores on linear scales, such as having too much Self Regard (arrogant) or being too Flexible (changeable). Instead, the user should look for other scales that may be lacking, such as Regard for Others to balance high Self Regard, and Goal Directedness to balance high Flexibility.

The second set of scales to be discussed (scales 11-15) are called multi-scales where middle scores represent higher EI. An example of a multi-scale is Balanced Outlook where people can be too high (Over Optimistic) or too low (Pessimistic) with the ideal being in the middle (Realistically Optimistic). Because the multi-scales consist of three separately scored sub-scales there are many different possible score combinations. For example, a person may score high on Over Optimistic (expecting too much) and high on Pessimistic (feeling disappointed when their expectations are not met). These multi-scale patterns are explained in Chapter 6.1.4.

Each of the EIP scales will now be discussed in turn from 1-16 within their sections on the EIP framework.

5.1 The Attitude scales

The Attitude scales of Self Regard and Regard for Others form the foundation of the EIP framework and therefore strongly influence all aspects of Emotional Intelligence.

Scale 1: Self Regard

Self Regard is the degree to which an individual accepts and values themselves.

Low score	Average score	High score
A tendency to ignore positive feedback and put oneself down.	Accepting of possible development areas without being too self-critical.	Authentic and non-defensive.
Self-confidence easily knocked by feelings of self-doubt and insecurity.	Generally self-confident with a reasonable sense of well-being.	Stays calm and centred, keeping challenges in perspective.
Possible need to continually prove oneself.	May give insufficient praise and recognition to oneself.	Easily flexes personal comfort zones.
May display defensive or rigid behaviour.	May be self-doubting when under pressure.	Strong sense of inner confidence and well-being.
Preoccupation or excessive worry about personal shortcomings.	Occasional worry about personal shortcomings.	Acceptance of weaknesses without being self-critical.

How Self Regard influences other scales:

Self Regard is the primary attitude underpinning EI, representing and influencing all of the EIP scales. Note that these interpretations assume a genuinely high Self Regard, which may be indicated by having a high Regard for Others.

- **Regard for Others:** *There are several links between Self Regard and Regard for Others as they form the Attitude Matrix described in Chapter 4.3. For example, a low Regard for Others and high Self Regard may indicate being more critical and blaming of others (masking low Self Regard).*

- **Self Awareness:** *People with a high Self Regard are more likely to accept and pay attention to all of their feelings (including painful feelings) and therefore be more Self Aware.*

- **Emotional Resilience:** *There is a high correlation between Self Regard and Emotional Resilience; an individual who feels OK about themselves is more likely to cope well with life's problems.*

- **Goal Directedness:** *People with higher Self Regard are likely to pay attention to their own needs, wants and goals.*

- **Flexibility:** *A high Self Regard will help an individual move outside of their comfort zones and therefore be flexible in their learning, behaviour and in how they respond to change.*

- **Personal Power:** *Having higher Self Regard will tend to create greater self-confidence and belief in one's capability (Personal Power). The close relationship between these two scales is explained in Chapter 7.8.*

- **Connecting with Others:** *Being open with others risks making oneself vulnerable which requires a degree of self-belief.*

- **Authenticity:** *A higher level of Self Regard may help a person be true to themself even if this may risk disapproval from others (Authenticity).*

- **Balanced Outlook:** *People with higher Self Regard are more likely to have an Optimistic outlook on things.*

- **Conflict Handling:** *Higher Self Regard will help an individual stand up for themselves and assert their wishes.*

Scales that influence Self Regard include:

- *Regard for Others*
- *Self Awareness*
- *Emotional Resilience*
- *Personal Power*
- *Conflict Handling*
- *Reflective Learning*

Scale 2: **Regard for Others**

Regard for Others is the degree to which a person accepts and values others (as distinct from liking or approving of what they may do).

Low score	Average score	High score
Less tolerant of and less inclined to listen to others' opinions.	Listens to people's concerns and responds to their needs.	Takes time to support and develop people.
Less likely to adapt and respond to people's needs.	Supportive and helpful when choosing to engage with others.	Listens well, pays attention and responds to people's needs.
A tendency to tell rather than ask questions.	Will occasionally use praise and personal encouragement to motivate others.	Will use praise and personal encouragement to motivate people.
Can be judgemental, critical or unsympathetic towards people.	May sometimes be critical or unsympathetic towards people.	Shows empathy, care and understanding towards others.
May frequently doubt other's competence or feel impatient towards people.	Tends to be more task than people focused.	Values people and builds strong relationships.

How Regard for Others influences other scales:

Regard for Others is the core attitude underpinning the interpersonal aspects of EI.

- **Awareness of Others:** *A person is more inclined to listen to others, understand their feelings and be aware of others if they have Regard for Others. They may also be less inclined to judge others and will be more open to seeing their point of view.*

- **Flexibility:** *A higher Regard for Others will help an individual be amenable and flexible towards the needs of others.*

- **Connecting with Others:** *People with higher Regard for Others are more inclined to see the good in others rather than being critical, which will typically help them build closer connections.*

- **Trust and Interdependence:** *People with higher Regard for Others are often more trusting and collaborative, although they should be cautious not to become Over Dependent or Over Trusting of others.*

- **Conflict Handling:** *Having Regard for Others will mean a person is more likely to understand the needs of others and take their opinions into account.*

Scales that influence Regard for Others include:

- *Self Regard*
- *Awareness of Others*
- *Conflict Handling*
- *Interdependence*

5.2 The Feeling scales

The Feeling scales of Self Awareness and Awareness of Others form the middle layer of the EIP framework and therefore strongly influence the upper level scales of Self Management and Relationship Management.

Scale 3: Self Awareness

Self Awareness is the degree to which a person is in touch with their physiology, feelings and intuitions.

Low score	Average score	High score
Less aware of own emotional states causing occasional reaction in others.	Tends to understand own emotional responses to different stressors.	Correctly interprets different emotional states and how they impact on own behaviour.
Limited range of emotional expression when communicating with others.	Displays reactive behaviour when not managing emotions effectively.	Clearly expresses own emotions when communicating with others.
Not fully incorporating intuitive feelings into decision making.	Could develop better use of intuition to support decision making.	Balances logic and intuition when making decisions.
Attempts to ignore, bottle up or compartmentalise emotions.	Sometimes ignore, bottle or compartmentalise emotions.	Understands own emotional responses to different stressors.
Lacks awareness of own values and needs.	Displays reasonable awareness of own values and needs.	Displays accurate awareness of own values and needs.

How Self Awareness influences other scales:

Self Awareness is the cornerstone to developing EI, as feelings influence behaviour and all of the EIP scales.

- **Self Regard:** *Self Awareness helps an individual notice how they feel about themselves and therefore recognise what thoughts, behaviours and circumstances help raise or lower their Self Regard.*

- **Awareness of Others:** *Awareness of Others is achieved partly through* empathy, which is experiencing the feelings of others within oneself (Self Awareness). Self Awareness can therefore help develop Awareness of Others.

- **Emotional Resilience:** Emotional Resilience requires Self Awareness to be bodily aware, notice feelings of anxiety and to learn how to relax.

- **Goal Directedness:** Self Awareness helps a person to know what they want and like and so helps them to identify their goals. Self Awareness also helps a person notice, and therefore manage their impulses that can distract them from achieving their goals.

- **Flexibility:** One reason people become rigid and inflexible is if they feel outside of their comfort zones. Recognising these feelings will help them to stretch their levels of flexibility.

- **Connecting with Others:** In order to be open with one's feelings (one part of Connecting with Others) a person needs to be in touch with how they are feeling (Self Awareness).

- **Trust:** Learning who to trust and when to trust someone is closely related to intuition, which requires an awareness of internal 'gut' feelings.

- **Balanced Outlook:** An aspect of Balanced Outlook involves not being carried away by feelings of excitement or being dragged down by negative feelings, both of which require Self Awareness.

- **Emotional Expression and Control:** By being in touch with their feelings (Self Awareness) people are better able to express and control their feelings as they see fit.

- **Reflective Learning:** Being aware of feelings in the present moment (Self Awareness) is an essential part of Reflective Learning. The more aware a person is of their feelings, the more they have to reflect upon and learn from.

Scales that influence Self Awareness include:

- Self Regard
- Emotional Expression and Control
- Reflective Learning

Scale 4: **Awareness of Others**

Awareness of Others is the degree to which a person is in touch with the feelings of others.

Low score	Average score	High score
May have less interest or curiosity in people.	Generally pays attention to and shows interest in others.	Shows a keen interest in and understanding of other people.
Can be unaware of the impact they have on others.	Reasonable understanding of individual's motivations and needs.	Displays tact, interpersonal sensitivity and empathy.
May find it difficult to empathise.	Sometimes lacks tact, interpersonal sensitivity and empathy.	Pays attention to and shows consideration for people's feelings.
Interpersonal style may be inflexible on occasions.	Not always aware of the impact they have on others.	Displays a flexible interpersonal style.
May form assumptions about others that are inaccurate.	May occasionally form assumptions about others that are inaccurate.	Develops a clear understanding of individual's motivations and needs.

How Awareness of Others influences other scales:

It would be difficult to develop any aspect of interpersonal intelligence without a reasonably well developed Awareness of Others. Reading how others are feeling is a vital attribute for developing the EIP relationship scales.

- **Regard for Others:** *Being aware of how other people are feeling (Awareness of Others) will help a person develop understanding and consideration towards others (Regard for Others).*

- **Flexibility:** *Being aware of individual differences (Awareness of Others) will help an individual adapt appropriately to people.*

- **Connecting with Others:** *Having Awareness of Others enables closer connections with others to be built.*

- **Trust:** *Knowing who to trust, when and by how much, requires an Awareness of Other's motivations and intentions.*

- **Conflict Handling:** *Being aware of the feelings of others will help an individual understand the needs of others, how to overcome conflict and find mutual agreement.*

Scales that influence Awareness of Others include:

- *Regard for Others*
- *Self Awareness*
- *Authenticity*
- *Connecting with Others*
- *Interdependence*
- *Reflective Learning*

5.3 Behaviour: the Self Management scales

Self Management is about how effectively people manage themselves to achieve their desired outcomes. There are six Self Management scales ordered according to their correlation with Self Regard, the foundation to EI, with Emotional Resilience being the first scale.

Scale 5: Emotional Resilience

Emotional Resilience is the degree to which an individual is able to pick themselves up and bounce back when things go badly for them.

Low score	Average score	High score
Tendency to exaggerate problems.	Generally positive about coping with situations.	Effectively manages energy levels during stress and anxiety.
Becomes easily despondent or takes things to heart.	Usually view mistakes as learning opportunities.	Takes a balanced view about what can be controlled, keep problems in perspective.
Takes a long time to bounce back from disappointments.	May become despondent with repeated setbacks.	Sees mistakes as learning opportunities and bounces back quickly from disappointments.
Tendency to ruminate on issues or be unforgiving.	Sometimes exaggerate problems.	Robust capacity to cope with setbacks.
Strong negative feelings such as anxiety or stress.	Can take a while to bounce back from disappointments.	Remains calm in a crisis and thinks through problems rationally.

How Emotional Resilience influences other scales:

If people do not cope well with pressure, stress and disappointment, this is likely to interfere with their capacity to think clearly, problem solve and therefore develop other EIP scales.

- **Self Regard:** *Emotional Resilience is closely correlated with and helps maintain Self Regard, as opposed to ruminating over problems and bringing oneself down.*

- **Personal Power:** *People are more likely to believe that they can determine their future (Personal Power) if they feel able to cope with the challenges they may face (Emotional Resilience).*

- **Goal Directedness:** *Higher Emotional Resilience will help a person to keep their focus and not be easily distracted from their goals when times get tough.*

- **Flexibility:** *Under stress people naturally become more rigid and inflexible. Being able to manage stress effectively (Emotional Resilience) will help a person to remain flexible in choosing how to behave when under pressure.*

- **Balanced Outlook:** *People are more likely to retain a positive outlook on the future (Balanced Outlook) if they feel able to cope with challenges that lay ahead (Emotional Resilience).*

Scales that influence Emotional Resilience include:

- *Self Regard*
- *Self Awareness*
- *Flexibility*
- *Connecting with Others*
- *Balanced Outlook*
- *Reflective Learning*

Scale 6: Personal Power

Personal Power is the degree to which a person believes that they are in charge of and take sole responsibility for their outcomes.

Low score	Average score	High score
Less likely to seek out opportunities for control and more responsibility.	Takes reasonable control and accountability for own decisions and actions.	Strong sense of control or influence over circumstances.
Some dependency on others to make decisions or take action.	Usually self-assured and knows how to get the result wanted.	Sees self as responsible for taking actions and accepts accountability for outcomes.
Can feel disempowered and frustrated by perceived constraints.	May seek out some opportunities for wider responsibility.	Identifies clear options and exercises high levels of personal choice.
May externalise responsibility e.g. not taking accountability for actions.	May lack confidence to influence certain situations.	Feels empowered and self-determined.
Sometimes sees self as a victim of circumstance or fate.	Can feel disempowered and frustrated by perceived constraints.	Quickly identifies scope of influence within most situations.

How Personal Power influences other scales:

Many of the EIP scales will be more easily developed if the person has confidence in their ability and takes responsibility for their personal development.

- **Self Regard:** *Personal Power is associated with higher self-confidence, which is a useful lever for raising Self Regard.*

- **Goal Directedness:** *Someone with Personal Power is more likely to have the confidence to set and work towards achieving their goals.*

- **Balanced Outlook:** *Being self-responsible (Personal Power) can lead a person to being more optimistic than pessimistic about their capacity to create a positive future.*

- **Interdependence:** *Personal Power will help an individual to be more self-determined rather than Over Dependent on others.*

- **Conflict Handling:** *Someone with Personal Power is more likely to act assertively by taking action.*

Scales that influence Personal Power include:

- *Self Regard*
- *Emotional Resilience*
- *Authenticity*
- *Balanced Outlook*
- *Conflict Handling*
- *Interdependence*

Scale 7: Goal Directedness

Goal Directedness is the degree to which a person's behaviour is aligned to their long-term goals.

Low score	Average score	High score
May seek new stimulation and lack focus on achieving personal goals.	Clear on most personal wants and goals.	Clear focus on achieving personal development goals.
Less aware of own wants and goals.	Engages in some long-term thinking and future planning.	Can maintain focus and not be easily distracted.
Can be impulsive, easily distracted and lack sustained concentration.	Can sometimes be distracted, impulsive and lack concentration.	Knows what gives them personal satisfaction and motivation.
May overly focus on achieving the goals of others.	At times may overly focus on achieving the goals of others.	Clear on personal wants and goals.
May lack long-term thinking and future planning.	May lose sight of broader aims and purpose when under pressure.	Engages in long-term thinking and future planning.

How Goal Directedness influences other scales:

Being Goal Directed will help a person know what they want to achieve and to set objectives in developing any of the EIP scales.

- **Self Regard:** *One of the factors that contributes to a person's Self Regard and happiness is knowing how to get what they want, which is a part of Goal Directedness.*

- **Flexibility:** *Flexibility is best balanced with Goal Directedness. Flexibility without Goal Directedness may lead to constant change, inconsistency and little clear sense of purpose.*

- **Authenticity:** *Higher Goal Directedness helps a person to be more consistent, reliable and dependable in their behaviour, which are also aspects of Authenticity.*

- **Emotional Expression and Control:** *Focusing on the longer term outcomes of what a person wants to achieve (Goal Directedness) can help them to develop Emotional Control and reduce impulsive behaviour.*

- **Conflict Handling:** *If a person knows what they want to achieve (Goal Directedness), they are more likely to be clear and assertive in asking for it.*

Scales that influence Goal Directedness include:

- *Self Awareness*
- *Emotional Resilience*
- *Personal Power*
- *Flexibility*
- *Authenticity*
- *Balanced Outlook*
- *Interdependence*
- *Reflective Learning*

Scale 8: Flexibility

Flexibility is the degree to which a person feels free to adapt their thinking and their behaviour to changing situations.

Low score	Average score	High score
May be slower to change or adapt personal ways of working.	Usually willing to explore options and experiment.	Able to quickly change or adapt personal ways of working.
Stays within own comfort zone or avoids new ways of doing things.	Able to change or adapt personal ways of working when required.	Willing to move outside of comfort zones and try new ways of doing things.

Low score	Average score	High score
Slow to innovate or embrace new ideas.	May be slower to innovate or embrace new ideas.	Open to new ideas and learning experiences.
Sticks to own preferences rather than situational requirements.	Will sometimes stick to own preferences rather than situational requirements.	Willing to explore options and experiment.
Less willing to adapt and accommodate to the needs of others.	May be less flexible and stay within own comfort zones when under pressure.	Willing to adapt and accommodate the needs of others.

How Flexibility influences other scales:

Flexibility will support self-development as people will be willing to move outside of their comfort zones and learn more rapidly. It will also support Relationship Management as people will be more willing to adapt to others.

- **Emotional Resilience:** *Being flexible by trying different strategies for coping with problems can help in coping with adversity, improving Emotional Resilience.*

- **Goal Directedness:** *Goal Directedness is best balanced with Flexibility. Goal Directedness without Flexibility may lead to rigid, driven and uncompromising behaviour.*

- **Conflict Handling:** *Adapting to others (Flexibility) will help find compromise and reduce unproductive levels of conflict.*

- **Interdependence:** *Being flexible towards others will allow a person to be more accommodating and collaborative.*

Scales that influence Flexibility include:

- *Self Regard*
- *Regard for Others*
- *Self Awareness*
- *Awareness of Others*
- *Emotional Resilience*
- *Goal Directedness*
- *Authenticity*
- *Interdependence*

Scale 9: Connecting with Others

Connecting with Others is the extent and the ease with which an individual makes significant connections with other people.

Low score	Average score	High score
May lack social confidence in some situations.	Fairly confident and comfortable engaging with people.	Confident and comfortable engaging with people.
Could invest more time into building relationships.	Invests some time in building relationships.	Invests time and energy into building and maintaining relationships.
Can appear guarded, closed or slightly detached.	Generally prepared to acknowledge and express feelings to others.	Open with people, being prepared to acknowledge feelings and express vulnerabilities.
May focus more on tasks than people.	At times may appear guarded, closed or slightly detached.	Listens to people and show appreciation toward them.
Takes time to form connections and engage with people.	May form close trusting relationships with a select few individuals.	Quickly forms close connections and trusting relationships.

How Connecting with Others influences other scales:

Connecting with Others is fundamental to building and maintaining relationships and therefore has an influence on all of the interpersonal scales.

- **Awareness of Others:** *Connecting with people will help a person to become more aware of others' needs, wants and feelings.*

- **Emotional Resilience:** *An important aspect of coping with adversity (Emotional Resilience) is having friends to talk to and connect with.*

- **Trust:** *Making connections with people is a vital ingredient towards building Trust.*

- **Emotional Expression:** *If a person struggles to express their feelings, then they may find it easier to do so having built closer connections with others.*

Scales that influence Connecting with Others include:

- *Self Regard*
- *Regard for Others*
- *Self Awareness*
- *Awareness of Others*
- *Authenticity*
- *Emotional Expression and Control*
- *Trust*
- *Interdependence*

Scale 10: Authenticity

Authenticity is the degree to which an individual invites the trust of others by being principled, reliable, consistent and known.

Low score	Average score	High score
Inconsistent, difficult to know or hard to read.	Usually reliable and can be depended upon.	Genuine, straightforward and easy to get to know.
Unclear about or not living in accordance with own principles and values.	Have reasonable integrity with some guiding values and principles.	Clear about own principles or values and acts in accordance with them.
Unpredictable and unreliable.	May change direction too readily in an attempt to meet others expectations.	Predictable, consistent and reliable.
Breaks promises and agrees to things that they do not do.	Some people may find them difficult to know or hard to read.	Displays integrity and behaves the same when on own as when observed by others.
Continually changes direction in an attempt to meet others' expectations.	May sometimes over-commit on what they can deliver.	Only commits to what can be delivered.

How Authenticity influences other scales:

Authenticity means a person is likely to be consistent with people which will support the relationship scales. They are also less likely to swing from one extreme to the other on the multi-scales.

- **Self Regard:** *Having integrity and being true to oneself is likely to help build a person's sense of self-worth and Self Regard.*

- **Emotional Resilience:** *Having inner principles is likely to help a person cope with setbacks and difficulties in life.*

- **Personal Power & Goal Directedness:** *Having inner guiding principles (Authenticity) means a person is more likely to be internally driven (Personal Power) and therefore less easily distracted from achieving their goals (Goal Directedness).*

- **Goal Directedness:** *Once an individual commits to making a change or to pursuing a goal, then they are more likely to see it through to the end and integrate this into their lifestyle if they have more Authenticity.*

- **Flexibility:** *Having principles should not be confused with rigidity. Authenticity is about doing what one believes to be right, which may mean moving outside of one's comfort zones (Flexibility).*

- **Connecting with Others:** *Being open with others will make it easier for people to develop trust in them, an important part of Authenticity.*

- **Emotional Expression and Control:** *Authenticity is about being sincere, which includes expressing and sharing one's feelings.*

104

Scales that influence Authenticity include:

- *Self Regard*
- *Goal Directedness*
- *Connecting with Others*
- *Emotional Expression and Control*
- *Conflict Handling*

5.4 Behaviour: the Relationship Management scales

Relationship Management is about how people manage their relationships to be interpersonally effective. These scales are scored differently from the linear scales as the most emotionally intelligent score is in the middle. A high score represents 'too much' of this scale and a low score represents 'too little' on this scale. Low, Average and High scores therefore have specific labels, each with its own separate sub-scale.

Scale 11: Trust

Trust is the tendency for a person to trust others. The key is not to be Over Trusting or be Mistrusting, but to get the right balance of Carefully Trusting.

Mistrusting	Carefully Trusting	Over Trusting
Reluctant to delegate and take too much work on personally.	Delegates responsibility appropriately.	Readily places belief in others abilities.
Questioning of people's motives.	Has a realistic expectation of other people's abilities.	May be taken advantage of or be let down by others.
Keeps people at a distance.	Accepting of others and will give them the benefit of the doubt where appropriate.	Accepting of people and tends to see the best in them.
Manages people's work very closely.	Monitors others progress in a supportive manner.	Prefers to leave others to decide how to deliver work.
May lack confidence in people's ability to complete tasks.	Will take action early if people are not delivering.	May avoid or feel uncomfortable challenging others.

How Trust influences other scales:

Trust is often a prerequisite for developing most other EIP Interpersonal scales and is developed largely through being authentic and consistent with people (see scale 10: Authenticity).

- **Connecting with Others:** *A lack of Trust can often get in the way of people being willing to open up and therefore connect with others.*

- **Balanced Outlook:** *Being able to know when to Trust others carefully may help avoid being let down by people, which often leads to feelings of disappointment and pessimism.*

- **Conflict Handling:** *Trusting others appropriately may help in negotiation (Conflict Handling), such as knowing when to trust a person and when to be more cautious.*

- **Interdependence:** *Trusting others appropriately may lead to greater collaboration, while Over Trusting can lead to Over Dependence and Mistrusting can lead to Over Independence.*

Scales that influence Trust include:

- *Regard for Others*
- *Self Awareness*
- *Awareness of Others*
- *Connecting with Others*
- *Authenticity*
- *Balanced Outlook*
- *Interdependence*

Scale 12: Balanced Outlook

Balanced Outlook is the degree to which an individual balances optimism with realism.

Pessimistic	Realistically Optimistic	Over Optimistic
Tendency to identify the negative aspects of events.	Demonstrates sound judgment and decision making.	Tendency to see all events very positively.
May generalise or exaggerate difficulties.	Keeps problems and difficulties in perspective.	May overlook, dismiss or ignore problems.
Focuses on identifying risks and problems.	Sets stretching but achievable goals and expectations.	Displays a tendency to take risks.
Tendency to use critical, negative or discouraging language.	Accurately assesses if ideas will work in practice.	Expresses initial enthusiasm and encouragement towards others.
May express less enthusiasm and encouragement to others.	Inspires confidence in others.	A tendency to make overly optimistic assumptions.

How Balanced Outlook influences other scales:

Having a Realistically Optimistic outlook will create a generally more positive orientation in how the individual manages their own behaviour and their relationships across all aspects of EI. Avoiding over optimism will help prevent disappointment and feelings of pessimism.

106

- **Emotional Resilience:** *Holding a positive outlook will help a person to cope with life's challenges.*

- **Personal Power:** *Having positive expectations of the future will help a person achieve what they set out to do (Personal Power).*

- **Goal Directedness:** *Being realistic and practical will support a person in setting achievable development goals.*

- **Trust:** *Being realistic can help a person avoid Over Trusting others.*

- **Reflective Learning:** *Being realistic will enable an individual to learn from past experience without being blindly Over Optimistic or unduly Pessimistic.*

Scales that influence Balanced Outlook include:

- *Self Regard*
- *Self Awareness*
- *Emotional Resilience*
- *Personal Power*
- *Trust*

Scale 13: Emotional Expression and Control

Emotional Expression and Control is the degree to which an individual achieves appropriate balance in the expression and control of their emotions.

Under Controlled	Free and in Charge	Over Controlled
Demonstrates less self-control over managing own emotions.	Demonstrates reasonable levels of emotional self-control.	May supress and 'bottle-up' their feelings.
May overreact, possibly upsetting or intimidating others.	Regularly uses emotions to motivate and inspire others, such as enthusiasm and appreciation.	Attempts to hide own feelings from others.
Strong emotions may interfere with their capacity to think clearly and problem solve.	Is comfortable when others display emotion.	May feel uncomfortable when others display emotion.
Emotions may overwhelm their behaviour.	Displays emotional maturity, does not overreact and expresses their emotions well.	Appears socially cautious, distant, very logical or business-like.
May be easily provoked or quick to anger.	Resolves differences with people quickly.	Refrains from overt expressions of enthusiasm or passion.

How Emotional Expression and Control influences other scales:

Emotional expression is mostly determined by what is going on inside for a person (their thoughts and feelings) but manifests externally and therefore influences many aspects of their relationships.

- **Self Awareness:** *Verbalising feelings can help a person to become more aware of and understand their feeling states.*

- **Connecting with Others:** *Being able to express oneself and one's emotions will help in building connections with people.*

- **Authenticity:** *By managing and controlling the expression of their emotions, others will feel they are more consistent and predictable, and invite their trust.*

- **Conflict Handling:** *Expressing oneself in an appropriate manner will help a person to be assertive rather than aggressive or passive.*

Scales that influence Emotional Expression and Control include:

- *Self Awareness*
- *Goal Directedness*
- *Connecting with Others*
- *Authenticity*
- *Conflict Handling*

Scale 14: Conflict Handling

Conflict Handling is how well conflict is handled; how assertive a person is.

Passive	Assertive	Aggressive
Less inclined to assert own wishes or opinions.	Comfortable communicating and expressing own needs.	Tendency to dominate others or take control.
Avoids or finds giving performance feedback uncomfortable.	Seeks to understand others needs and takes them into consideration.	Less inclined to listen or take into consideration the needs of others.
Capitulates easily or overly accommodating.	Deals with poor performance or confrontation in an assertive and respectful manner.	Tackles difficult conversations in a confrontational or hostile manner.
Does not fully express own needs or puts them second to the needs of others.	Less inclined to express anger.	Resists compromise, even when appropriate.
Avoids conflict and finds disagreement uncomfortable.	Comfortable with compromise and negotiating win-win outcomes.	Relies on a directive style of management and may be seen as 'bossy'.

How Conflict Handling influences other scales:

Conflict Handling is a good scale for illustrating some of the main aspects of EI such as having Regard for Others and managing one's emotions. When people are Aggressive or Passive it can have negative consequences on their relationships or getting their needs met.

- **Self Regard and Regard for Others:** *Assertive behaviour is a good demonstration of balancing one's own interests with the interests of others.*

- **Personal Power:** *By being assertive, a person will be better at making happen what they want to happen.*

- **Authenticity:** *Being consistent and calm in how conflict is managed, rather than aggressive or passive, will gain the trust of others (Authenticity).*

- **Emotional Expression and Control:** *If a person is effective at handling conflict these skills should support them in managing how they express their emotions.*

- **Interdependence:** *Minimising aggressive conflict will help to create more harmonious and productive relationships (Interdependence).*

Scales that influence Conflict Handling include:

- *Self Regard*
- *Regard for Others*
- *Awareness of Others*
- *Goal Directedness*
- *Flexibility*
- *Trust*
- *Emotional Expression and Control*
- *Interdependence*

Scale 15: Interdependence

Interdependence is how well an individual manages to balance taking themselves and others into account.

Dependent	Interdependent	Over Independent
May seek regular reassurance, guidance or approval from others.	Values others contributions and fully considers their perspectives.	Comfortable making own decisions and relying on self.
May be easily influenced by others opinions.	Works effectively as part of a team. Comfortable making own decisions and relying on self.	May not consult or consider others' perspectives fully. May be seen as a reluctant team player and as individualistic.
Finds it difficult or uncomfortable to make decisions on own.	Takes responsibility and acts decisively.	May take on too much responsibility.
Dislikes working on own. Less inclined to stretch comfort zones or take risks without support.	Consults and seeks advice when necessary.	Strong preference to work independently.

How Interdependence influences other scales:

Collaboration and teamwork is an important element to building relationships, but it is equally important to be able to work independently when required.

- **Regard for Others:** *Including others in one's decision making and actions (Interdependence) demonstrates Regard for Others.*

- **Awareness of Others:** *Collaborating with others will help in understanding others and what matters to them (Awareness of Others).*

- **Personal Power:** *Not being Over Dependent upon others and being willing to make independent decisions will demonstrate and build Personal Power.*

- **Goal Directedness:** *Being able to work and act independently is likely to help a person remain focused and not be distracted from their goals.*

- **Flexibility:** *Being able to adapt between working with others and working alone shows Flexibility.*

- **Connecting with Others:** *Interdependence is an important element for Connecting with Others.*

- **Trust:** *Working with others or in a team is likely to build Trust.*

- **Conflict Handling:** *Not being Over Dependent on others will help develop Assertiveness.*

Scales that influence Interdependence include:

- *Regard for Others*
- *Personal Power*
- *Flexibility*
- *Trust*
- *Conflict Handling*

Scale 16: Reflective Learning

Reflective Learning is the degree to which Emotional Intelligence is enhanced by the individual reflecting on what they and others feel, think and do, noticing the outcomes these produce, and altering their patterns accordingly.

Low score	Average score	High score
May not know what to develop or how.	Aware of what to develop and how.	Clear on and takes responsibility for personal development.

Low score	Average score	High score
Relies on current or narrow skill set.	Open to developing or broadening their skill set.	Seeks opportunities to develop and broaden their skill set.
Slow to adjust or adapt to changing circumstances.	Reasonably adaptive to changing circumstances.	Adjusts and adapts to changing circumstances.
May not seek or listen to constructive feedback.	Receptive to constructive feedback.	Seeks and is receptive to constructive feedback.
May believe in development but claim to be 'too busy'.	Recognises the benefits of personal development.	Plans and actively organises their personal development.

How Reflective Learning influences other scales:

Reflective Learning is a scale specifically for developing EI and all of the EIP scales. Practicing Reflective Learning is therefore an essential part of personal and interpersonal development.

- **Self Regard:** *Reflective Learning will help an individual identify what it is that erodes or develops self-esteem.*

- **Self Awareness:** *Reflecting on personal learning will in itself involve reflecting on moments of awareness and therefore help develop cognitive Self Knowledge (described in Chapter 4. 2.1) and emotional Self Awareness.*

- **Awareness of Others:** *Reflecting on how others feel and respond to the individual's behaviour is core to enhancing their Awareness of Others.*

- **Emotional Resilience:** *Reflective Learning will help an individual to learn from experience and how to cope with adversity.*

- **Goal Directedness:** *Incorporating past experience into deciding on future actions is fundamental to a person knowing what they want (Goal Directedness).*

- **Authenticity:** *In order to be authentic a person must know their values and guiding principles, and review whether they are acting in accordance with these (Reflective Learning).*

Scales that influence Reflective Learning include:

- *Self Awareness*
- *Balanced Outlook*

5.5 Interpreting scale patterns

The scale descriptions given above explain the relationship between pairs of scales which is a useful starting point when interpreting scales. However, when interpreting a profile it is usually necessary to consider the relationship between several scales together. With sixteen EIP scales there are too many combinations and permutations to provide a list of all possible interpretations. One way to look at scale patterns is by using the EIP framework and the Matrix reports, as described in Chapter 4.

Another method for interpreting several scales together is to consider the profile in relation to a specific matter or issue that the client wishes to address. This will make the search for patterns more manageable and relevant to the client's needs. The ten scenarios given below explain scales that are possible causes of the issue and scales that will support the individual's development by addressing the causes.

Scenario One

An individual is having difficulty standing up to their boss.

Possible causes may include:

- **Conflict Handling:** *The most relevant scale may be Conflict Handling and checking whether they are too Passive and lack Assertiveness.*

- **Self Regard:** *Underlying this may be a low Self Regard and high Regard for Others (Submissive on the Attitude Matrix).*

- **Self Awareness:** *Sometimes people lack assertiveness because they don't pay attention to their own needs or wants.*

- **Goal Directedness:** *They may not have specific goals or have expressed their intentions clearly to their boss.*

- **Emotional Over Control:** *Perhaps they also have difficulty expressing themselves and bottle up their feelings.*

Scales that may support their development

- **Self Awareness and Emotional Expression:** *Helping the individual to develop awareness of what they want and rehearsing how to express themselves will help to raise their Self Regard and Assertiveness.*

- **Awareness of Others:** *Are they aware of what their boss is feeling about them and what their boss wants from them?*

- **Trust:** *Have they gained the Trust of their boss?*

- **Connecting with Others:** *Have they invested time in building a personal connection with their boss?*

Scenario Two

An individual is not coping with the pressure of their work.

Possible causes may include:

- **Emotional Resilience:** *The immediate scale to consider here is Emotional Resilience as they would probably benefit from developing their coping skills.*

- **Self Regard:** *Underlying this may be a lower Self Regard indicating a longer-term and more pervasive issue affecting their wider self-esteem.*

- **Balanced Outlook:** *Also look at their Balanced Outlook, to see if they tend to assume the worst and exaggerate or generalise problems.*

Scales that may support their development

- **Conflict Handling:** *It would be useful to explore what causes them to feel under pressure. If they are not managing their workload they may consider developing their Assertiveness by learning to push back and delegate work.*

- **Goal Directedness:** *They could develop their Goal Directedness so as to focus on what is most important to them and prioritise this.*

- **Connecting with Others and Interdependence:** *If they need more support from others then they could develop their Connecting with Others and their Interdependence.*

- **Personal Power:** *A common cause of dissatisfaction and stress is not feeling in control. Helping them to recognise that they have choices in their life and reminding them of their strengths will empower them.*

- **Self Awareness:** *Help them to notice the signs of stress early such as mild worry, or feelings of uncertainty, so that they can deal with them sooner before they become less manageable.*

Scenario Three

A newly appointed leader is failing to motivate their team.

Possible causes may include:

- **Interdependence:** *Several scales may be worth looking at here. Are they working closely enough with their team?*

- **Connecting with Others:** *Are they building close working relationships with individuals?*

- **Trust:** *Consider their leadership style; do they micro manage (Mistrusting) or leave people with little direction on what to do (Over Trusting)?*

Scales that may support their development:

- **Personal Power and Goal Directedness:** *Do they display confidence and conviction to others?*

- **Authenticity:** *As a leader are they seen as consistent, fair and dependable by their team?*

- **Regard for Others:** *Importantly, do they believe in, appreciate and value their team members as individuals?*

Scenario Four

An individual upsets their colleagues and is resistant to change.

Possible causes may include:

- **Regard for Others:** *It depends on how they have upset their colleagues; are they a bully and arrogant (high Self Regard and low Regard for Others)?*

- **Awareness of Others:** *Are they insensitive to others?*

- **Connecting with Others and Interdependence:** *Do they lack interpersonal skills?*

- **Emotional Under Control and Aggressive:** *Do they suffer from sudden emotional outbursts and anger?*

- **Goal Directedness and Flexibility:** *Upsetting colleagues combined with their resistance to change may indicate that they are highly driven but inflexible (high Goal Directedness and low Flexibility).*

Scales that may support their development:

- **The above scales:** *Once they have identified the cause, developing the appropriate scales above will help.*

- **Awareness of Others:** *They may benefit from becoming more aware of how their own behaviour impacts on others.*

- **Reflective Learning:** *Also, taking time to reflect on their actions and consider how they could behave differently.*

Scenario Five

A middle aged individual is feeling demotivated and unfulfilled by their work.

Possible causes may include:

- **Self Regard and Self Awareness:** *People often attend coaching who have invested greatly in their family and their work but in doing so haven't paid sufficient attention to what they also want for themselves (low Self Regard, high Regard for Others and low Self Awareness).*

- **Goal Directedness:** *Maybe they get too easily distracted from achieving their own goals.*

- **Pessimism:** *Perhaps they have lost their sense of optimism and excitement about the future.*

Scales that may support their development:

- **Reflective Learning:** *Help them to reflect on their past, present and future.*

- **Self Awareness:** *Identify what makes them feel happy, motivated and excited.*

- **Flexibility:** *Encourage them to look at their options and be creative.*

- **Goal Directedness and Balanced Outlook:** *Set realistic goals and objectives for their future.*

- **Personal Power, Emotional Resilience and Connecting with Others:** *They may also need some support in building their confidence to make what may be quite significant life changes.*

Scenario Six

An individual who is highly productive is let down by being unreliable and inconsistent at work.

Possible causes may include:

- **Goal Directedness:** *It is not unusual that a person's strength can also be their 'Achilles' heel'. If someone is drawn outwardly to pursue ideas and possibilities they are less likely to focus on details and completion. Being unreliable and inconsistent is the hallmark of the scales below.*

- **Goal Directedness (low):** *They may be easily distracted and have poor impulse control.*

- **Authenticity:** *They may want to please others so make promises they are* *unable to complete. They may also be unpredictable and changeable.*

- **Over Optimistic:** *They may be unreliable due to having unrealistic expectations that don't get achieved.*

Scales that may support their development:

- **Self Awareness:** *The skill is not to curb their creativity but to help them to become more structured, realistic and focused when appropriate to be so. This may come from improving their Self Awareness and building the scales listed above.*

- **Flexibility:** *Ironically, they may also need to develop their capacity to change as being constantly unreliable and inconsistent is an unhelpful and rigid habit that indicates low Flexibility.*

Scenario Seven

An individual has difficultly managing their emotions and has occasional aggressive outbursts.

Possible causes may include:

- **Emotional Expression & Control and Conflict Handling:** *Learning to separate feelings from behaviour and choosing how to express feelings is a basic life skill developed as a child. One reason people have aggressive outbursts is because they ignore or try to repress their feelings. Rather than disappearing, emotions will build up eventually becoming too powerful to contain. This is indicated in the EIP by the 'rebound' profiles, such as being high on both Passive and Aggressive or being high on both Emotional Over Control and Emotional Under Control.*

- **Regard for Others:** *Aggressive behaviour may also suggest an underlying low Regard for Others masking a low Self Regard.*

- **Emotional Resilience and Personal Power:** *Being emotionally under controlled may also be the result of high anxiety (low Emotional Resilience) and a fear of not being able to cope (low Personal Power).*

Scales that may support their development:

- **Self Awareness:** *Rather than encouraging people to control their emotions more and hold in their feelings, they may benefit from learning how to notice them sooner before the feelings grow, by developing their Self Awareness.*

- **Emotional Expression and Assertiveness:** *By reducing their Emotional Over Control and Passivity they will, as a consequence, also reduce the rebound effect from this of Emotional Under Control and Aggressiveness.*

Scenario Eight

An individual has experienced a sudden drop in performance and is feeling despondent.

Possible causes may include:

- **Self Regard:** *Where there is a sudden change in a person's behaviour it is useful to find out how they were previous to this and what has happened to cause their drop in performance. It is likely to be reflected in a perceived low Self Regard and possible low Regard for Others ('Blocked Potential' on the Attitude Matrix).*

- **Balanced Outlook:** *They may have created a 'negative loop' where a drop in performance creates despondency (pessimism) and despondency creates a drop in performance.*

- **Personal Power:** *Performance is often related to feelings of control and competence. Look for any aspect in their life that may have lowered their Personal Power such as negative feedback, less autonomy and stress at work.*

Scales that may support their development:

- **Emotional Resilience:** *It may help them to increase their Emotional Resilience and focus on their inner resources, to minimise a downwards decline.*

- **Self Awareness:** *An understanding of what motivates them will provide them a more positive focus.*

- **Goal Directedness:** *Focusing on solutions (Goal Directedness) could improve their performance and feelings of optimism.*

- **Personal Power:** *Recognising their strengths and what they can do may increase their feelings of control.*

Scenario Nine

An individual was surprised to receive negative 360 feedback from their colleagues about being difficult to get along with.

Possible causes may include:

- **Awareness of Others:** *If the feedback is surprising to the individual it may* indicate a lower Awareness of Others. This may suggest that they do not listen sufficiently to others or notice their own impact on others.

- **Regard for Others:** *Being difficult to get along with could be due to a host of different reasons, such as not showing others sufficient respect.*

- **Flexibility:** *They may be too rigid and uncompromising.*

- **Trust:** *Any of the above behaviours can break down Trust.*

- **Conflict Handling:** *Low Trust can lead to conflict.*

- **Interdependence:** *Conflict and Mistrust can interfere with effective teamwork.*

Scales that may support their development:

- **Self Regard:** *Negative 360 feedback can be damaging to a person's self-esteem. It is important they get specific feedback so that they can verify its accuracy and also decide if it is something they wish to develop in themselves.*

- **Reflective Learning:** *Being aware of this feedback can help them to improve their relationships by seeking more specific feedback from others.*

- **Connecting with Others:** *They could also invest time in repairing and maintaining their relationships.*

Scenario Ten

An individual scores high on most aspects of the EIP and gets consistently positive feedback from others. They are unsure what they can develop.

Possible causes may include:

- **Self Awareness and Reflective Learning:** *If a client is unsure as to what they can develop they may benefit from heightening their Self Awareness and spending more time reflecting on their experiences.*

- **Balanced Outlook:** *They may also be Over Optimistic and not notice potential problems or miss opportunities for their own development.*

- **Self Regard and Regard for Others:** *Check also their Attitude is not coming from the Critical position, 'I am OK, others are Not OK' which may suggest they have an inaccurate self-perception.*

- **Self Awareness and Flexibility:** *Even when all scores are high there will still be room for further improvement. If they scored a '9' ask them to imagine what a 'ten' would look like. If they responded 'agree' to any positive items ask them why they didn't respond with 'strongly agree'. Notice if they spend time justifying themselves; which may indicate they are less open to exploring how they can change (Flexibility) or to their deeper level feelings (Self Awareness).*

- **Goal Directedness:** *Personal development does not have to be about dealing with problems and weaknesses. A person may also be looking for continuous improvement, aspiration, fine tuning enhancement, future goals and going from 'good to great'.*

This chapter has given an interpretation of the EIP scales and some of the most common relationships between scales. The next section looks at how to apply this learning through using the EIP. It is through practical application of the product that all the learning taken from Section Two will be consolidated.

Summary points from Chapter Five

- Of the sixteen EIP scales, eleven are linear, where high scores represent higher EI, and five are multi-scales, where middle scores represent higher EI.

- The sixteen EIP scales have some degree of inter-correlation as they all stem from the same single construct, scale 1; Self Regard. The relationship between scales is described in this chapter.

- The interpretation of scale scores given in the EIP reports should be treated as potential hypotheses (as opposed to facts) that need to be explored with the client. Interpreting combinations of scales is an art that requires knowledge of the scales and subjective skills acquired through experience.

- Eight skill levels of interpretation are recommended. Over time the user can develop their skills and move up through the eight levels. For example, it is easier and advisable to start by combining single scales before combining multiple scales.

- One way to look for themes between scales is to cluster them within the six parts of the EIP framework, as described in Chapter 4.

- When looking at the whole profile it is easier and more relevant to have a specific question or objective in mind, such as; why does my client have difficulty asserting themselves? Then to examine and interpret the profile from this perspective. Several example scenarios are given in this chapter.

- Learning to interpret the meaning of the EIP scales begins with understanding the scale definitions. The user can develop deeper skills of interpretation through practical experience of coaching clients with the EIP. Section Three considers the practical application of using the EIP for coaching in personal and leadership development.

●　　●　　●

Section Three

Applying the Emotional Intelligence Profile

The first two sections of this book have been largely theoretical and knowledge based: explaining the theoretical nature of EI, how this led to the development of the EIP, and an interpretation of the EIP scales and framework. With an understanding of EI theory and knowledge of the EIP product, Section Three explains how to apply this to coaching and business.

The EIP may be used for different applications, including team working, talent development, leadership training, customer support, culture change, conflict resolution, personal counselling, group work and 360 feedback. The most frequent application of the tool is for personal development coaching on an individual basis, which will be the context for describing how to apply the EIP in this section.

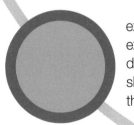

There is no single way to use the EIP and it is expected that users will also draw upon their own experience as coaches. Qualifying to use the EIP does not equip the user to be a coach, rather they should see this as a tool they may include within their suite of existing interventions.

Chapter Six

Coaching with the EIP

Introduction

This chapter describes best practice and gives advice on how to administer, interpret, explore and coach clients using the EIP. A six step process is recommended when using the EIP for coaching individuals and some key coaching skills of particular relevance to EI are explained.

6.1 How to prepare for coaching with the EIP

6.1.1 Preparation

Before deciding to use the EIP the coach needs to consider the purpose, benefits and implications of doing so. Typically the EIP is used to support an individual's personal development; often as part of a coaching programme or group development event.

The EIP is not and should not be used as part of a selection assessment. As a self-report questionnaire the EIP is open to faking and therefore using it for selection would be inaccurate and could adversely contaminate the comparison database.

The coach may initially consider how the EIP will fit within the entire process, for example:

- *What is the specific purpose for using the tool?*
- *Is the EIP the only source of feedback or will it include other data such as 360 feedback?*
- *How much time is available for exploring the results? (An hour is usually a minimum requirement).*
- *Which version of the EIP report will be used?*
- *Who will have access to the results?*
- *When will these be shown to the client?*

It is the first question in particular that needs to be agreed with the client. Ideally the coach will find out before using the EIP what the client wants to achieve from the coaching programme and what their specific goals for development are. Without a clear agenda, using the tool can be likened to a 'fishing expedition' as in seeing what turns up, rather than giving the client what they want or adding value. Establishing client objectives prior to the exploration session enables the time available to be focused and productive.

6.1.2 Administration of the EIP

A question often asked by clients before completing the EIP is; *should I be thinking specifically about work?* The advice on this is that whatever comes to mind for the client on each question is what matters, whether this is work or non-work related, as the EIP is designed to measure the *whole person*. Unlike most other questionnaires, changing any aspects of a person's EI (as defined by the EIP scales) will change them in all aspects of their life. Learning to be a better IT programmer, for example, will do just that, but developing an individual's Emotional Resilience will help them cope better with setbacks whatever the context.

Therefore, to prepare people for completing the EIP, it is important to help them access an appropriate mindset. If the client is feeling highly anxious about something that happened that day, this may have a strong influence on their responses and how they presently perceive themselves. For the purpose of self-development it is useful for them to consider other aspects of their life. Ask the client to recall four events; one positive, one negative from both their work and their non-work life, then to reflect on what happened and how they were feeling at the time. This activity helps the client to take a broader perspective on themselves when responding to the EIP questions.

It is recommended that the individual undertakes the EIP questionnaire in a quiet place without distractions and that they allow themselves at least thirty minutes to complete it in a single sitting. If, however, they need to complete the questionnaire in more than one sitting, any completed questions will be saved and they can log on to finish the questions at a later date.

6.1.3 Interpretation of the EIP report

The full EIP report is called the *Executive Report,* which is also available as two separate reports; the *Narrative Report,* which includes all sixteen scale scores, and the *Development Summary Report* which includes the EIP framework scores and matrices.

Once the client has completed the EIP questionnaire the administrator can instantly generate the selected report. Before sharing this with the client the coach may choose to spend time examining the report and forming hypotheses about the results in relation to the client's objectives. For example, if the client's objective is to deal more effectively with conflict, the coach may pay particular attention to the Conflict Handling scale. The purpose of forming hypotheses is to be able to discuss and check this out with the client. The most comprehensive of the EIP reports is the *Executive Report* described below.

The cover page of the EIP includes the client's name, the date of completion and the selected comparison group.

The first page has an introduction and list of contents followed by an explanation of Emotional Intelligence and the EIP framework (refer to Chapter 4.1). It is important to explain the EIP framework to the client in terms that relate to them, such as linking it to their work competencies.

The profile pages list the client's scores on each of the 16 EIP scales. These are ordered according to the EIP framework below:

Attitude scales:	1	*Self Regard*
	2	*Regard for Others*
Feeling scales:	3	*Self Awareness*
	4	*Awareness of Others*
Behaviour scales		
Self Management:	5	*Emotional Resilience*
	6	*Personal Power*
	7	*Goal Directedness*
	8	*Flexibility*
	9	*Connecting with Others*
	10	*Authenticity*
Relationship Management:	11	*Trust*
	12	*Balanced Outlook*
	13	*Emotional Expression and Control*
	14	*Conflict Handling*
	15	*Interdependence*
Developing EI scale:	16	*Reflective Learning*

The first profile page lists the *linear* scales 1-10 where higher scores represent higher EI. All scales are scored in decile bands from 1-10, so that someone scoring 6 would have scored higher than or equal to 60% of the comparison group and lower than 40%. It is important to remember that as with all psychometric measures the EIP is open to error. As a rule of thumb it is standard practice to accept 1.5 deciles either side of their scores so as to account for error (extend this to 2 deciles either side of their score for the red and green sub-scales as these scales have fewer items within them and therefore a greater standard error of measurement). Error is most likely to creep in through the EIP being a self-report measure. To mitigate against this, during the exploration process the coach should seek to validate the client's scores by:

- *Gauging the clients level of self-awareness*
- *Checking scores in relation to their background*
- *Seeing if the scores fit their expectations*
- *Exploring if the scores help explain their circumstances*
- *Discussing the accuracy of their answers to specific questions*

Looking at the entire profile containing large amounts of data can initially be quite overwhelming, so the five step approach described below is recommended:

1 *Look for key features: are there any scales that stand out as being particularly high or low and are there clear strengths and development areas?*

2 *Look for themes across scales: It may help at this stage to look at the EIP framework scores; are they stronger on Self Management or Relationship Management scales? Are there differences between the levels; Attitude, Feeling and Behaviour?*

3 *Begin to look for overall patterns between scales; for example a high score on Emotional Resilience, Goal Directedness and Personal Power may suggest the client is quite strong-minded and confident.*

4 *Look more carefully at specific scales of interest; by reading the Narrative section later in the report and examining their answers to specific questions in the Item Analysis section.*

5 *Throughout this process keep in mind the client's objectives (if known) when making interpretations.*

The key here is to be open and creative when considering possible interpretations. The coach is not expected to have all of the 'answers' before the coaching session; being over-prepared can be a barrier to fully listening to the client. Remember, this stage is only about forming hypotheses in preparation for the coaching session. The coach should be willing to abandon or form new interpretations in the coaching session depending on what transpires from their exploration.

6.1.4 Multi-scale scoring

The second page of *The profile* lists the Relationship Management scales which are all multi-scales. In these scales 'more' is not necessarily better as it is possible to have 'too much' as well as 'too little' on a scale. For instance, Conflict Handling is about getting the correct middle balance of being Assertive; i.e. not being Passive (too little) and not being Aggressive (too much). Multi-scale scoring measures all three levels separately; the 'too much' and 'too little' scales are shown in red because high scores on these scales are not desirable, hence middle scores are shown in green because these are desirable.

An EI tool with three sub-scales is unique. Typically other measures have a single scale with opposite ends, such as: Passive at one end, Aggressive at the other and Assertive in the middle. Difficulties can arise in using this single scale approach if people score in the middle. Consider someone who is usually Passive until they can no longer contain their frustration and then becomes Aggressive. On a single scale, the two extremes (Passive and Aggressive) would balance each other out and the score would appear in the middle of the scale as Assertive. Since people's behaviour and emotions are variable it is necessary to have scales that measure this variation. In this example, where a person rebounds from being Passive to Aggressive, it would show on the EIP as being high on both the red sub-scales and low on the green sub-scale. Due to its shape this is called the *tuning fork* or *rebound* profile, as shown below. A rebound profile can occur on all of the multi-scales: Over Trusting someone (too high) can lead to being let down and becoming Mistrusting (too low); or being Over Optimistic (too high) may lead to disappointment and then feeling quite Pessimistic (too low). A rebound may be likened to a see-saw where a person bounces from one extreme to the other.

Fig. 6.1 Example of a 'rebound/tuning fork' profile

Clients often comment that the multi-scales are very insightful as they show patterns of their emotions and behaviour that have often been missed by previous conventional measures. There are other multi-scale patterns to look for, such as the *rifle* profile where a person scores high on the 'too little' scale, average on the middle scale and low on the 'too much' scale. On Trust this would indicate that they are typically Mistrusting and rarely Over Trusting. The reason for this may not be that they want to be Mistrusting, but that they fear being Over Trusting, such as a police officer who doesn't want to be 'taken in' so errs on the side of suspicion. The opposite pattern to this is the *step* profile; scoring high on Over Trusting and low on

Mistrusting. One possible reason for this is if they fear being Mistrusting and consequently fall into being Over Trusting, such as a manager who doesn't want to appear Mistrusting of their team. The *ideal* profile however is to score high in the middle (Carefully Trusting) and low on the extremes.

Fig. 6.2 **Example of a 'rifle' profile**

Fig. 6.3 **Example of a 'step' profile**

Fig. 6.4 **Example of an 'ideal' profile**

Two other possible multi-scale profiles are to have all low scores or all high scores. A person scoring low on all three multi-scales may not have related well to the questions or they may be feeling 'flat' and disengaged. Alternatively, scoring high on all three multi-scales may suggest they are quite changeable and possibly inconsistent in their behaviour, something that could be verified by scale 10; Authenticity.

The above descriptions account for most of the nine possible permutations of high, average and low multi-scale score combinations. The multi-scales are scored from 1-10, which for three sub-scales gives 1000 possible permutations of scores for each multi-scale. To help with the interpretation of this, the reports include a narrative description, one of forty-eight permutations. However, any computerised interpretation is objective and purely based on the limited information collected from the questionnaire. In addition to this a coach will need to use their subjective skills by being aware of, listening to and exploring alternative interpretations with their client.

The multi-scales are summarised by a blue bar which shows the overall balance between all three sub-scales. High scores on the blue bar indicate that the client gets a good overall balance on this scale; i.e. more green than red on the multi-scales. Low scores on the blue bar indicate the client has a poor balance on this scale; i.e. more red than green. In which case, they may choose to examine the sub-scales to identify where specifically they are out of balance. The blue bar is calculated using a simple formula (green minus red which is divided by 2). Red scores are divided by 2 because there are two of these scores. Note that this calculation is done on the raw scores not the decile scores, and the resulting raw score is then compared normatively to derive the blue bar decile score.

The next large section of the profile is the *Narrative* which provides an interpretation of each scale for the reader, plus some short summary and development points. It is important to remember that these interpretations are hypotheses only for the reader to consider, and that the development points are suggestions that should act as a starting point. The *Narrative* is also based on of the individual's scale scores and is only as relevant as their scores are accurate.

6.1.5 The Item Analysis

Another original feature of the EIP is the item analysis section that lists the client's answers and scores to each question that can be found at the back of the EIP report. One reason the items are listed is that the EIP is designed specifically for development and therefore the items are intended to be provocative discussion points about the scale construct. Listing the items is very valuable for personal development; it enables detailed discussion about the scales and the opportunity to explore the meaning of the client's answers, helping them to see exactly why they scored as they did. Ultimately the results of any self-report questionnaire only measure what the person meant by their responses to the questions, which can only be discussed if the respondent has access to their answers. The client is the expert on themselves, not the coach, and is therefore best placed to interpret their own scores and answers. All too often ownership is taken away from the client and the coach is seen as the expert with the answers. This is comparable to the traditional medical model where the Doctor diagnoses and prescribes, effectively disempowering the patient. Having the items available to the client gives them ownership of their report, allows them to understand and give their own interpretation of their responses, and so encourages greater self-responsibility for their development. In this way the coach models emotionally intelligent Interdependence (scale 15).

6.1.6 The Summary Profile

The *Summary Profile* appears at the back of the Executive Report but also exists as a separate report in itself (the Development Summary Report). It shows the EIP framework which is colour coded as red, amber, or green to give a quick visual representation of the scores in each of the six parts of the framework. The six parts are made up of three separate sections or pairs that represent each level of the EIP framework; Attitude, Feeling and Behaviour.

Each of these levels is also shown as a 2x2 matrix with a blue ball indicating where the person scored in comparison to the norm groap selected. These matrices are explained in detail in Chapter 4 and provide the coach with a useful tool. Important questions for the coach to ask their client are; *what percentage of time do you spend in each of the four quadrants? What causes you to fall out of the 'ideal' (top right) quadrant into each of the other three? How do you move back to the 'ideal' quadrant once you have dropped out of it? What feelings (or what behaviours) are associated with being in this quadrant for you?*

The final page of the Summary Profile includes three development points, based on the individual's three lowest scale scores, and three strengths based on their three highest scale scores. This page may be used separately as a brief summary report, and for when there is only limited time available for coaching.

6.1.7 Sharing the profile with a client

Having prepared an analysis and interpretation of the EIP, the coach will be ready to begin the coaching session. There are different ways in which to reveal the EIP scores and results to the client, each having different merits and drawbacks. One method is to give the report to the client, for them to go away and read for a while. This may be quite provocative and typically gets a strong reaction. The benefit of this is that it can provoke discussion and the individual will inevitably have questions to direct the process. The potential downsides are that they may misunderstand the information, they may only focus on the highest and lowest scores and they could be swamped by too much information. This need not be a problem with an experienced coach who can answer questions confidently and reassure the client.

A more structured approach would be to address scale sections in turn; Core Attitudes, followed by the Awareness scales, followed by the Self Management scales and then the Relationship Management scales. This allows the coach to gradually build the client's understanding of each section and is therefore less likely to overwhelm the client. This process works particularly well when working with groups. It may involve covering a section like Self Management over a day and having the group or individual complete a range of activities specifically for developing these scales.

A third approach to presenting the profile involves asking the client to first self-rate against each of the scales then to provide them with feedback on how they scored on the EIP. This provides an interesting comparison between their general self-perception and how they compare to the norm group. An 'exploration guide' produced by JCA is specifically designed for this purpose, giving the individual their 'results' without overwhelming them with data and interpretative text.

Alternatively, the client may not be interested in reviewing single scales but would prefer to look at the big picture. This can be done by exploring the EIP framework in the Summary Profile section.

Each coach will find the way that works for them, and their approach can be adapted to suit their client, which may be any variation of the above. Within each approach there are recommended steps which are described below.

6.2 Exploring the EIP with a client

The feedback process is referred to as an 'exploration' rather than 'feedback' as this more clearly reflects the nature of the process. This process has been split into six steps and provides the coach with a structure for exploration.

Step 1 Agree the purpose and contract

In practice these steps may not take this particular order, as there is much to be said for going with the flow and energy of the client. It is important early on to agree a contract which includes; what the client wants from the process, who will see their information, what the role of the coach is and how long the process will take.

From the outset the skilled coach will approach the coaching session with an emotionally intelligent mindset of high Self Regard and Regard for Others. This is one reason why the process is described as an *exploration* rather than *feedback*. Some traditional ways of using personality questionnaires have been from a more *judgemental* position, where the coach is seen as the expert, giving feedback and interpreting the client's results for them. The *exploration* process assumes that the individual is the expert on themselves and the coach asks the client to explain and interpret their results. When using the EIP it is essential that the client knows what answers they gave to each question and what scales each question relates to. Only the individual knows why they answered the question as they did and what they meant by this. The role of the coach is to ask the questions that will help the individual make sense of the information in relation to their own life.

Step 2 **Build rapport and gather information**

Building a good rapport early on is essential as this will help define the level and quality of communication the coach has with the client. As the discussion progresses a skilled coach will gradually help their client to reflect more deeply, like peeling off layers of an onion; starting with their current situation, then their behaviour, their thoughts, their feelings and finally their deeper attitudes. It is often easier for the client to start by talking about their present situation on a topic they can easily relate to and feel comfortable sharing; *tell me what you are doing currently in your job?* And then to track backwards; *how did you come to be doing that?* The conversation can then drift into discussing their behaviours; *what did you enjoy doing and how did you do that?* As the client becomes more relaxed and in touch with their thoughts and feelings, the coach can go deeper and ask them to share their feelings, attitudes and motivation; *how were you feeling at that moment? What was going through your mind? Why was that important to you?*

While building rapport the coach can observe and notice the client's behaviour and interaction with them. It may be useful to feed this back to them; *I notice your whole body became tense when you were describing this*, but be careful not to make them feel uncomfortably self-conscious.

Building rapport also allows background information to be gathered on the client that will then help them understand their circumstances and place their objectives for the session in context; *tell me more about why you find it difficult managing your new team?* This may be drawn upon and referred to when exploring their EIP scores; *what links might you see between your low score on Connecting with Others and the issue you described earlier with your team?*

Note that building rapport can easily move into Step 4 (exploration). It may be appropriate to suggest a pause to introduce the EIP (Step 3 below) before exploring the EIP scales with the client.

Step 3 **Explain the EIP report**

It is important to give the client an understanding of Emotional Intelligence early on in the process. As with most things, this is best explained simply without going into too much detail; *Have you come across the term Emotional Intelligence before? What does it mean to you?* Refer them to the EIP framework; *this is JCA's model of EI which looks at how you manage your own behaviour (point to the left column) and your relationships (point to the right column). You will see that it is separated into three levels, the deepest level (point to the Attitudes) which is your attitude towards yourself and others, the middle level which is your awareness of your own and others* feelings *(point to middle layer)*, and the top level which is your behaviour and what you actually do *(point to top layer)*. *Self Management (point to this) includes things like coping with setbacks, motivating yourself and adapting to change. Relationship Management (point to this) looks at areas such as trusting people, managing conflict and working as part of a team.* It can be useful at this stage to refer to examples from the client's organisational competencies so they can see the clear relevance of EI to their work; *Relationship Management relates to your work competencies such as team working, communicating effectively and influencing others*.

The client may wish to discuss some aspects of the EIP framework further, such as how the arrows connect to the different aspects of EI. Again, be prepared with a practical example, and point to the relevant boxes; *Regard for Others (bottom box) underpins all of the Interpersonal scales. For example, if you have a negative and critical attitude towards others, then you may be less open to hearing what they have to say, so are less Aware of Others (middle box). This may be because you have already formed your opinion of them, which may make it more difficult for you to trust and get along with people, which will therefore lower your Relationship Management (top box)*.

Before moving on to explore the results, it is important to emphasise and reiterate throughout that all aspects of EI are changeable; people are not born with them and that they can all be developed. Also emphasise that EI is not one thing; people are likely to be stronger in some areas than in others, that the EIP is a self-report questionnaire and is only one source of feedback (and therefore open to error).

At this point the coach may choose to explain how the EIP is scored using the norm comparison group and scale deciles (alternatively they may wait until discussing the first scale); *we have compared your answers to the answers from a large sample of senior managers. How your answers compare is represented on a scale from 1-10. If you scored 1, this means that 90% of people in this group rated themselves higher than you rated yourself. If you scored 8, this means that 80% of this group rated themselves equal to or below how you rated yourself, or 20% of people rated themselves higher than you rated yourself*. It is important to rehearse this explanation as it can easily become confusing and cause the client to lose confidence in the process or their coach.

The coach may continue their explanation; *if you scored lower than the comparison group there are three possible reasons. One, you are lower than other senior managers in this scale; two, that you under-rated yourself in this area or three, that most senior managers tend to over-rate themselves in this area. This is what we will now explore.*

Another area that will require explanation are the multi-scales as these are less familiar to people than linear scales; *the Relationship Management scales are what we call 'multi-scales'. This means it is possible to have too much as well as too little on each scale. For example, with Trust, people can be Mistrusting and Over Trusting, but the ideal is to be in the middle, Carefully Trusting. This is why we measure this scale in three parts. The ideal is to score high on the green bars and low on the red bars. The overall score is summarised by the blue bar on top. A high blue score means you have the right balance of Trust. Think of the ideal like a see-saw, that you want to keep in balance and avoid swinging from one extreme to the other.*

Step 4 **Explore the EIP report with the client**

Many of the coaching skills for exploring the EIP are covered later in this chapter. A few essential aspects include:

- *Be client led and ask questions; which scales are of interest to you? What does this mean to you? How is this scale relevant? What would you like to explore next?*
- *Relate scales and results to the client's circumstances.*
- *Look for scale patterns and themes to draw out key points.*
- *Test out hypotheses; could this mean that you...?*
- *Validate the accuracy of their scores through discussion.*
- *Avoid getting too focused on the scores or data and bring conversation back to the client.*
- *Keep focused on their objectives and keep it relevant.*
- *Allow time for reflection.*
- *Include activities within the process such as drawing a 'life-line' of key events.*
- *Open up exploration at this stage rather than seeking solutions.*
- *Allow them to interpret results; it is an exploration, not feedback.*
- *Draw upon all relevant aspects of the report, such as the item analysis, matrix reports and narrative interpretations.*

The exploration phase is about opening up the discussion to consider all the information, discuss hypotheses and explore possibilities. The aim is to draw out meaning from the EIP in terms of scale patterns and insights that relate to the client's life. This may also involve exploring themes in more depth such as the client's thoughts, feelings and attitudes. For example, a client may identify a pattern of being emotionally closed and inhibited, reflected in scale 13, (Emotionally Over Controlled), which may make it more difficult for them to Connect with Others (scale 9) and people may find them more difficult to read (Authenticity; scale 10). Further discussion may reveal that they are inhibited because they feel anxious around people they do not know well, they think that people will not be interested in them and their attitude is; *it is better to be quiet than to risk making a fool of myself*. It is important to explore the client's circumstances in sufficient breadth and depth before progressing to Step 5 of setting goals and turning 'exploration' into 'action'.

6.2.1 Discussing the relative difference in high and low scores

Unlike personality measures, the EIP is evaluative, presenting the client with scores that represent higher (better) or lower (worse) levels of EI. Although having a 'score' may be a useful benchmark for individuals, scores should only be used as indicators to provoke useful conversation for the benefit of the client. It is essential that the coach and client both remember that EI is changeable and the scores represent a person's self-perception only.

The EIP is a normative based instrument as people are generally interested in how they compare with others. It is important to reassure the individual early on about norm based scores; *people often become concerned by low scores, but remember that they reflect your own answers to the questionnaire (which you can review on page... of the report), also the group that you have been compared against is already at a high level (managers/leaders) so for example, a scale score of 5 would be considered high relative to the general population.*

There is an alternative to using the scores normatively, and that is to compare the scores between scales (idiographically). It can be more relevant and useful to compare the relative higher and lower scores for the individual regardless of how they compare to the norm group. A person may score low on all scales compared to the norm group, but relative to themselves, some of the scales will be higher than other scales. The purpose of the EIP is for personal development and therefore the relevant benchmark for this is themselves.

Another reason for recommending a 'self' comparison is that people will have their own perception and benchmark for each question they answer. If a person has particularly high standards for themselves and tends to mix with people who do the same, then they are likely to be tougher on themselves in their response to each question. This is something the coach should consider when discussing the client's scores; does the client over-rate or under-rate themselves?

One factor that determines whether people rate themselves more positively or negatively will be their level or stage of personal development:[1]

Stage 1 **Unconscious incompetence**
   (the client is unaware of what they do not know)

Stage 2 **Conscious incompetence**
   (the client is aware of what they do not know)

Stage 3 **Conscious competence**
   (the client has learnt something new)

Stage 4 **Unconscious competence**
   (the new learning has become automatic and habitual)

People who are at Stage 1 are more likely to over-rate themselves. They may lack Self Awareness and self-knowledge and possibly come from a Critical life position (I'm OK, You are Not OK) tending to blame others rather than accept self-responsibility.

Getting people to Stage 2 can require considerable input from the coach through means such as 360 feedback and is often met with resistance from the client. As the client moves through the stages they typically take on more responsibility for their own development and the coach has less input. Sometimes people who have completed the EIP questionnaire rate themselves lower the second time around because through their coaching they have become more aware of what they want to develop in themselves. One of the reasons for asking people to practice some self-reflection activities before completing the EIP is to move their level of awareness from Stage 1 up to Stage 2. This is particularly important for people who do not engage in much self-reflection. These individuals are more likely to over-rate themselves on the EIP and may not develop greatly until they are compelled to do so. Stage 2 may be accompanied by a reduction in self-confidence as the individual drops some of their defences which may have served to protect them from uncomfortable feelings. This drop in confidence is only temporary, as in Stage 3 the individual will develop more effective, non-defensive behaviours to replace them.

Once the client implements their learning and makes changes (competence stages 3 and 4) then they will usually start to rate themselves higher again on the EIP, there being a sense that they are now achieving the development goals they set for themselves. In other words, a person scoring low may be at the start of their current development journey (conscious incompetence) and a person scoring high may be at the end of that phase in their development journey (unconscious competence). Therefore people may move up as well as down on their EIP scores as they progress through Stages 1-4 and repeat this each time they move on to a higher level of awareness in their personal development.

In practice, the stages continue indefinitely as Stage 4 is followed immediately by Stage 1, but at a higher level. This may be explained to the client as follows: *Personal development is an on-going journey where ever increasing levels may be attained. Some highly emotionally intelligent people score themselves quite low on the EIP questionnaire because they set themselves a high target they wish to achieve. Equally, scoring high doesn't mean a person has nothing more to develop, just that they have neared the end of this phase in their journey and will soon be ready for the next phase. The next phase will begin when they become aware of other things that they want to develop and consequently their scores may drop again on the scale. Therefore the real benchmark for personal development is oneself. Think of scale scores as an 'emotional barometer', scores may move up and down depending on where a person is on their journey of personal development.*

It is important therefore that the coach considers the client's level of personal development and encourages them to look at their relative scores in addition to their normative scores.

Step 5 Set personal development goals

Personal development coaching is about making changes that will help the individual improve and develop in what they do. It is therefore important that the client and coach continue through from Step 4 'exploration' to Step 5 'taking action'. Some coaches will place little emphasis on setting goals, assuming it to be an automatic consequence of the exploration phase. Unfortunately, unless the client leaves the coaching session with a clear commitment for action, it is highly likely they will return to their day to day habits and put the coaching session to the back of their mind.

Step 5 moves the client from the Feeling (Awareness) part of the EIP framework into the Behaviour (Management) part. EI is sometimes criticised for being too soft and just 'navel gazing' when, in fact, EI is really about doing the 'hard stuff' as it involves making difficult changes.

There are perhaps two main reasons why people do not carry out their development goals; one being that they do not truly want the chosen goals for themselves and the second is that the goals are too large and unsustainable. Once back in their routine habits of daily life, a person's motivation to carry out their development actions will soon wane. Therefore it is essential to set objectives that are focused, practical and easily achieved. The development goals must also be something the person is motivated to do for themselves.

Following the exploration phase, it is a good idea to invite the client to write down all of their thoughts and reflections from the exploration in enough detail to act as a reminder should they come to revisit them in the future. They can then identify from this what they want to develop.

The next step is to prepare the client with an action plan that they will implement after completion of the coaching session to facilitate their personal development. The following activity has been found to work very well for this:

A **Select one aspect or scale from the EIP that interests you right now.**
Example: Conflict Handling - being too Passive.

B **Describe a behaviour you wish to change.**
Agreeing to do things for people that I don't have time for and don't want to do.

C **Describe what the pay-offs and drawbacks of this behaviour are.**
Pay-offs - people like me and I avoid conflict.
Drawbacks - I am overworked, I let people down and I feel bad about myself.

D **Describe a behaviour you would like to do instead?**
To be more assertive and say 'no' to people.

E **What would be the pay-offs and drawbacks to this?**
Pay-off - I would get more work done and I would get more respect from people.
Drawback - people may not like me and I may be seen as aggressive.

F **Write down one specific action you can take by completing the following phrase:**
Every day for the next 21 days I will…
Say to people 'can you give me a moment to think about that?' when they ask me to do something.

There are several aspects of this exercise that can help make it successful:

It is important to ask the client to select something that interests them right now, because this is something they will have energy for. Also start with a broad area, such as Conflict Handling which will mean the specific behaviour they choose to change will relate to and affect the whole aspect of Conflict Handling. Asking about the client's pay-offs and drawbacks helps to check how much they want to make the change and explores any other barriers to them making this change. It may be necessary at this stage to change a deeper blocker first; for example, if someone wants to be more Assertive but doesn't feel they have the confidence (Personal Power) to do so then building their confidence should become their first goal.

The commitment the client makes should be short and easy for them to understand. The reason for a 21 day commitment is that habits are created mostly through repetition, research has shown that it takes 21 days to start forming habits[2] and up to 66 days for these to become embedded as new neural networks.[3] It also helps if the client is encouraged to declare their commitment (tell people about it) as other people may support them and create more of an incentive for them to follow it through. Finally, it helps to find a person who will act as a 'buddy' and check that they are doing their commitment on a daily basis. The buddy's role is mainly to get the client 'back on the wagon' if they should relapse. Giving up after a setback is one of the most common reasons for people not making an initial change into an enduring habit.

The very action of the client successfully making one single change will provide considerable reinforcement to them that they have the capacity to change, and by adopting this attitude (EI attitude No. 7; *Change is possible - see Chapter 1.5*) they will find it easier to make changes in the future.

One other benefit of the behavioural habit change technique is that it will also help change the client's underlying attitude. It has already been explained how attitude change leads to behaviour change (see Chapter 3) but the reverse can also be true, a concept originally defined by Festinger as cognitive dissonance.[4] Behaving in a way that contradicts a person's attitude creates a state of anxiety (dissonance) compelling them to either change their behaviour to be consistent with their attitude or change their attitude to be consistent with their new behaviour. This explains why it can be quite uncomfortable to change a behavioural habit and why doing so requires prolonged repetition. In the example above, passive behaviour may be linked to the individual's attitude of low Self Regard, assuming others know better, and holding a 'Please Others' condition of self-worth. It is helpful for the client to become aware through coaching of the attitudes that drive their behaviour. By continually reinforcing a specific behaviour that is incongruent with their attitudes this will create doubt and uncertainty in the emotional (limbic) brain opening their attitudes up to question from the higher thinking brain so that new attitudes may be formed. (Refer to Chapter 7.3 for suggestions on how to change attitudes).

Step 6 **Close the session**

Having advised the client of the time frame at the start of the session, it is helpful to let them know when they are approaching the end. Allow them time to wind down gradually rather than having a sudden finish. Check if there is anything they would like to pick up on or ask. If there is a lot to discuss, plan how this could be carried forward in a follow up meeting. Ask them how, in summary, they feel about the process. Confirm agreed actions they are going to take between now and the next meeting and how these relate to their objectives. Confirm arrangements for the next meeting and how they can contact you, their coach, if they have any concerns or questions. Remind them of what happens to the results and about confidentiality. Finally, close with a positive and encouraging comment, such as; *I think you made some excellent progress today in identifying your priorities and setting yourself a clear objective.*

6.2.2 **Summary checklist for the exploration process**

Prepare:
Produce the correct reports
Examine the data and generate hypotheses
Review the development suggestions in the EIP

1 Agree contract:
Make introductions
Confirm the time frame
Agree the process
Check what the client wants to achieve from the session
Explain this is a two-way process; an exploration not feedback
Confirm aspects of confidentiality

2 Build rapport:
Discuss their circumstances and relevant context
Start with easy opening questions (about their situation and their work behaviour)
Listen and be aware of their body language
Use appropriate follow-on questions (about their thoughts, feelings and attitudes)
Review their objectives

3 Explain the EIP:
Explain why the EIP is being used
Explain Emotional Intelligence

Describe the exploration process

Explain scoring, measurement error, multi-scales and norms

Explain that scores are self-perceptions and represent
a stage in their development journey

4 Explore the EIP: Explore the client's interpretations and reactions

Provide guidance on interpretation

Challenge and explore

Clearly explain the scale meaning

Refer to specific items

Work at a client-led pace and structure

Look for themes

5 Set goals: Allow time for reflection (have them record this)

Consider development themes and specific goals

Create a personal development plan

Identify one area they will action

6 Close: Summarise outcomes (by the client or the coach)

Discuss any final questions

Agree the next steps

Confirm confidentiality

Leave them with a positive message

6.2.3 Handling client resistance

With the EIP, the information on the scale sores, interpretations and implications can be challenging for a client to understand and explain and may elicit some resistance. There are several ways the coach can make the EIP results more manageable and less threatening.

Has rapport been established? Without this it will be very difficult to have an open and non-defensive conversation. Equally, the coach needs to be non-defensive and model EI behaviours and attitudes.

Have the objectives and purpose been agreed? Be sure the client wants to explore the report and that their general questions or concerns have been discussed. It may be that they are very cynical towards psychometric testing, for instance if they had a negative experience of receiving test feedback or were not selected for a job that applied psychometric assessment.

Do they understand the limitations of the questionnaire? The EIP is a self-report questionnaire and is based on their self-perception only. As with all forms of measurement there is room for error. If they want to understand a score, refer them to their item analysis, they can then judge for themselves what they meant by their answers. Also, remind them that the EIP is not an exact measure of EI as this can vary moment to moment, but serves to support them in becoming more emotionally intelligent.

Do they understand how the EIP is scored? Remind them that the EIP is norm referenced and which norm group was used. Usually these are higher than the general population and an average score compared to senior leaders may be very high when compared to the general population.

Discuss their implicit benchmark. When answering the EIP questions some people have a high internal benchmark, particularly if they have lower Self Regard, a 'Be Perfect' driver or if they have engaged in a significant amount of personal development. Therefore it is often more useful to consider their relative higher and lower scores than how they compared to a norm group.

Help them learn how to use the reports. Explain that the EIP results should not be considered in isolation but in combination with all other forms of feedback they have had. Encourage them to look at strengths as well as development areas.

Explain that EI development is a continuous cycle. Remind them that EI development is a journey, there is no final 'score' and people can be quite content scoring themselves low and enjoy the process of continual growth. A high score may mean they are ready for the next phase in their development of that scale, and a low score may mean they are beginning a new phase in their development.

People's reactions to the EIP report can be informative to the coach, some people will score high but be self-critical and disappointed in themselves, others will score low and be curious, positive and engaged in their learning. The scores are there to create the conversation and to raise awareness; they are not what define a person or their performance.

Is it a repeat completion of the EIP? Discuss how scores can go up and down for different reasons, such as personal development or raised awareness (conscious incompetence) and explore what happened following their last EIP exploration.

6.3 Applying the EIP in groups

The EIP is mainly applied through one-to-one coaching; alternatively it may be used as part of a group workshop for EI development. An advantage of using the EIP within a group is that individuals can practice developing their EI in pairs or groups and they can co-coach and support one another whilst in a safe learning environment.

Facilitating a group EI workshop is outside the realms of this book and requires expertise in group facilitation. Given below is some general guidance on delivering the EIP within group settings.

At the outset, before releasing the EIP results, it is important to create an open atmosphere within the group where individuals are willing to communicate honestly and will take responsibility for their own development. As with individual feedback, the facilitator would give a general explanation of EI, describe how the scales are scored and how to interpret the report. To make group feedback manageable and to structure the workshop process, it is recommended to explore the EIP scales by sections based on the EIP framework (Awareness scales, Self Management scales, Relationship Management scales and Attitude scales). For each section, provide practical and relevant activities to help individuals process the information and set appropriate actions for their development. It is generally recommended exploring the Attitude scales later in the process as these are deeper constructs and easier to put into context having explored the other scales. It is advisable to offer individuals the opportunity for a one-to-one conversation about their profile with the facilitator, such as at the end of the workshop or by including a second facilitator. In general, to explore EI Profiles in a group setting (of up to 10 people), run appropriate activities and identify development actions would take a minimum of two days.

The Group Reporting/Management Information function of the EIP makes it possible to group several individual EIP results into a single report, which may have various applications:

- **Viewing the average profile for a group of people:** *It may be useful to identify on which scale a particular group (e.g. managers or an organisational cohort) score higher or lower. This could then be used to build a bespoke management development programme.*

- **Comparing different group profiles:** *It may be used to examine whether there is a difference in EI between different groups. For example, sales people in different regions or between senior and middle managers.*

- **Comparing pre and post results for a group:** *It can be used to demonstrate the added value of an EI intervention programme for a group or for an organisationally wide intervention.*

6.4 Applying the EIP with other products

The EIP is not a panacea but a product and model that will support personal development. EI is one part in the process of personal development and is sandwiched between personality and behavioural competence. As described in Chapter 1, EI is what turns personality and potential into effective performance.

It would therefore make sense to measure both the input (personality) and the output (behavioural competence) of EI.

The JCA Development Hub provides an integrated online platform for measuring all three areas:

- **Personality Type Profile:** *Helps the individual understand their personality and potential.*

- **Emotional Intelligence Profile (EIP):** *Enables the individual to understand how well they manage their personality and potential and what to do to improve this.*

- **Behaviours 360:** *Shows how effectively the individual is performing in the workplace (as measured by the organisation's behavioural competencies).*

The key ingredient for turning personality into effective behaviour is Emotional Intelligence. Consider the metaphor of a jet engine (Emotional Intelligence) that sucks in air (personality) turning this into power and performance (effective behaviour). This is presented by the formula:

Personality + Emotional Intelligence = Effective Behaviour

In summary, the suite of products measures how effectively a person manages their personality to sustain effective behaviour and performance in the workplace.

Where possible, it is generally recommended that the coach uses a combination of these three assessment products to help their client obtain maximum benefit from their coaching. The coach may choose to explore the feedback from the Behaviours 360 questionnaire (competency) first as this will help the client set their objectives, define what is going well and what they would like to improve. The Personality Type Profile may then be used to help the client understand how their typical style and characteristics may be influencing how they behave and perform in the workplace. At this stage the client may be seeking more insight into *why* they behave in this way (their feelings, thoughts and attitudes that drive their behaviour) and *what* they can do to develop this. The EIP will help explain how they can manage their personality to improve their performance in the workplace.

It is quite usual for clients to complete the Behaviours 360 questionnaire (competency) again at a later date, to measure what impact the coaching has had on their behaviour and performance. It is also recommended they repeat the EIP as this will identify how their EI has developed and which aspects of EI may be helping or hindering their personal development. It may not be necessary to repeat the Personality Type Profile as personality type is unlikely to change.

Learning to use JCA's Personality Type Profile and the Behaviours 360 questionnaire requires additional specific training to learn about the models. However, the coaching skills for using both tools are not dissimilar to using the EIP and are discussed below. More information describing the relationship between the EIP and Personality Type Profile is given in Appendix 3, and the relationship between the EIP and competencies (Behaviours 360) is given in Chapter 8.2.3.

6.4.1 Exploring the 360 degree Emotional Intelligence Profile

One further product that is often used in combination with the EIP is the EIP 360. This is shorter than the EIP, with fewer items, whilst still measuring the six parts of the EIP framework. Used in combination with the EIP, the client can make a direct comparison between their self-perception and others perception of them on the EIP framework.

The reason that the EIP 360 is shorter than the EIP is that it would be unreasonable to expect other people to complete the whole EIP questionnaire on someone else, because of the time and also the detailed knowledge of the other person required for some of the items (especially on items about their feelings).

The 360 questionnaire can be used separately or in addition to the EIP questionnaire and is especially useful for raising a person's Self Awareness and self-knowledge. If a person lacks Self Awareness then their self-reported answers to the EIP may be less accurate. Also, feedback from others is particularly important on scales such as Authenticity (the degree to which you tend to be reliable, consistent and knowable to others) which may be more accurately measured by others rather than by the individual. Using 360 feedback also provides an additional source of evidence to confirm or challenge one's self-perception.

All feedback may be useful in providing different perspectives. There is sometimes a danger of assuming psychometric questionnaire data is more valid than other sources of feedback. Psychometric measures add particular value in that they provide objectivity, but each approach is of value for different reasons. Applying several types of feedback is recommended for coaching, as this will help identify themes, challenge assumptions and avoids over reliance on one set of data. Some alternative methods of feedback may include:

- *A person's general self-perception*
- *Observing and noticing their behaviour and feelings*
- *Noticing other people's reactions to them*

- *Asking people for immediate feedback on them*
- *Completing standardised questionnaires*
- *Visualisation or guided imagery activities*
- *Role-play scenarios*
- *Reflecting on their experiences*
- *Assessment style activities*

The EIP 360 is designed to gather information quickly from several respondents. This is both quantitative (from the scales) and qualitative (from people's comments). Most approaches to 360 place emphasis on keeping results anonymous to encourage people to give their honest opinions. Unfortunately, this also leads to the recipient spending time trying to work out who said what about them. An ultimate goal of 360 feedback is to achieve a level of openness where individuals or groups can sit face to face and share their thoughts, feelings, wants and concerns with each other in a compassionate and non-defensive manner. This would demonstrate an emotionally intelligent level of communication and this is what is typically facilitated during an EI development workshop.

A challenge that may occur with 360 feedback is when the feedback does not match one's own self-perception. There are several possible reasons for this from the individual's (Self) or from others' perspective.

Table 6.1 Self and others' perspectives on feedback

Self	Others'
The individual does not know themselves well	Others under-rate the individual or do not like them
The individual is closed and difficult to read	Others over-rate the individual or idolise them
The individual presents a false image of themselves	Others do not know the individual very well
The individual over-rates themselves	The questionnaire is inaccurate
The individual under-rates themselves	

As a rule of thumb the client is encouraged to consider the possibility that 1% of the feedback may be true, as a way of encouraging them to consider it rather than discount it entirely. Although feedback from others can be particularly uncomfortable, exploring the 360 profiles follows the same principles as the EIP.

- *Before sharing the 360 data with the client check the results for any potentially difficult feedback (such as where they were rated lower by others than they rate themselves, or for any harsh and negative comments).*

- *If using the EIP and the EIP 360 together look at whether the results are consistent or different.*

- *Decide on what order the feedback will be given; providing 360 feedback first usually helps the client identify their development goals, while the EIP helps them understand how to develop.*

- *When examining the results look first at the overall scale difference between the client's responses and the rater's responses, and where the client rated themselves higher or lower than others did.*

- *Then consider differences between groups of raters; line manager, peers and their direct reports. The EIP 360 report also highlights items with the greatest difference including where they rated themselves higher than others rated them (blind spots), and where they rated themselves lower than others rated them (hidden potential).*

Typically, individuals will have a tendency to focus on the negative feedback, but it is important to encourage them to balance this with positive feedback and their 'hidden potential'. The 360 report also shows the exact rating given by each rater on each item should they choose to explore the spread of responses. For example, do all raters score them the same, or is there wide variation. If there is a wide range of ratings then it could be that the individual gives a different impression to different people and is inconsistent. Perhaps the most valuable part of the 360 report is the qualitative comments, which provide a personal insight from the raters, as to why they gave the scores they did on the scales.

In summary, exploring the EIP 360 is similar to using the EIP in that it helps the client to understand the scale meaning, look for patterns in the data, identify specific development actions, and focus on specific strengths that they can exploit.

6.5 Effective coaching skills when using the EIP

Following the recommended steps when using the EIP will help structure the coaching session. However, the ultimate success of coaching will depend upon the skills of the coach and the commitment of the client to make these changes for themselves.

There are four key ingredients to make coaching with the EIP successful. These are written in ascending order of importance, as each ingredient is dependent upon the next one if it is to achieve the ultimate outcome of helping the client develop their EI.

1   **The application of the EIP report:** *The EIP report and results should be seen as only the start of the process; to provoke thinking and discussion rather than an end in itself.*

2 **The knowledge of the coach:** *The EIP results will only be useful if the coach is fluent in EI knowledge. The effective coach will have a sound understanding of the theory behind the EIP results, the EIP framework, the EIP scales, and how to develop EI.*

3 **The skills of the coach:** *Having in-depth knowledge of the EIP will only be useful when exploration is client-centred. Behind this sit the skills of the coach in building rapport, engaging the client, asking helpful questions, challenging appropriately and creating solutions.*

4 **The client's commitment to developing their EI:** *All the above are resources to facilitate change in the client. Change in the client may be defined in terms of how the client feels and acts as a consequence of the coaching process. It is ultimately the client's responsibility to commit to making any changes.*

So far this chapter has examined the first two of these points, enabling the coach to explore and interpret the EIP with their client. The rest of this chapter provides more generic information on becoming a skilled and emotionally intelligent coach (point 3). This is followed in Chapter 7 by a discussion on how to develop EI in oneself and others (point 4).

6.6 The skills of the coach

As the skills of the coach are a key factor in the success of the EIP, here follows a concise section, to serve as an overview of the key coaching skills required when working with a client using the EIP.

Be an emotionally intelligent coach: Before helping others to develop their EI, it is of vital importance that the coach has engaged in and developed their own EI to a high standard. All scales on the EIP are of importance to being an effective and emotionally intelligent coach. In particular, having an attitude of high Self Regard and Regard for Others (I+ U+) underpins and filters through to all other scales.

Table 6.2 Relevance of EIP scales to coaching

Scale	Relevance to being a coach
1 **Self Regard**	*To be open and genuine with clients and avoid being defensive.*
2 **Regard for Others**	*To have compassion for and a desire to help the client develop.*
3 **Self Awareness**	*To self-monitor feelings so as to manage one's behaviour with the client.*
4 **Awareness of Others**	*To notice and pay attention to the client's needs and feelings.*
5 **Emotional Resilience**	*To persevere when facing set-backs with the client.*
6 **Personal Power**	*To have and demonstrate confidence in the coaching process.*

7	**Goal Directedness**	*To keep the coaching and the client focused on their objectives.*
8	**Flexibility**	*To adapt to the needs of the client and be willing to try different approaches.*
9	**Connecting with Others**	*To build rapport and engage with the client.*
10	**Authenticity**	*To be able to separate oneself from the client's issues and have a set of inner guiding principles.*
11	**Trust**	*To build a trusting relationship with the client, but also be open to challenging them.*
12	**Balanced Outlook**	*To focus on positive outcomes and not be drawn into negative thinking.*
13	**Emotional Expression and Control**	*To demonstrate interest and compassion without being overly drawn into the client's emotions.*
14	**Conflict Handling**	*To question, challenge and debate with clients in a calm and respectful manner.*
15	**Interdependence**	*To work in partnership with the client while retaining an appropriate degree of separation.*
16	**Reflective Learning**	*To continually develop as a coach and not to become complacent.*

It is also important for the coach to develop their Self Knowledge so they become aware of their own needs and do not use the coaching session as a means of getting their own needs met for say, attention or status. For example, a coach with the 'rescuer' defence may invent or exaggerate client problems, want to be seen as providing the 'cure' and create client dependence on them. Taken to an extreme they may fall into the realm of being manipulators, cult leaders or self-appointed 'gurus'.

Be a self-aware coach: Exploration of the EIP is a two-way process between the coach and the client. The dynamics of this interaction depends upon both personalities and, despite following a well prepared approach, some pairings will work more smoothly than others. It is important for the coach to be aware of their own preferences and habits and the type of clients they find more difficult to work with. If they feel intimidated by certain people, or if they prefer coaching people of a certain age or gender. The coach should recognise how they respond to these clients; do they become too self-conscious and stop attending to what the client is saying? Do they try to rush the process? Do they try to assert too much control or avoid challenging the client? As a general rule it is recommended that the coach has experienced personal development at the level to which they are coaching their client, as this will help build their confidence and expertise. The coach should be experienced and comfortable in discussing their own feelings, if they are to be asking clients to do the same, or if they are helping the client to change their habits, they will have done this with themselves. This does not mean that the coach needs to be an expert in everything they are coaching, such as being an effective leader, but having relevant experience is valuable and adds credibility.

Prepare fully: A primary skill for effective coaching is to prepare before meeting the client. This will help the coach organise their time, anticipate any challenges and keep focused on the client rather than thinking about what they will be doing next. This is particularly important for the less experienced coach or if they have had less practice with the EIP. Preparation may include aspects such as:

- *Reviewing the client's profile*
- *Preparing some questions to ask*
- *Having a clear structure to follow*
- *Having a range of activities that they are confident at using and know tend to work well*
- *Having a range of useful references for the client's development*
- *Also refer to section 6.1 above on Preparation*

A caveat to good preparation is not to fall into the trap of becoming over-rehearsed or so familiar with a routine that the coach stops paying attention to the person in front of them and the client needs. The coach must be sure to work within the client's frame of reference rather than expecting them to fit within their expectations, theories or the EIP framework.

Build rapport: There are various factors that will make the coaching experience more natural, relaxed and productive. One of these is building rapport with the client. Rapport exists between two people when they are both synchronised in their communication and there is a natural 'ebb and flow' in conversation. This is usually recognisable in that both people will automatically adopt similar behaviours, such as posture, breathing and tone of voice. It is possible to induce rapport more quickly by adopting similar actions to the other person, known as 'matching and mirroring'. A natural benefit in gaining rapport is that it lowers people's arousal level, as the emotional brain can anticipate a person's actions and will not perceive them as a threat. Once in rapport, people are reluctant to break it and a skilled coach will use this to lead the client into a positive emotional state. The coach may prepare their physiology before meeting with the client so as to feel relaxed and unhurried, which will show in their posture, voice and breathing, which will be automatically detected by the client. The coach can also observe the client's emotional state when they meet; if the client is anxious it may help for the coach to slow down and relax gradually, so allowing the client to naturally relax with them.

Create an atmosphere for change: The rapport created by the coach will determine the atmosphere (the emotional state) of the coaching session. This can take a little while to instil, but once the client feels relaxed and has a positive and open mindset, then personal change will tend to happen far more rapidly. An important element in creating an atmosphere for change is for the client to slow down and relax. This will help them to engage with their feelings and reduce the amount of mental distraction (self-talk). Simple ways to do this are:

- *To agree from the outset the timings and process*
- *Turn off mobile phones*
- *Use a quiet and comfortable room with natural light and comfortable chairs*
- *Talk in a calm way and don't appear rushed*
- *Ideally be away from their office*

Also, don't seek out solutions too soon as this will tend to restrict how deeply the coach listens to their client and gets to understand their circumstances and underlying needs.

Listen at a deeper level: An essential element to coaching is effective listening, which may seem obvious but is difficult to do well. Most conversations between people involve a small amount of listening before the other person gives their opinion or shares something about themselves. A deeper level of listening involves the coach focusing their full attention on the talker, reflecting back what the person has said (possibly in a more positive way), asking for more information, clarifying questions, probing about their feelings or simply allowing for silences. The challenge in doing this for the coach is to suspend any tendency to interpret and find immediate solutions, which would reduce their capacity for open and non-judgemental listening.

Keeping an open mind and tolerating ambiguity will allow for deeper intuitive insights to emerge, to hear patterns in what the client is saying, to understand their feelings better and to notice subtleties such as what the client is not saying that may be important. By focusing attention on the client and what they are saying, the unconscious brain will sooner or later supply the answers. Suspending judgement or at least being aware of inner self-talk is an advanced skill that requires continued practice by the coach.

Listen for underlying needs: Clients will often present innumerable issues and problems which seem too many or insurmountable and it is all too easy to be drawn into a long discussion attempting to 'solve' each 'problem' in turn. This approach is often futile as each time a solution is presented the client will search for reasons why they are right and entrench their own negative thoughts. Rather than seeking to resolve each issue, the coach can listen to the client without forming judgements or answers. The longer the coach suspends their judgement the more their intuition will identify common underlying patterns across the client's related issues. Beneath many apparent problems are basic human emotional needs that are not being met, such as the need for connection, autonomy, control, attention, meaning and challenge (these are described further in Chapter 7.4). Reflecting back the underlying need to the client; *It sounds like you are presently experiencing a lack of control in your life,* can help the client focus, simplify and get to the core essence of their issues.

Look for simple solutions first: It may be tempting for the coach to show off their psychological expertise to a client and demonstrate great insight and wisdom. However, complex problems do not necessarily require complex solutions. Sometimes they are best solved with simple practical approaches; small changes are easier to implement and can have a domino effect on other related problems. For example, a person may be suffering from low self-esteem due to a difficulty in forming relationships because they have never learnt the basics of how to make small talk. Teaching them some simple ground rules of communication; such as remembering a person's name, to ask people open questions and to listen to their response, could be far more effective than lengthy discussions about their childhood.

Notice the client's behaviour during coaching: Identifying areas for the client's development will often become evident through observing the client's behaviour, language and how they interact during coaching. For example, a client who has received feedback for being unreliable at work turns up late for the coaching session; a client who is not connecting with their team does not express their feelings during coaching; a client who at work has few clear personal goals constantly digresses in conversation during coaching; or a client who as a leader is struggling to gain the trust of colleagues uses critical and blaming language when discussing others. It is extremely powerful to make the client aware of this in a tactful and helpful manner; *I notice you used the word 'incompetent' several times to describe your colleague. How do you feel towards them?*

Be skilful in the use of language: Words are tools of the trade for a coach, used knowingly they can help the client access and use different parts of their brain. Asking the client; *What do you think?* will access their left analytical brain, an important resource for problem solving. Asking them to use feeling words, will get them to pay attention to their body and to self-observe, both are important aspects of EI.

154

Using more abstract language will tend to activate their right brain hemisphere, which makes connections by processing information metaphorically. This can be a highly effective way of influencing the unconscious and deeper emotional parts of the brain that form a person's attitudes that drives much of their behaviour. The following suggestive statements would engage the client's imagination to initiate positive and proactive thinking, feeling and behaviour; *can you imagine how it would be for you if you felt more confident? If you didn't have this concern how would your life be then? I am wondering whether you will use this approach often or just occasionally? How do you feel now you are starting to relax?*

Avoid colluding with the client: As a coach there is a natural tendency to want to agree with and maintain harmony with the client. The job of the coach is not to be their friend but to help them move forward, this often requires pushing them outside of their comfort zone. The client is likely to want to spend the coaching time doing what they feel most comfortable doing, which is often the thing they least need to develop. If the client enjoys exploring their feelings deeply, then they may benefit more from taking action; if the client likes goal setting then they may benefit more from stepping back; if they are highly analytical and cognitive then they may develop more from noticing their feelings. Notice what the client prefers to discuss; do they focus mostly on the past and avoid discussing the future, or are they mostly looking ahead without learning from past experience?

The tendency to collude may come from the coach having similar preferences to the client; such as both preferring to explore ideas and not being very realistic, or both getting stuck on details and not considering the wider picture. It is entirely possible to have what feels like a very enjoyable dialogue because the coach and client both enjoy discussing the same thing, yet the client gains very little personal development.

Notice the client's resistance: Managing one's own behaviour as a coach is one side of the coin; the other side is getting the client to take responsibility for their own development. Clients may intentionally or unconsciously attempt to avoid or sabotage the coaching process and their own chances of success. This may be in practical ways, such as not completing the questionnaire, turning up late or being interrupted during coaching. If so, consider whether this is an aspect for the client's personal development, for example, does the client often let people down? Do they like to assert control? Are they very disorganised? Do they avoid feedback and self-reflection? Also be observant of any behaviours that distract from their personal development such as:

- They may choose to debate the technical aspects of the questionnaire or the definition of the items. Giving them confidence in the product is important, but remind them that the purpose of coaching is to focus on them and avoid being drawn into long technical discussions. Refer them instead to the EIP technical manual that they may read after the session.
- A client may be over-enthusiastic and keen to embrace everything the coach says; be careful not to be drawn into becoming their 'guru' and encouraging over dependence. If they do seem to be overly dependent then reflect this observation back to them.
- Some clients are more difficult to open up and expect the coach to be the expert and do all the talking, this may be driven by a suspicion and fear of the process. It may be necessary to go back to rapport building and an explanation of the EIP. Also check if they have any concerns and re-contract the process if needed.
- Listen to the client's language for signs of not taking responsibility and reflect this back to them. Do they detach by saying *'you'* instead of *'I'* when talking about themselves? Do they focus externally and blame others rather than what they can do about it; *It's just the way I am, I can't help it*? And do they use vague or non-committal language *I will try, I suppose so*?

Tactfully push clients with high scores: Sometimes clients will find it extremely difficult to identify anything that they want to change or develop and will have rated themselves very high on nearly all of the scales. This may be because they lack awareness or they feel resistant to showing a weakness (a 'Be Strong' or 'Be Perfect' defence). Ask their permission to challenge them (which they may like) and put these hypotheses to them. An alternative strategy for challenging them is to emphasise how highly they rated themselves but that there is always room for improvement, as opposed to there being a 'weakness' and ask them how they could make even better use of their strengths and move from 'good' to 'great'. The important thing is for the client to experience the benefit of active self-development. If they are constantly making excuses or justifying themselves then push them to consider the possibility of some improvement; *If there was room for a 1% improvement what would it be?* Look more carefully at the Item Analysis section, it is unlikely they 'Strongly Agree' with every positive item and 'Strongly Disagree' with every negative item. Look also at the scale scores, if they scored '9' ask them what a score of '10' would look like for them. Also remind them that having a high score indicates they are near the end of this phase in their development journey and ready now for the next phase and to set their benchmarks higher.

Focus on solutions: The EIP is designed to identify what blocks a person from reaching their natural potential and starts from the assumption that *people have a natural propensity towards growth and health* (EI attitude No. 8, Chapter 1). From this premise it is important that the coach focuses the client on what they can do to develop their EI, and does not get drawn into the unhealthy trap of continually discussing (and therefore unconsciously reinforcing) the client's issues, problems, weaknesses, difficulties and challenges, etc. The coach may start by finding out what the client's inner resources are and how it is they have managed to cope so well despite these challenges. Ask questions that will elicit their strengths and focus on solutions, such as; *which scales are your relative strengths? What would make this a worthwhile session for you? How have you coped with these problems? How did you manage before this happened? Talk me through this step by step. Describe to me the future you want to create. How will you know when you have it?* Using *how* rather than *why* questions tends to be more constructive, asking about the *future* rather than the *past* is more progressive, and talking about what *is* rather than what *is not* is more positive.

Psychology often encourages people to unpick problems and understand the reasons 'why', which intellectually may be interesting, but understanding the causes does not necessarily enable people to change. However, knowing what works and putting this into practice does make a difference. For example, keeping solution diaries instead of problem diaries, doing something different instead of repeating the same mistake, and taking action instead of putting up with things will lead to more successful outcomes.

Set realistic expectations: An important skill of being an effective coach is setting the correct level of expectation; too much and the individual may fail and become disheartened, too little and they may become bored and under perform. There is an optimal level of expectation and motivation described by Csikszentihalyi[5] as *flow*. This is when a person feels challenged but not stressed in working towards their goal, allowing them to meet or slightly exceed their expectations (releasing the feel good neurochemical dopamine). One of the reasons people fail to move towards their goals is because they are waiting to feel motivated or inspired before taking action. This is a common misconception as motivation comes from taking action. The first small step can be difficult but it creates energy and motivation which in turn makes the next step easier to take and so the cycle continues of action-motivation-action.

Help the client integrate change: Life is a continuous process of change. Part of being emotionally intelligent is learning to integrate changes into one's life to create balance. A metaphor for this is like 'riding a bicycle', where a person must keep moving to stay in balance. Along the journey there will be rocky terrain and sometimes the person may fall off or need to carry extra things in their basket. Whatever happens, the journey is always changing and the person must learn how to adapt, incorporate and integrate the changes in themselves and their environment. A useful model to help with change is described by Prochaska and DiClemente's[6] stages of change. Working through this with the client and the related EIP scales will provide a useful structure.

Table 6.3 Stages of change and the EIP

This chapter has provided an explanation on how to apply the EIP, the process for exploring EIP reports, and the skills for coaching with the EIP. .

Stage of change	Relevant EIP scales to progress to the next stage	Reason for these EIP scales	Example
Pre-contemplation (Not Ready)	Self Awareness	To become aware of the need to change.	Receiving negative 360 feedback on having poor organisational skills and noticing how they feel about this.
Contemplation (Weighing up options)	Flexibility Balanced Outlook Reflective Learning	To start to consider why they behave as they do and decide what they want to change.	Reflecting on why they got this feedback; is it true? Do they want to change?
Preparation (Planning)	Flexibility Goal Directedness Connecting with Others Balanced Outlook	To be willing to change. If the change involves others they may also need to develop some of the interpersonal EIP scales such as Connecting with Others so as to get support from others.	Choosing to do something about this such as deciding to: ● *Discuss it with their line manager.* ● *Model someone who is a good organiser.* ● *Buy a book for prioritising activities.*
Action (Doing the plan)	Emotional Resilience Personal Power Authenticity	To build resilience to cope with setbacks and to have the conviction to see change through.	Implementing the above decisions.

Stage of change	Relevant EIP scales to progress to the next stage	Reason for these EIP scales	Example
Maintenance	All of the above EIP scales. For example, if a person lacks Self Awareness they may never get to the Contemplation stage.	To keep on track. To integrate the new behaviour to be congruent with underlying attitudes, values and their self-concept.	During change it is usual to have a relapse, for example, if at the Preparation stage the individual buys their 'activity book' but doesn't fill it in. The individual may benefit from repeating and reinforcing the earlier stages, such as Contemplation, so as not to become stuck again at Pre-contemplation.

The next chapter explains specifically how to develop Emotional Intelligence using the EIP

Summary points from Chapter Six

- Before using the EIP, the coach needs to acquire the relevant knowledge and skills to administer, interpret and explore all parts of the EIP reports.

- The coaching process is an exploration rather than feedback. Emphasis is placed on the client being the expert on themselves, not the coach. For example, the Item Analysis section gives all of the client's responses to the EIP, enabling them to explain and interpret their own scores.

- Each user of the EIP will develop their individual style of exploration. However, a recommended six step process is given to ensure all aspects are covered by the coach. This includes agreeing the purpose, building rapport, explaining the EIP, exploring the EIP results, setting development goals and closing the session.

- Although the EIP uses normative scoring, for development purposes it can be just as useful and relevant to consider the client's relative balance of scores such as where they score higher and lower relative to themselves.

- It is important to recognise that the client's scores are relative to their own self-perception and personal benchmarks. People may score low because they set their own benchmarks fairly high when answering the questions or because they are self-critical. Equally, they may score high because of limited self-knowledge or because they have a high ego, so tend to over-rate themselves.

- A low score may also indicate a person is at the start of their developmental journey (conscious incompetence). A high score may indicate they are close to completing their development (unconscious competence) and are ready to progress to the next phase. The next phase of awareness would put them back into 'conscious incompetence' but at a higher level (as they become aware of what else they could develop). For this reason a person's scores may rise and fall (like an 'emotional barometer'), even though their personal development is on a continuous upwards spiral.

- It is worth recognising that a strong indication of an individual's EI is how positively they view their EIP report and engage in their personal development, regardless of their scores being high or low. As this would reflect high Self Regard (valuing oneself unconditionally), which is the essence of EI.

- The EIP may be used in combination with other products. EI is what turns personality into effective behaviour, so combining the EIP with the Personality Type Profile and Behaviours 360 provides a comprehensive assessment of the individual to support their personal development. (Sample reports may be downloaded from www.jcaglobal.com).

- In addition there is also a 360 degree version of the EIP. When used in combination with the EIP the client can make a direct comparison between their self-perception and other's perception of them, against the EIP framework.

- The EIP can be explored within a group setting. It is recommended that group exploration is broken down into chunks based on the six parts of the EIP framework. Such as, a separate module on Relationship Management combined with relevant experiential activities.

- The EIP is a tool to facilitate the coaching process. The success of coaching will depend largely on the skills of the coach (rather than the EIP product alone) and ultimately upon the client's willingness to take responsibility for their own development.

- Coaching with the EIP requires some core skills including; the ability to build rapport, the skills to listen at a deeper level, the experience to create an atmosphere of change, and the techniques to focus the client on solutions and taking action.

- The skilled EIP coach will also have developed their own EI. They should be sufficiently self-aware to notice their own resistance and defences as a coach, whilst also being sufficiently aware of their client's resistance and defences to their development.

●　　●　　●

Chapter Seven

How to develop Emotional Intelligence

Introduction

The very process of a client completing the EIP and reflecting on their responses can help raise their self-knowledge and knowledge of others. By exploring their EI Profile with their coach they will be able to interpret their scale scores, draw out meaningful insights, and define what they want to develop and change in their behaviour, thinking, feeling and attitudes. The next stage is to make these changes happen through taking action. To some degree this will take place spontaneously through exploring the EIP results; however it is easy to become stuck at the middle Awareness (Feeling) level of the EIP framework and for this not to be followed through to the Behaviour level by implementation. This chapter provides suggestions on how to make this happen so that good intentions are turned into enduring habits and attitudes. These suggestions are not intended to be step by step instructions, but rather a guide for the coach to help draw upon their existing set of skills and techniques.

The first part of this chapter describes how to develop Emotional Intelligence through the six psychological stages of EI (SAFE-TBO), which were described in Chapter 2. The second part of this chapter gives more specific suggestions that can be given directly to the individual, on how to develop EI in each of the sixteen EIP scales.

7.1 Processes for developing Emotional Intelligence

Of the many human attributes that differentiate higher performance in the workplace, the majority may be summarised by the acronym KASH; Knowledge, Attitude, Skills and Habits.[1] When organisations are asked which of these they invest in most for people development, the answer is usually *skills and knowledge*, but when asked which of these are more long-term predictors of performance and make a sustained difference, the answer is typically *attitudes and habits*. These are both the province of Emotional Intelligence and the answer to sustainable change. Skills and knowledge on the other hand, can more easily be developed when people hold complimentary attitudes and habits.

Attitudes and habits form part of a psychological process by which people perceive, interpret and act upon their experiences. Each part of this process, including their thinking and feeling, fall between the initial stimulus of an event and the resulting outcome of their behaviour, as illustrated in the example below.

Table 7.1 Example of the six EI stages

#	Stage	Description
1	Stimulus:	A manager calls out to their PA; *where are those files?*
2	Attitude:	Their PA perceives this as being told they are too slow.
3	Feeling/Emotion:	They feel annoyance.
4	Thinking:	They think to themself; *you don't appreciate how hard I work for you.*
5	Behaviour/Habit:	Their automatic response is to shout back; *I can only do one thing at a time!* A few minutes later they slam the files down on the Managers desk.
6	Outcome:	The result being that they don't talk and avoid one another for the rest of the day.

This six part model (SAFE-TBO) for how people process their experiences is drawn from the neuropsychological explanation of EI described in Chapter 2. This provides a useful structure for understanding the various mechanisms by which coaching interventions can be made. All of these stages are interconnected therefore changing one of them is likely to produce a change in the others and ultimately in the final outcome. For example. The recommended development suggestions given below for each stage will also be relevant to many of the other stages. These interventions are based on a wide experience of using the EIP with individuals and groups, and have been found to produce effective results for making change sustainable.

7.2 How to respond to or change the stimulus

The first stage in psychological processing will be initiated by a stimulus, whether this is external such as the telephone ringing, or internal such as feeling thirsty. Stimuli may provoke several automatic responses in a person including attitude pattern matches, thoughts, feelings and behavioural habits. Therefore, by changing, removing or creating new stimuli a person can trigger an entirely different set of responses. The emotionally intelligent individual will learn to identify their triggers and to manage these accordingly as described below.

Change the stimulus: A stimulus can be anything from the environment that triggers a response in a person; therefore by changing the stimulus a person may also change their response. This may be as simple as the individual avoiding people or situations that bring out the worst in them, or choosing to be with people or environments that bring out the best in them. An individual can also learn how to create the response they want from others which in itself will act as a stimulus. For example, by making an effort to engage with people, others are likely to reciprocate by being more responsive which in turn will create a more positive atmosphere (a new stimulus). In other words, the stimulus-response effect is cyclical as one will initiate the other.

Create emotional anchors: In the early twentieth century psychologists demonstrated how animal behaviour is largely the result of conditioned responses. For example, Pavlov[2] demonstrated how if a dog was repeatedly given food when a bell rang, the dog would soon start to expect to be fed and salivate at the sound of the bell alone. This was termed a 'conditioned' response whereby through repetition (reinforcement) an emotional and behavioural response could be created. A similar technique, known as 'anchoring',[3] has been used to help people manage their emotional state. For example, a person may rehearse recalling happy memories and their associated feelings while clasping their hands together. After sufficient repetition the action of clasping hands together becomes an anchor for the associated feelings of their happy memories. Rather like the dog's response to the bell, the individual will only need to activate the stimulus (clasping their hands together) to trigger the conditioned response (the happy feelings). This principle can be widened to any set of feelings or behaviours, and is similar in principle to how habits are formed through reinforcement, discussed later in this chapter.

Block the stimulus: At a neurological level it is possible to intervene between the stimulus being fired and the person's response. Libet[4] showed that there is half a second gap between the signal (an 'action potential') and the automatic response. It takes 0.3 seconds before a person becomes aware of the desire to act, giving them 0.2 seconds to intervene and block their automatic response. In other words, by developing good emotional Self Awareness (scale 3) a person can learn to stop their automatic response allowing them time to then choose a different behaviour. This inhibitory system is activated by the ventrolateral prefrontal cortex that helps a person to inhibit their impulses. Such as, not being distracted from a task, resisting an emotional outburst and thinking before acting. There is a caveat however, as each time an individual tries to inhibit an impulse the next impulse will be more difficult to stop. Research done by Baumeister[5] found that people who had to resist the urge to eat chocolate were less able later on to resist their impulse to eat chocolate. This would suggest that self-control is a limited resource that should be used sparingly.

Self regulate the heart: In Chapter 2.8 it was explained how the heart is a primary stimulus that activates responses within the brain and the rest of the body. It is possible to influence this relationship by directly attending to the heart so as to stimulate emotional and cognitive change. Several approaches have been created for this by the HeartMath Institute (www.heartmath.org). One such technique involves focusing attention on the heart (by placing a hand on this area), and then to imagine breathing in and out though the heart. This is then accompanied by recalling positive feelings and experiences, and paying attention to how the body feels. Ideally this is supported by biofeedback of the individual's heart rate and rhythm. The outcome of focusing on the heart in this way is to improve cortical functioning and create a more relaxed physical state.[6]

Minimise the threat response: The brain's primary purpose is to keep a person alive and it does this by scanning the environment (about five times every second) for possible threats. Threat (pain) stimuli can make people more rigid and defensive and therefore less emotionally intelligent. Evidence shows that some of the most powerful motivating threat stimuli are social stimuli, which have even been found to activate the same pain and pleasure receptors as physical stimuli[7] (this contrasts with Maslow's classic need theory[8] that suggests social factors are lower down the hierarchy of needs). To this extent, people are primarily motivated to maximise certain social reward stimuli and will resist any threat to losing them. Rock[9] identifies five social stimuli (SCARF) that will activate the reward or threat response. Learning where these stimuli appear in a person's life will help them minimise defensive behaviour (threat response) and maximise emotionally intelligent behaviour (reward response).

The five social stimuli (SCARF):

1 **Status:** *People compare themselves to others mostly within their localised groups, such as the workplace. Performance appraisals, unskilled feedback and competitive work environments are likely to activate the threat response. Appropriate praise, reward for competence (rather than seniority) and promoting values such as respecting others, are likely to activate the reward response.*

2 **Certainty:** *The brain is hardwired to anticipate and predict what will happen, so managers who are consistent and reliable (Authenticity; scale 10) will create a calmer and more productive environment (reward stimuli). A manager who is inconsistent and unpredictable on the other hand is more likely to activate the threat response in others.*

3 **Autonomy:** *Giving individuals choice and control over their work life (reward stimuli) will increase their sense of Personal Power (scale 6). Removing autonomy (threat stimuli), however, will increase stress and impair performance. One study in a nursing home found that residents who were given greater choice over small matters, such as where to place a plant and when to have a meal, lived longer and healthier lives.[10]*

4 **Relating to others:** *The brain automatically makes friend (reward response) or foe (threat response) decisions on meeting others. An important aspect of relationship management is learning how to read others (Awareness of Others; scale 4) and to give off subtle 'friend' signals such a smiling, some eye contact and a calm tone of voice (Connecting with Others; scale 9).*

5 **Fairness:** *A perceived sense of unfairness and inequality (threat stimuli) will stir up strong feelings of mistrust, anger and hostility. The boss who is open and fair with others (reward stimuli) is likely to foster an environment of Trust (scale 11) and collaboration (Interdependence; scale 15).*

These social needs are also emotional needs discussed in Table 7.2.

Change the internal triggers: Stimuli may be either external, such as people, situations and the environment, or internal, such as a person's feelings, thoughts and attitudes. Each of the psychological processes being discussed in this chapter are internal stimuli; a negative attitude may trigger negative feelings, negative feelings may trigger critical thinking, and critical thinking may trigger defensive behaviours and habits. The most direct form of internal stimuli affecting a person's behaviour is their feelings. One of the EI attitudes that underpin the EIP is that *feelings and behaviours are separate.* Individuals who have difficulty separating their feelings (stimulus) from their behaviour (response) will usually be impulsive (low Goal Directedness, scale 7) and emotionally under-controlled (scale 13). It is important that a person learns to differentiate between their thoughts, feelings, behaviour and attitudes if they are to develop their EI. This may be done by the individual first becoming aware of these different elements. Such as, noticing their feelings in the body, becoming aware of their self-talk (thoughts), understanding the attitudes behind their feelings and seeking feedback on their behaviour.

The remainder of this chapter looks at attitudes, thoughts, feelings and habits, all of which are interrelated and therefore act as stimuli and responses to each other. Learning how to manage these different psychological elements is what constitutes being emotionally intelligent.

7.3 How to develop constructive attitudes

It has long been known that people are drawn to behave in ways that are consistent with their attitudes, otherwise they experience anxiety (known as cognitive dissonance) compelling them to change how they behave.[11] Attitudes create people's emotional responses through a pattern matching process in the emotional brain (described in Chapter 2.4), which in turn fuel their thinking and lead to their behaviour. Therefore in the long-term to change behaviour people must also shift their attitudes. For example, teaching a person to say *no* assertively will not last for long if underneath they still feel inadequate (their attitude). Or introducing a set of customer service competencies is unlikely to achieve the desired outcome if the person concerned does not want to be of service to others (their attitude).

The first step to changing attitudes is to become aware of them. Attitudes are intended to help simplify life in order that people do not need to consciously process and choose every action they make. Once a person becomes aware of their attitudes they cease to be unconscious and automatic and become open to question, deliberation and change. Many of the methods described in this chapter help challenge, create doubt in and undermine negative attitudes, whether this is by changing emotional states, adapting thinking, or creating new habits, all of which are connected with and influence the underlying attitude.

Create doubt in negative attitudes: Changing attitudes does not require deep psychological therapy; rather a person needs only to create an element of doubt in their attitudes for them to be open to change. This is because attitudes operate categorically, such as like/dislike, good/bad or right/wrong. Once attitudes become open to question they are then no longer automatic responses, but conscious thoughts open to debate. This is particularly useful when people hold deeply ingrained attitudes such as; *nobody likes me*, *I am bound to fail* or *nobody can be trusted*. The skill of the coach is not to challenge the person's attitude directly, as this will often result in the person thinking of reasons why they are right and entrenching their attitude further. But instead, to engage the individual in an exploration of their attitude, to discuss how it helps them and hinders them and what may be a more useful alternative attitude to hold.

One such approach, called *the continuum method*,[12] is to ask the client to place their attitude on a 0-10 scale with 0 being the lowest; *I am a failure,* to 10 being what they would like to see; *I am a success*. Then to ask them to list what they would see in someone scoring a 10 (*I am a success),* such as; they would have friends, money and qualifications, etc. Then ask the individual to score where they are on each of these criteria on a 0-10 scale. The likelihood is they will be higher than zero (zero being no friends, no money and no qualifications). By moving them away from a zero the attitude ceases to be categorical; by breaking down their attitude to specific parts they are less able to generalise, and by using a 0-10 scale the attitude becomes open to debate. Also, using 0-10 scales with specific outcomes is an excellent way of setting targets for their goal setting and behaviour change.

Start with a positive mindset: In nature the animal that lives to pass on its genes will be the one that has well developed survival instincts and can instantly focus attention on any perceived threat. Human evolution is no different and people will naturally focus their attention more on the negative than on the positive. For example, people are drawn more rapidly to bad news, they have a better memory for negative events than positive events, they do more to avoid loss than to get a comparable gain and they put more weight on negative information. Kahneman & Tversky,[13] who won the Nobel Prize in Economics, found that the psychological impact of loss is two and a half times as powerful as that of gain, and research on the EIP has shown EI to rise and fall in line with the economy.[14] One reason for this may be that during difficult times the brain switches to *survival* mode; to protect and conserve, even though the best way to survive in difficult times can be to look for opportunities and be creative, that is, to have a *thrive* not a *survive* attitude.

Knowing that people have a natural propensity to focus their attention on the negative is an important consideration when developing EI. Personal Power (scale 6); feeling responsible for oneself, and Balanced Outlook (scale 12); feeling realistically hopeful, are two scales from the EIP that are strong indicators of a positive mindset. By adopting and habitually practicing a positive mindset, people can develop these scales and counter the brain's negative default setting. This includes activities such as actively choosing to focus on positive memories and expectations, investing time in friendships, recognising that people are doing the best they can, having compassion towards oneself and others, replaying the caring rather than critical messages received in childhood and engaging in humour and laughter which have been shown to boost the immune system and be good for people's health.[15]

Apply positive abstract language: When the creators of Neurolinguistic Programming (NLP), Grinder & Bandler,[16] started to model the behaviours of exceptional communicators they observed that one of the key characteristics of influential therapists was the use of positive abstract language. Some examples of positive abstract language used in the coaching context may include; *you will soon be ready to make the changes you wish, ...the next step you make will be significant, ...you can use your inner confidence to grow and develop, ...you can create the future you desire, ...your experiences and knowledge will guide you through,* and *...you have access to your innate capabilities and gifts.* Such statements can be very powerful, because the human brain can't help but search for meaning (pattern matches) from the positive abstract words. In all these examples, the individual will draw out their own positive meaning which will reinforce existing positive attitudes. However, negative abstract language can be equally influential. Statements such as ...*this is hopeless, ...I have depression* and ...*my motivation has gone*, are vague generalisations that create negative attitudes. In contrast therefore, when describing negative experiences it is important to avoid abstract and vague generalisations but to be specific and concrete.

Use metaphors and stories: Similar in process to abstract language are metaphors and stories, which engage the right hemisphere of the brain in a search for meaning. The right hemisphere of the brain is involved in new learning, linking ideas, imagination and being creative. Metaphors and stories capture the imagination causing a type of trance state whereby attitudes are formed and adapted (as described by the REM state in Chapter 2.4). This can be seen in children who quickly go into a daydream when they hear something interesting said, as their pattern matching brain makes meaningful sense of it. A skilled coach will often leave the ending of a metaphor open for the listener's imagination to draw their own conclusions. They will also make the metaphor analogous to the individual's circumstances (such as stories of overcoming adversity, morality and perseverance) and may draw parallels with other parts of the person's life such as their hobbies and sports, where they have demonstrated being effective. Some common metaphors used to help people in their personal development include climbing a mountain (putting things into perspective), taking the stabilisers off a bicycle (letting go), learning to drive a car (developing automatic skills through practice), learning to walk or read as a child (the first steps are the most challenging) and going on a journey (life is unpredictable). Such metaphors can become powerful unconscious motivators, influencing a person's attitudes and behaviour.

Disassociate from negative feelings: There are a growing number of therapeutic and developmental interventions that focus directly on changing the emotional response attached to a person's attitude (a pattern match). Some of these include the Rewind Technique by The Human Givens Institute,[17] Disassociation; an NLP technique,[16] Thought Field Therapy (TFT) also known as 'tapping' by Callaghan,[18] Eye Movement Desensitisation (EMDR) by Shapiro,[19] and Amygdala Depotentiation by Ron Ruden.[20] These techniques all have one thing in common: they require the individual to re-experience an event that triggers their emotional response whilst maintaining a more positive or calmer emotional state. This allows a new and more positive emotion to be attached to the underlying attitude. For example, replacing anxiety with feeling confident when making an important sales pitch, replacing anger with calmness when receiving critical feedback, and changing feelings of pessimism to optimism when faced with a setback. Learning these techniques requires specific training provided by these institutes. Other techniques for calming down emotionally and managing feelings are described in the next section of this chapter.

7.4 How to manage feelings

Feelings are the direct consequence of a stimulus pattern matching with an attitude and are the primary influence on a person's thoughts and behaviours. Feelings are the key mediator between how attitudes determine behaviours, which is illustrated by the three levels of the EIP framework (Chapter 4.1) where Feeling sits in-between Attitude and Behaviour. Feelings drive a person's behaviour in the form of motivation, expectations, needs, wants, fears, likes, hopes and intentions. If a person decides to improve their relationships, develop their confidence or enhance their performance, it is their feelings that will drive this change, which is why feelings are integral to developing EI.

Notice feelings early: All feelings are useful in that they are the 'messenger' telling a person how they are doing, what needs they have and the attitudes they hold. If a person does not notice or attend to their feelings they will manifest in other ways, usually growing in strength until the person is unable to manage them appropriately. An important aspect of EI is learning to notice feelings early, then to accurately label the feelings and understand what they are telling the person. The longer a person ignores, represses and denies their feelings the more likely it is that they will be unable to manage them later on. For example, if a person notices when they feel a mild sense of frustration then they can do something to manage this feeling such as to breathe deeply, consider why they feel this way, or take some positive action to address the cause of their frustration. If not, the feeling may grow until the person feels consumed with anger, by which time they will be less able to process the feelings calmly and rationally and are more likely to overreact.

Pay attention to feelings: There are several stages to becoming aware of one's feelings (and the feelings of others) and acting upon them appropriately.

- *They must first notice the feeling (for example, a tension in the neck).*
- *Then pay attention to this feeling and give it some significance rather than ignore it (why do they have this feeling?).*

- *Then think about what this feeling means (maybe they feel anxious about their presentation).*
- *Then decide how to act upon it (they could practice delivering their presentation to a colleague).*

If people do not pay attention to the initial feelings, as many people do not, they will be unable to move to the next stage of this process. Paying attention to feelings also gives people an insight into their underlying attitudes. For example, if they feel nervous about making a presentation this may indicate they have doubts about their competence in this area, or they have a pessimistic outlook, or they hold a self-critical attitude. Being aware of feelings also gives people access to their intuition. For instance, if they notice feeling uncomfortable about a decision they have made, it may be that they have missed something important, or if they notice feeling uneasy being with a person it may be that they do not trust them.

Learn relaxation techniques: A key skill in developing EI is learning how to be emotionally and physically relaxed. There are several very effective ways of doing this, many of which will involve techniques for breathing, using the imagination, relaxing all parts of the body and focusing attention on calming thoughts. The sequence usually involves the individual closing their eyes, sitting comfortably and minimising any external distractions. This is followed by focusing attention on their breathing and taking longer out-breaths than in-breaths, which helps activate the parasympathetic nervous system which in turn relaxes the body. The individual may then start to become aware of their body by relaxing their muscles, moving up from the feet, into the legs, the torso, up to the shoulders, the head and finally through the arms, hands and fingers. They may continue to relax by using their imagination to visualise walking in a place that they find calming, such as on a beach, in the countryside or on a mountain. Repeating this technique will reinforce the experience and make it easier and quicker to reach the same level of relaxation each time they use it.

Calm down the emotional brain: When a person practices relaxation techniques they are effectively calming down the limbic system which is the part of the brain that triggers emotions. Too much emotion can have significantly negative effects on a person's performance, as in the case of an emotional hijack (described in Chapter 2). This is when the brain perceives a dangerous threat even though none may exist, such as freezing during an important presentation, panicking when late for a meeting or losing one's temper during a discussion. Under such conditions a person's performance can sink to hopeless incompetence, their IQ drops dramatically and reasoning and judgment are easily lost. There are several reasons why poor management of strong emotions can impair a person's performance in this way:

1 *Strong emotions narrow a person's attention and therefore make them less aware and able to consider all of the options.*

2 *They make a person more judgemental in their thinking, as emotional brain thinking tends to be more categorical and less refined.*

3 *They block access to a person's rational thinking brain so reducing their capacity to think things through. This is an evolutionary fight/flight/freeze response to danger.*

4 *They make a person more certain and decisive and less flexible, which can be catastrophic if they are in the grip of the three points above.*

5 *They make a person less self-aware and less aware of others. The individual may not realise how they are behaving and acting, resulting in them pursuing reckless actions and being oblivious to feedback.*

6 *Furthermore, everyone else around them is aware of and impacted by how they are behaving, which may greatly damage their relationships.*

However, if people learn how to manage their emotional state effectively by noticing what causes them anxiety, remaining calm in a crisis, being aware of their feelings in the moment and listening to feedback from others, all of these negative behaviours will be reversed leading to greater awareness, higher intellectual functioning, more flexible behaviour, better decision making and improved relationships. Many techniques for calming the emotional brain are explained later in this chapter.

Reduce levels of stress: The effects of excessive emotion and stress are cumulative. Feelings of stress and anxiety are triggered instantly through the sympathetic nervous system, but it takes the parasympathetic nervous system 3-4 hours to fully calm down after a stressful event.[21] Over time, if people experience regular stress then this will not allow them sufficient recovery time and they could spend much of their time in a state of heightened arousal with the negative consequences this has on their thinking, behaviour and physical health. The danger is that this becomes the individual's typical daily experience, where they feel generally anxious, despondent and unhappy or depressed. People who experience regular stress may benefit from slowing down, reflecting on their experiences and learning how to relax in order that they can change their patterns of behaviour and cope better with life's challenges.

In order to recover from long-term stress they may need to re-evaluate what is important to them and how they want to live their lives. EIP scales that can help in this respect are Emotional Resilience (scale 5), Goal Directedness (scale 7) and Reflective learning (scale 16). Developing these scales is discussed later in Chapter 7.9.

Make time for sleep and recuperation: In Chapter 2.4 it was explained that one of the main ways that arousal and anxiety are reduced is through the natural process of dreaming while asleep. This is the REM phase of sleep, whereby unfulfilled emotional expectations are metaphorically acted out and therefore completed during the dreaming stages of sleep.[22] If an individual does not get sufficient REM sleep they will wake up feeling tired and less able to deal with the challenges of the day ahead. One of the key ways to support sleep is to lower anxiety during the waking day by learning how to relax. A few essential guidelines to aid restful sleep are to avoid caffeine and alcohol before bed, keep to regular sleeping patterns wherever possible, do some physical activity during the day, do not go to bed until feeling tired, do not sleep-in excessively and avoid anxiety provoking thoughts (such as worrying about tomorrow) before bedtime.

Make change experiential: Feelings are the primary drivers of behaviour. To change behaviour it is necessary to change the feelings behind them. Feelings are created in the limbic brain which learns largely through stimulus-response conditioning, which is experiential (practical and emotional) reinforcement, i.e. repetition. This contrasts to the higher parts of the brain, the neocortex (or thinking brain), which learns more through acquiring knowledge and information. For example, people can become very knowledgeable about themselves by reading books, getting feedback, going on courses or being coached, but behavioural change will only happen if it is backed up by putting this knowledge into actual physical practice. All too often people know what they 'should' do but don't do it in practice. What is learnt during a coaching session will only lead to behaviour change if the individual implements and practices it after the coaching has taken place.

This difference between the emotional and thinking parts of the brain is illustrated by the case of an amnesic patient whose emotional memory remained intact despite having no knowledge recall of past events.[23] On one occasion his doctor placed a tack in his hand which caused the patient some pain when they shook hands. The following time when they met, the patient had no recollection of ever having met his doctor but did not want to shake the doctor's hand. Despite the patient having no conscious cognitive explicit memory (in their thinking brain), he still held an unconscious emotional implicit memory that associated shaking hands with the doctor as painful (in their emotional brain). Much of what drives a person's behaviour does so at an unconscious emotional level.[24]

Provide opportunity for interaction: One way to make change experiential, is for it to be done interactively with a group of people. People are innately social and are fundamentally drawn to interact, so it would be hard to justify how EI could be developed without involving some interaction. The changes that take place are often far more dramatic and powerful when carried out collectively rather than individually, this is because other people provide a sense of context and reality to a person's experience. This does not discount the benefit of one-to-one coaching, but this is often only a prelude to the action of putting EI into practice with others.

Meet the basic emotional needs: All living things have essential needs that must be met in order for them to thrive and flourish, for plants it is the need for sunlight, water and soil, for humans it is their emotional needs that will determine their emotional health and well-being. When people do not get their emotional needs met in sufficient balance they become unhappy, angry, unstable, over emotional, anxious and greedy. The Human Givens Institute has identified a set of basic emotional needs that should be met in balance if people are to be emotionally and socially healthy. The EIP scales that help meet these emotional needs are shown in the table below.

Table 7.2 The basic human emotional needs

Basic emotional need	Description	Helpful EIP scales
Security	People need to feel secure and able to cope with the demands and challenges of life. This may be achieved by using and developing their innate resources (described below).	• Self Regard • Emotional Resilience • Personal Power
Emotional connection	Having the capacity and opportunity to connect openly and intimately with others is a basic human need.	• Awareness of Others • Connecting with Others • Emotional Expression and Control
Control	People need a sense of influence and choice over how they live their lives. This should be balanced with their capacity to adapt to changing circumstances.	• Personal Power • Flexibility • Emotional Expression and Control
Community and Status	Humans are social beings and need to belong to groups where they feel valued.	• Regard for Others • Connecting with Others

Basic emotional need	Description	Helpful EIP scales
		● Trust ● Conflict Handling ● Interdependence
Privacy	Having the opportunity for personal time and space where the individual can reflect and be alone is a basic emotional need.	● Interdependence ● Reflective Learning
Achievement	The human brain and body are like muscles that have evolved to be at their healthiest when being utilised and stretched.	● Goal Directedness ● Personal Power ● Balanced Outlook
Attention	The degree to which people receive attention and the form of attention they receive throughout their lives will strongly influence their self-esteem. This is described later in Chapter 7.8; *How to raise Self Regard through effective communication.*	● Self Regard ● Connecting with Others
Meaning and purpose to life	Having meaning and purpose to life is an essential element for emotional well-being. It is derived from three criteria: being stretched and personal growth; being needed and serving others; and from connecting with something bigger than oneself, such as through philosophy and spirituality.	● Self Awareness ● Goal Directedness ● Authenticity

Learn to use the innate resources: Humans possess a set of innate resources that equip them to meet their basic emotional needs (described above). The skill of being emotionally intelligent is in learning how to manage these resources so as to achieve one's potential (just as not learning how to manage one's innate resources represents low EI). Some of the key innate resources, examples of their use and misuse, and how they may be developed through the EIP scales are given below.

Table 7.3 **The fundamental human resources**

Innate resource	Example of effective use	Example of misuse	Related EIP scales
Imagination	Visualising positive outcomes.	Picturing only what could go wrong.	● Goal Directedness ● Balanced Outlook
Creativity	Being insightful and finding solutions to complex problems.	Being entirely unrealistic and impractical.	● Self Awareness ● Flexibility ● Personal Power
Logic and objectivity	Working through problems step by step.	Ignoring feelings, values and sensitivities.	● Self Awareness ● Emotional Resilience

Innate resource	Example of effective use	Example of misuse	Related EIP scales
Self-observation and self-awareness	Noticing one's feelings and how they affect motivation.	Being totally self-absorbed and unaware of others or the environment.	• Self Awareness • Reflective Learning • Authenticity
Sleep and recovery	Being able to rest and recuperate both physically and emotionally.	Feeling constantly tired and run-down, unable to be alert and engaged.	• Self Awareness • Emotional Resilience
Empathy (being in rapport with and reading others feelings)	Adapting and responding to others' individual differences.	Making assumptions about how others are feeling. Or letting others negative feelings bring you down.	• Awareness of Others • Connecting with Others • Trust • Interdependence
Relaxation (calming down physiologically)	Breathing techniques to help reduce anxiety.	Being over relaxed, bored and demotivated.	• Self Awareness • Emotional Resilience
Self-choice (choosing how to respond to feelings)	Developing appropriate impulse control.	Lacking spontaneity, fun and openness.	• Personal Power • Goal Directedness • Emotional Expression and Control • Conflict Handling
Expectation (thinking about the future)	Planning and preparing for a meeting.	Focusing only on the future rather than learning from the past or enjoying the present.	• Goal Directedness • Balanced Outlook • Reflective Learning
Learning (reflecting and learning from past experience)	Modifying a behaviour based on previous experience.	Constantly reflecting (navel gazing) but not putting learning into action.	• Authenticity • Reflective Learning

The suggestions given above are about how to manage feelings, which is closely connected with the next section on how to manage thinking, in that feelings trigger thoughts and thoughts fuel feelings and both direct a person's behaviour. Or, as defined by the EIP: *EI is achieved through the habitual practice of thinking about feeling and feeling about thinking to guide one's behaviour* (refer to Chapter 1.4).

7.5 How to manage thinking

Most techniques for 'managing thinking' focus on changing and interrupting irrational and generalised thinking patterns. Irrational thinking is largely the result of excessive emotion; neurochemicals stimulated by the deeper limbic system that interfere with higher brain functioning. If sufficiently strong, emotions such as joy, desire, hate, and fear can prevent the individual from engaging their rational thinking brain to make a more fine-grained analysis of their emotional feedback. One sign of this is when people use generalised language such as; *can't, must, have to, never, and always,* which may indicate they are locked into their emotional brain which leads to exaggerated and inappropriate thinking and behaviour. Calming down the emotional brain from excessive arousal to enable clearer thinking is an essential aspect of Emotional Intelligence and was discussed in the previous section on 'How to manage feelings'. This section on 'How to manage thinking' includes a range of cognitive techniques, such as *reframing,* that help the individual to use their thinking capacities to understand and manage their feelings so as to be more rational, objective and self-managed.

Quieten the rational thinking brain: Calming the emotional brain (see previous section) may be complimented by learning how to quieten the rational thinking brain which allows for more insightful, creative, intuitive and inspired levels of thinking. People tend to do their most insightful thinking when relaxed and not trying to think. One study by Rock[9] showed that only 10% of people did their best thinking at work and that their most insightful thinking was during non-work activities such as at play, when resting, during physical exercise, in down time, whilst reflecting and when experiencing something new. All these activities share a number of criteria that are often present at times of quality thinking:

1 *The person is not trying too hard to solve a problem, which helps them to switch off the noise (distracting thoughts, inner dialogue, self-conscious inhibition, etc.)*
2 *The activity is non-demanding allowing their mind to wander and make insightful connections.*
3 *They have slowed down their thinking, giving more time for ideas to connect. Rather like taking the scenic route instead of the motorway on a car journey.*
4 *They may be doing something different from their routine which connects different neurons and forms new associations.*
5 *They are focusing internally which helps them reduce external stimulation and access deeper insights. Intuition and insight come from connecting with deeper level patterns (accumulated wisdom) and the quieter brain signals.*
6 *They have a positive (but not over excited) mindset, which prevents their threat response from being alerted (which would block clear thinking) and activates quieter circuitry in the brain.*

7   *They are in a focused state of attention (a trance state) where their interest and imagination have been captivated, allowing for longer and deeper levels of concentration.*

Developing this deeper level of insightful thinking has several benefits:

A   *It is often the only way by which more complex problems can be solved.*
B   *It creates new neural networks so the learning acquired is more permanent.*
C   *The individual is more likely to take ownership and be motivated by learning through self-discovery.*
D   *The instant euphoria gained from an insight releases energy helping the person to take action.*

Use positive reframing: Reframing is a technique often used by the coach to feedback what their client expresses but in a more positive way. For example; *I can't do anything right*, may be reframed by the coach as; *I see there are some things you are finding quite challenging at the moment*. The word *can't* has been replaced by *challenging,* the word *anything* by the words *some things* and adding *at the moment* implies that the situation is temporary. More often than not the client will accept the reframe, and their emotional (limbic) brain will unconsciously create new expectations and patterns to match this more positive description. People can also apply this technique to reframing their feelings. For example, feelings of 'anxiety' may be reframed as 'anticipation', and 'boredom' may be reframed as 'relaxation'. Reframing is particularly useful in areas such as sports motivation, mood enhancement and building self-confidence. However, the skill of the coach is to balance positive reframing without discounting what the client is saying and to fully acknowledge how they are feeling.

Challenge negative thinking: Other methods for changing negative thinking are more direct than reframing and aim to consciously challenge the individual's excessively emotional and categorical thinking by applying a more analytical and rational approach. For example, a client may be asked what advice they would give a friend who was in a similar situation to themselves. People are often very good at giving sound, rational and sensible advice to others but are less adept at applying it to themselves. This is because people are less emotionally involved with others than they are with themselves and can therefore think through problems more clearly. (This is described in Transactional Analysis as coming from the Adult ego state rather than from the Parent or Child ego states).

Another way in which people can challenge their negative interpretation of events is to think of several alternative explanations. For example, one reason why their boss didn't reply to their email was because *he doesn't respect me* (a negative assumption). Alternative reasons may include; *he didn't receive it, he hasn't had time to reply, or he did reply but the email has been lost*. Rather than assume the worst the individual could be encouraged to choose an explanation that is more probable and will help them to feel better. A modification of this method is to ask the client to think of the very worst possible explanation, then the very best possible explanation and then what is the most realistic, typical and likely explanation. To help the individual think of the most realistic explanation they could be asked to recall past experiences where they have been in similar situations and to describe what happened. For example, they may fear that they will freeze at their next presentation, yet their previous presentations have been well received. Or they may expect their colleague to become very upset at their appraisal yet they have previously handled such difficult conversations very well. To help the client challenge their negative thinking further, the coach may draw upon more tangible evidence such as feedback from others, performance data and using the continuum method (described in Chapter 7.3). Once the individual recognises that in the past their overly negative assumptions turned out to be false they may start to appraise situations more realistically.

There are many other techniques to help individuals challenge their irrational thinking patterns that may be found under titles such as cognitive-behavioural techniques, rational emotive therapy, solutions focused coaching and positive thinking.

Unpack the problem: It can sometimes help an individual to examine a problem in detail so as to identify the sequence of events and common errors in their thinking and interpretation. For example, it may be a situation they did not handle very well in the past such as getting into an argument with their line manager. The following questions will help them to examine and learn from the specific event:

- *Describe what happened.*
- *What was the initial trigger?*
- *How were they feeling immediately prior to this event?*
- *What were they thinking at the time of the event?*
- *How did they feel during the event?*
- *What do they think the other person (if relevant) was thinking and feeling?*
- *Was this a one-off or a common pattern for them?*
- *What did they do after the event?*
- *What would they have done differently, before, during and after the event?*

It is also important when discussing the situation that the individual is feeling calm. People often try to resolve their problems when feeling anxious and tired, rather than waiting till they are more relaxed and able to think things through more clearly.

Use the language of choice: People's negative thinking is often reflected in their use of words and language. Negative language typically reflects low choice, low control and rigid behaviour. Positive language typically reflects high choice, self-responsibility and flexible behaviour. Below are some examples of how to use high choice words and language.

Table 7.4 Examples of using high choice language

Suggestion	Low choice examples (negative language)	High choice examples (positive language)
Say 'I' instead of 'you' when referring to oneself	*You don't like to speak up when you are in a group*	*I don't like to speak up when I am in a group*
State if something is an opinion rather than claiming it to be a fact	*That's true* *This is difficult*	*I think that is true* *I find it difficult*
Use self-empowering words rather than disempowering words	*I should* *I will try* *I must do* *I have to* *I need to*	*I will do* *I can do* *I shall do*
Be specific rather than generalising	*It is always like this* *I never win* *Nobody likes me* *I have nothing* *Everyone says so*	*On this occasion* *I was unsuccessful this week* *I don't think Jane likes me* *I no longer have this* *Four people in the group agree*
Use committed language rather than too many non-committal or downplaying words	*Interesting* *Possibly* *Maybe* *Sort of* *I suppose* *I guess so*	*I agree/disagree* *I like it/dislike that* *In my opinion*
Avoid confusing feelings with thinking	*I feel that is correct* *I feel we should do x.* (Both of which are thoughts not feelings) *I think you are an idiot* *You are wrong* (Both may be masking feelings)	*I feel angry, happy, upset, etc.* *I feel annoyed when you* *I am unhappy with your decision because*

Repeated use of either negative or positive language will over time become an automatic, unconscious and ingrained habit for a person. Learning how to change a negative habit and to reinforce positive and constructive habits is explained in the next section.

7.6 How to create useful habits of behaviour

Habits are automatic responses that may include behaviours, emotions and thoughts. For example, a person may have a *behavioural* habit of not listening to people, an *emotional* habit of becoming upset by confrontation, and a *thinking* habit of assuming the worst when things go wrong. Emotional and thinking habits have been explained above, and behavioural habits are discussed below.

Replace negative habits: Behavioural habits are mostly automatic and unconscious, therefore the first step in creating new habits is for the individual to become aware of their existing habits and start to notice which behaviours are constructive and which they may wish to change. The next step is then to replace the unhelpful habits with positive habits. For example, replacing blaming others with showing appreciation, blaming oneself with valuing oneself, demanding constant attention with listening to people, avoiding people with initiating conversation, compulsively working with taking time for relaxation, over-eating with taking exercise, watching too much television with being outdoors, and being tired with setting personal goals. One of the difficulties in changing a habit is making it stick as the existing neural pattern must be replaced by a stronger alternative.[25] This can be achieved through repetition, rehearsal and reinforcement of the new behaviour pattern to avoid reverting back to the old behavioural habit.

Use conscious thinking sparingly: One of the key benefits of developing habits is they free up the higher thinking parts of the brain (the prefrontal cortex or the 'boss') for more demanding mental activities such as understanding new information, prioritising and decision making. This is because habits are carried out in a deeper region of the brain called the basal ganglia which, unlike the prefrontal cortex, is highly energy efficient, having the capacity for hours of constant activation and multi-tasking with relatively little effort (an example of this would be driving a car).[26] The basal ganglia is also a fast learner that will store routine functions quickly and start to take over after only a few repetitions of a task. Conscious thinking on the other hand is resource intensive requiring a lot of glucose and oxygen, particularly when switching between tasks. It is therefore recommended that, whenever possible, repetitive and multitask activities are embedded as habits and that conscious thinking is reserved for high quality thinking, ideally done in short bursts and on single tasks.

Be motivated to change: Making the initial change in behaviour can be relatively easy but maintaining it and not changing back can be far more difficult to sustain. All too often when people are under pressure or the initial motivation for change has gone they revert back to their old behaviours. One reason for this is that the person does not really want to change. At an unconscious level they may even want to hold on to their negative and defensive behaviour because it still provides them with some benefit. The solution to this is to make sure that the person really wants to change and that the pay-off for doing so outweighs the sacrifice for giving up the old habit. For example, an individual who behaves aggressively may not want to change their habit since doing so may mean that people will pay them less attention or that they do not immediately get their own way on matters.

It is also important to be sure that the new behaviour is something the person wants for themself rather than to meet other people's expectations of them to do the 'right thing' or to keep others happy (such as their parents or their coach). Motivation to change is largely unconscious, so if an individual is relying solely upon conscious willpower to change, they will often revert back over time to what they unconsciously wanted to do (their underlying attitude).

Focus on one specific behaviour: Another reason why people fail to achieve their goals is that they aim to change too much in one go such as new year's resolutions; *I will be nice to everyone from now on, …I will only eat healthy food, …I will always remain positive and happy,* are all unlikely to succeed. More specific alternatives to these could be; *…doing one good turn for someone each day, …eating one whole piece of fruit every day,* and *…making a point to laugh with someone once a day.* It is tempting during the enthusiasm of a coaching session to set noble and ambitious goals, but after a day or two back into the daily demands of life the motivation wanes and people slip back into their automatic habits. The technique of habit change involves making sure it is focused on something highly specific that will be easily completed and repeated over a period of time so that the new habit is stronger than the old one. Any specific behaviour change will also have a wider impact than the specific change itself. For example, getting a client to develop the habit of remembering people's names may help improve their relationships with people, which may then raise their self-esteem. In addition, success breeds success; by learning that habit *change is possible* (EI attitude No. 7) and that it works, the individual may continue to practice it and become more skilled at changing their habits, which will allow them to develop their EI.

Link habits to attitudes: It was explained in the section on changing attitudes that people's behaviour generally reflects and is consistent with their attitudes. It is therefore important that the specific habitual behaviour being changed is congruent with their underlying attitude. If not, the person will soon revert back to their original behaviour. For example, assertiveness skills training often fails because underneath the individual still holds the attitude that they are submissive (I am Not OK, you are OK). It is possible to change attitudes by changing behaviour. To do so, the behaviour change must be highly specific and consciously linked to the attitude. Over time the new specific behaviour will begin to undermine and erode the attitude, allowing it to be replaced by a more congruent attitude to the behaviour. This is explained in more detail with a related habit change technique in Chapter 6.2 (Step 5; Set personal development goals).

Practice a different behaviour response: Habits are unconscious automatic responses to stimuli that happen on a daily basis. Consider these examples:

- *When answering the telephone the individual expects the worst.*
- *When opening the fridge they take out a piece of chocolate.*
- *When meeting a friend they start by talking about themselves.*
- *When in a hurry they become irritable.*

Simply becoming aware of these habits of association can help the person change their automatic response if they choose to do so. This may be done by consciously deciding to respond differently and repeating the new behaviour until it also becomes an automatic response. In the examples above;

- *When answering the telephone they could stand up and smile.*
- *When opening the fridge they could take out a piece of fruit.*
- *When meeting a friend they could ask about them first.*
- *When in a hurry they could pause to take six slow deep breaths.*

To do this requires two steps; first becoming aware of the habit and second choosing and repeating a new behavioural response.

Develop healthy lifestyle habits: Much of Emotional Intelligence focuses on developing the psychological skills described above, but a healthy mind is also dependent upon a healthy body. Physical health has many benefits for stress reduction, mental stamina and work performance.[27] There are three main ways of building and maintaining a healthy body; rest, nutrition and exercise. Rest, which includes sleep and recuperation, has been discussed in Chapter 2 and is crucial for de-arousal and physical recovery. Nutrition and exercise along with emotional well-being are the other key factors influencing a person's physical health. People are usually aware of the importance of exercise and healthy nutrition but struggle to put this into practice. One reason for this is people's preference for quick fix solutions which often do not work, such as dieting which by design is temporary and therefore does not keep weight off permanently. Making healthy eating and regular exercise into daily lifestyle habits is far more likely to lead to long-term success. This can be achieved in the same way as developing psychological habits discussed above; through regular repetition of specific changes in behaviour.

Changing a behavioural habit is not the final stage in the process of developing EI. How a person behaves will also lead to consequences and outcomes. By focusing on the outcomes the person wants to achieve they are more likely to develop the habits and behaviours that enable them to attain their goals. How this is done is discussed in the next section.

7.7 How to create positive outcomes

The basis to a person achieving the outcome they want is to firstly identify what it is they want, which requires Self Awareness (scale 3), followed by the ability to focus on and not be distracted from achieving it, which requires Goal Directedness (scale 7). A number of useful suggestions for creating positive outcomes are given below.

Have clear intentions: In order to develop EI it is important for an individual to have clear intention as to what it is they want to achieve, as reflected by scale 7, Goal Directedness. In neurological terms this means creating expectations that will orientate the individual consciously and unconsciously towards the outcome they want to achieve. The brain is a pattern matching organ and is constantly scanning the environment for matches. This is why, for example, optimistic people will often spot opportunities and pessimistic people are more inclined to focus their attention on barriers and problems. A powerful way of setting positive expectations is through visualisation, guided imagery and mental rehearsal, described below.

Plan each step: As well as focusing on the end outcome it is important for the individual to plan *how* they are going to achieve it. Sometimes people know what they want but go about it in the wrong way, such as not building rapport before making a request, or making a decision without consulting those who may be affected by it. When broken down into sequences of action there are a surprising number of steps that lead to an outcome; just boiling a kettle takes about twenty steps, building a trusting relationship with someone will take several more. Often a client will leave the coaching session with clear goals and objectives but without a specific plan on how they are going to achieve them. It is important that the client has thought this through otherwise they may not even start the process or they may go about it in the wrong way, and then find it doesn't work and give up.

Access the imagination: Guiding someone to use their imagination to set positive expectations and intentions is quite simple but with several subtleties to it. The first step is to help the individual to relax physiologically, cognitively and emotionally. This can be done by getting them to focus on their breathing, to relax every part of their body and to imagine being in a peaceful place (relaxation is described previously under 'how to manage feelings' in Chapter 7.4). Also, speaking to them in a gradually softening voice using vague and abstract positive language helps create positive feelings (see 'how to create constructive attitudes' in Chapter 7.3). Once relaxed, the person can be guided to visualise whatever outcome they wish to achieve, such as giving a confident presentation, succeeding in sport, or feeling calm and relaxed after a stressful day. The more texture people put on their image, such as sound, colour and smell, the stronger and more compelling the image becomes. Having created a positive expectation people are unconsciously drawn to make this happen through their attitudes, thoughts and feelings. This is why people who anticipate success tend to succeed, and those who expect to fail are more likely to be unsuccessful. Imagination has the capacity to create negative as well as positive expectations, so it is important that people learn how to use and manage their imagination rather than letting their imagination control them.

Role-play and rehearse success: An extension of imagination/visualisation is to use role-play and rehearsal. This makes the experience real and at the same time safe and non-threatening to rehearse. Imagination and role-play act as a 'reality generator' firing off the same neurons as if the action were completed for real. For example, if someone feels anxious about a meeting they could visualise how they would want it to go and then role-play it several times with a trusted colleague. They may build on this by role playing their anticipated concerns, which will help them to feel more in control and relaxed, and their rehearsed behaviour will free up spare capacity in their thinking brain to help handle the actual meeting. A step on from imagination and role-play is to have the real life experience but to treat it as a learning event (like having learner plates for a new driver). This takes the pressure off the person and allows them to learn from their mistakes without having high expectations.

The few suggestions given above will help the individual create positive outcomes which in turn will build confidence and self-esteem. Creating positive outcomes is the final stage in the six part process for developing EI. One other factor that strongly influences all of these processes is effective communication which is fundamental to raising Self Regard and Regard for Others, the two Core Attitudes that underpin EI. Techniques for communicating effectively to raise Self Regard in oneself and others are described below. The coach may apply these techniques to build their client's Self Regard or teach their client how to use them for themselves.

7.8 How to raise Self Regard through effective communication

The ultimate purpose of raising EI is to enhance Self Regard (unconditional self-acceptance), the cornerstone of the EIP framework. Self Regard is largely determined by the communication people experience throughout their lives.

In Transactional Analysis theory (TA) communication is referred to as a 'stroke' or a 'unit of attention'. An important distinguishing feature of a stroke is whether it is conditional (for a person's behaviour) or unconditional (for a person's being) and whether it is positive or negative. Combining these two essential elements of communication produces the stroke/communication grid,[28] which may be used to help individuals understand how to communicate so as to influence and build their own and others Self Regard.

Table 7.5 The communication grid

	NEGATIVE STROKE	POSITIVE STROKE
UNCONDITIONAL **For Being**	Put-Down	Expressed Value
CONDITIONAL **For Doing**	Feedback	Praise

Let positive strokes in: One of the most powerful ways to raise someone's Self Regard is by Expressing Value towards them (positive unconditional strokes) and by avoiding Put-Downs (unconditional negative strokes). Value is often expressed through the small things people do such as acknowledging others through a smile, saying *good morning* or offering them a drink. Equally, Put-Downs can be easily transmitted through a scowl, raising the eyebrows, or by the absence of Expressed Value (not saying *good morning*).

The most frequent form of communication a person receives is not from others but from oneself and their own self-talk. It is a person's capacity to accept Expressed Value and to reject Put-Downs from oneself and from others that will largely determine their level of Self Regard from moment to moment and throughout their lives.

Praise people for what they do: A distinction should be made here between Self Regard (the feelings people have towards themselves) and confidence (what they believe they are capable of), as a person can be confident but still have low Self Regard. For example, an individual may think they are good at using spread-sheets (confidence) but not feel good about themselves (Self Regard). Conversely, an individual may think they are hopeless at using spread-sheets (confidence) but still feel good about themselves (Self Regard).

Providing someone with Praise for what they do well is likely to raise a person's confidence but will not necessarily increase their Self Regard. Praise is not a substitute for Expressed Value. There is even a risk that if an individual is only praised when they do something that others want, such as performing well or making a profit, then they may feel their value is conditional upon their performance or profit making. This could have the reverse effect of lowering their Self Regard as they begin to feel their Self Regard is conditional *(I am only OK if...I perform well or make a profit etc.)*, rather than unconditional *(I am a valuable and worthwhile human being)*. Value is often expressed through spontaneous acts of kindness, consideration and forgiveness, and demonstrates the feelings a person has towards the other *(I like you for who you are)* rather than with any expectation of reciprocation or reward.

Praise others to reinforce positive behaviour: Apart from raising confidence in others. Praise is also a powerful way to reinforce and encourage desirable behaviours, and is generally more effective than negative Feedback at influencing change. If a person is poor at time keeping and often late it may be more effective to show them appreciation on the occasions they are on time or early than to criticise them when they are late. As a general rule people will want to be praised and are likely to repeat behaviours that elicit positive reward. An important skill in showing appreciation is noticing when people are doing something well, which requires developing Awareness of Others (scale 4). The more a person notices and praises others the more habitual this behaviour becomes and the more they will start to automatically recognise the positive in others.

Express lots of value: A concern sometimes raised about showing appreciation is that a person can be given too much Praise and start to 'over-rate' themselves. This may be true, as Praise is conditional and becomes meaningless and unappreciated if not related to something a person has done to 'deserve' it. However, this is not true when expressing Value towards others, a person cannot receive too much Value (so long as it is sincere). It is not possible to feel 'too OK' or to have too much Self Regard (remember that Self Regard is a linear scale not a multi-scale). People sometimes mistakenly attributed arrogance to having too much Self Regard, when in fact it usually indicates a low Regard for Others which is masking low Self Regard.

As a general rule, the recommended ratio of Strokes is to give 3 Values and 2 Praises for every single Feedback and to never give Put-Downs (to oneself or to others). One useful technique to raise Self Regard is to write down 3 Values, 2 Praises and 1 Feedback at the end of each day for oneself. And to raise Regard for Others find 3 Values and 2 Praises about the other person to combat every critical thought towards them.

Distinguish Feedback from Put-Downs: Feedback is essential if people are to learn and develop as without it they are likely to repeat the same mistakes. Receiving Feedback also shows that the person cares enough about the other person to help them learn and develop. People are different and have different strengths and weaknesses. Some may be faster, slower, more academic, less academic, musical or less musical, etc. The important point is that people grow to learn that they are unconditionally OK, that is, they are still OK regardless of them being slower, faster, taller, shorter, more musical, less musical, or whatever. Experiencing negative Feedback and failure (conditional Feedback) does not mean *they* are a failure (an unconditional Put-Down), but that they are a valuable human being who has not been successful at a particular task. If children are not exposed to this reality; that *people are different* and *however you and others are, is OK* (two of the EI attitudes; see Chapter 1) through life experiences such as competitive activities, then they will not learn to distinguish Feedback from Put-Downs. This may mean that every piece of future Feedback they receive will be experienced as a Put-Down (I am Not OK) lowering their Self Regard. One way to prevent an individual turning Feedback into a Put-

Down is to show them Expressed Value alongside the Feedback. For example, a parent may explain to their child that they have done something naughty (Feedback) but show them that they are still loved by giving them a hug afterwards (Value). Or a manager may give Feedback to a team colleague that their performance was poor but show them that they are still a valued member of the team, that they think highly of them and that they will continue to support them.

If a person does not learn to distinguish their behaviour (conditional self) from their being (unconditional self) it can become very difficult in later life for them to accept negative Feedback without interpreting it as a Put-Down and consequently it affecting their Self Regard. For example, negative Feedback such as; *the calculation you did was incorrect,* may be interpreted as; *you think that was a stupid mistake,* which is interpreted as; *you think I am stupid,* and reinforces their feelings that*; I think I am stupid,* (a Put-Down from themself). This then becomes the message the individual replays to themselves when receiving Feedback in the future. Three effective ways of preventing individuals from interpreting negative Feedback as Put-Downs are described below.

1 *Be aware of others:* Firstly, be aware of others, notice how they like to be appreciated and what they may not like. Some people will experience humour and banter as a Value, while others will experience it as a Put-Down. For someone who, in the past, has experienced few positive strokes, a lot of sarcasm and inconsistent messages (such as Value followed by Put-Downs), it will be more difficult for them to accept Expressed Value. In such cases it may be necessary that the other person gains their trust, demonstrates that they mean what they say, consistently gives high quality Feedback to them and, when they do give Praise, does so in a genuine and sincere way.

2 *Have positive intentions towards others:* Secondly, to stop people turning Feedback into a Put-Down, the individual providing the Feedback should check their intentions towards the other person; that they value and respect them. If they hold resentment, hostility or dislike towards the other person, they will need to look for reasons to feel tolerance, compassion and understanding towards them as a human being. This is about learning to separate out what the person has done (which may be totally unacceptable behaviour) from who they are (having unconditional Regard for Others). If not, the Feedback giver's attitude will leak out unconsciously in their behaviour, tone of voice and body language even if they are very skilled at giving Feedback.

People are highly attuned to detecting incongruity between a person's behaviour and their attitude. On the other hand, those people who have high Regard for Others will be able to give Feedback to others without them turning it into a Put-Down or raising their defences, leaving the other person's Self Regard intact. Even if they lack Feedback skills and are slightly clumsy, the person receiving the Feedback will detect that the other person is on their side, cares about them and has positive intentions towards them.

3 *Combine Feedback with Expressed Value:* People in organisations are often taught to 'sandwich' negative Feedback between two pieces of Praise. This tends to fail in that people soon begin to anticipate that every compliment is going to be followed with a 'but' *(that was good, 'but' you didn't…).* A more effective option is to sandwich negative Feedback between two Values such as asking; *do you have time to talk* (Value), then sharing the Feedback, and then thanking them and asking for their reaction and feelings (Value). Many businesses tend to use Praise and reward to motivate people, gain their commitment and improve their performance. However, evidence suggests that people are far more motivated when they feel valued.[29] For example, feeling supported during difficult times not just when things are going well, feeling that their boss is interested in them personally rather than just their performance, and that their emotional as well as job needs are being considered.

Learn how to receive Feedback and Praise: Communication is a two-way process, and involves being able to receive as well as give Feedback. Some key guidelines to receiving strokes are outlined below:

- Don't accept Put-Downs. These are toxic (rude or insulting comments usually say more about the attitude of the person giving them). Understand the Feedback being given and who specifically is giving it. Ask for clarification on the Feedback if required. It is only conditional if specific and supported by clear evidence and examples.
- Distinguish opinion from fact; *you have poor communication skills* may be better phrased as; *I think what you said to Bob was unclear because…*
- When receiving Value or Praise, slow down, take a deep breath and allow this feedback to sink in.
- Accept positive strokes. People will often discount a stroke by thinking; *they are just being nice to me,* or bounce it back with; *you are looking good too!* By discounting or dismissing a positive stroke the person giving it may feel they have

not been heard and interpret this as a Put-Down, and be less likely to offer positive strokes in the future.

- Say *thank you* when receiving a positive stroke. This acknowledges the feedback and also gives a positive stroke back to the other person.

A key principle in receiving feedback is to keep one's Self Regard intact and to remember that being an OK human being is unconditional and not, therefore, dependent on what a person does. Using affirmations such as; *even though I made a mistake or behaved inappropriately I am still a valuable and worthwhile human being* can help reinforce this attitude.

This concludes the guidance on how to develop Emotional Intelligence through each of the psychological stages of EI. The next section, 7.9, provides more specific suggestions on how to develop EI in each of the sixteen EIP scales.

7.9 Specific guidance of how to develop the EIP scales

The following suggestions on how to develop the sixteen EIP scales are presented to help the individual with their self-development. They have been written in order that the coach may give them directly to their client to read. These are by no means definitive and the individual may also be directed to other references for each scale, as well as be encouraged to be creative in generating their own ideas. Guidance on how to set development goals is given in the previous chapter. It is recommended that exploration and interpretation of the EIP is undertaken before considering what to develop. In addition to the suggestions made below, refer to Chapter 5 for other scales that will influence and support the development of each scale.

1 Self Regard

- Take a few minutes once a day to notice your 'inner critic' and challenge what it says with the question, *Is that really true*? Ask others who know you well for their opinion on what you doubt about yourself; they are likely to have a valuable perspective.

- Reject any 'Put-Downs' that come your way. A 'Put-Down' is when someone (including yourself) criticises something about who you are as a person rather than what you have done. Every time you say something negative about yourself counter it with something positive.

- Rather than disregarding compliments or feeling uncomfortable when others give you compliments, really let them in and notice the positive effect on how you feel. Also, get used to asking for positive 'strokes' – they count too.

- Each day allocate uninterrupted time for yourself to do what you want both in work and outside of work.

2 Regard for Others

- Notice and recognise when others do something well and show your appreciation.

- Notice your judgements – check that when you challenge or disagree with others it is for what they do or say, and not for their being. For example, notice when you are thinking *I don't like X*, and modify this to *I don't like what X did/tends to do*.

- If you tend to form quick judgements of others, pause for a moment and seek to understand them first. See things from their point of view. What are their concerns? How may they be feeling? What do they want? Understanding others makes it easier to feel compassion and respond appropriately.

- Try to do the small things that can make a big difference, for example, remembering a person's name, a smile, saying *good morning* or asking them a question.

3 Self Awareness

- Keep a record of your emotional responses to stimuli. This helps to identify and name your emotional reactions which provide a first step to managing them.

- Choose to share your feelings with someone you trust. Talking through your feelings may help you to learn your patterns of behaviour and their impact on your performance.

- Be prepared to listen to and trust your gut reaction. Next time you make a work related decision, check whether it feels like the right decision as well as if it is logically the right decision.

- Consider how your feelings from yesterday may still be affecting your feelings and/or your behaviour today. Ask yourself how this might impact on your self-management and how others view you.

4 Awareness of Others

- When exploring how a person is feeling about a situation, reflect this back to them to demonstrate that you have listened and to check the accuracy of your understanding with them.

- Seek out opportunities to enquire about what others are thinking and feeling. For example, about a decision during a meeting, are they positive, concerned or excited?

- Increase your empathy by imagining yourself in the other person's position and openly acknowledging the feelings of the other person during the conversation.

- During conversation, observe body language and tone of voice; notice how people talk to you and their facial expressions. Subtly mirror body language to see what that tells you about their feelings and to help build rapport.

5 Emotional Resilience

- If you are feeling the effects of stress on your physical health, particularly if you are living an unhealthy lifestyle, look after yourself physically, for example, through exercise and nutrition.

- Ask for support from a trusted individual. Talk through your feelings and concerns to gain a different perspective and establish a rounded view of the issues.

- Distract yourself from stressful situations temporarily by doing physical activity, such as going for a walk, have an informal conversation, or close your eyes and breathe deeply for twenty seconds.

- Attempt to understand what causes you negative stress by writing down those situations in which you felt under pressure. Note down how you reacted and the events leading up to the stressful situation. You may then choose to ask for help or delegate during these situations.

6 Personal Power

- When there appears to be no choice, stop and challenge yourself to identify at least three options that have desirable consequences. If you find it difficult to identify clear options, elicit advice from someone who can help.

- Note down every time you start a sentence with *I should* or *I must*. Consider replacing *should* and *must* with *will* or *am responsible for*. Then begin to action the statement.

- Recall a time when you felt empowered for taking on responsibility, not just organisationally but also socially, physically and mentally. Remind yourself of this when faced with challenging situations.

- Explore the option of getting involved in slightly more challenging work that will stretch you and increase your confidence and capability.

7 Goal Directedness

- Work out what it is you really want. One way to do this is to pay attention to your feelings and notice what things in life give you pleasure and satisfaction. If you are not getting much satisfaction in your life think of what you have enjoyed in the past, what you would like to be doing tomorrow, next week, next year and in five years' time.

- Notice if you tend to put your own needs behind others and rarely do the things that you want to for yourself. This may be because you have a lower Self Regard than Regard for Others. Recognise that it is also OK to do things for yourself and by doing so you are more likely to feel positive about yourself and others.

- Develop impulse control over those things that give you immediate gratification but do not meet your longer term goals (such as eating chocolate or being angry). In these moments you may feel you have no control, but you do. It is possible not to act upon your immediate feeling and choose your behaviour (refer to Chapter 7.1.1).

- If you set clear goals for yourself but find it difficult to stay on track, identify what distracts you and aim to eliminate the distraction, for example, find somewhere quiet to work and set yourself short periods of concentration time followed by a break.

8 Flexibility

- Before making a decision or reacting to a proposed organisational or role change, spend a few minutes considering alternative ways of responding.

- Consult the views of others and consider each opinion and suggestion from the perspective that it could be the best way forward. Also consider the advantages for the change.

- Check that you are not rejecting change for the wrong reasons, such as a fear of the unknown, feeling outside of your comfort zone or stuck habits.

- If you find changing your behaviour difficult, start with small changes which hold no risk, for example, move your watch from the wrist you normally keep it on to the other wrist for a few days. Notice your initial reactions and the time it takes for you to feel comfortable.

9 Connecting with Others

- Make a deliberate effort to initiate contact with people and communicate with them face-to-face.

- Make it part of your daily routine to spend time getting to know people at a deeper level than only discussing tasks/situations. What do they value? How do they feel?

- Notice what you don't share when talking with people; risk being more open about your feelings than you would usually. For example, when appropriate, share something about yourself on a personal level, express your feelings and share your vulnerabilities.

- Identify which areas of relationships are stronger for you - 'depth' or 'breadth'. Experiment in developing the area that is the least strong.

10 Authenticity

- Ask a range of people who experience you in different settings whether you are consistent and reliable with them in all situations. Ensure that you extend your reliability to all people in all situations. Ask them what they would like you to do to improve on this even further.

- You could help others get to know you more quickly by telling people about your principles, for example, what is important to you, what your values are, what you expect from others and what are your likes and dislikes. Invite them to share this with you to maintain a balanced interaction.

- Be reliable and keep your promises, only agree to deliver on things if you have made an assessment of your workload and priorities to ascertain how achievable it is.

- Write down your top three values. On a scale of 1-10 rate how much you live by each of them, identify examples of when you have done so. If you struggle with examples then consider whether you need to change something in your life to be more true to your values.

11 Trust: Mistrusting

- Notice your feelings towards other people, do you tend to be suspicious of people or feel threatened by them? If so, consider why you feel this way towards them.

- Check yourself for over-generalising about people or situations, for example, if a person didn't deliver on one task you may think they never deliver on any task.

- Calibrate your expectations of others (and yourself); are they fair and realistic? Allow room for others to learn from their mistakes. Provide training where necessary.

- Check whether you have provided people with the right information and communicated your expectations accurately and clearly before assuming they will not deliver.

Over Trusting

- Combine your subjective view with objective information before making a decision about how much trust to place in people. Identify what is factual and what is more hopeful.

- Learn to listen and pay attention to your intuitive feelings about people, such as when you meet someone new or someone invites you to trust them.

- When coaching and managing others use the appropriate level of challenge to enable them to deal with difficult situations, and to learn, grow and improve.

- Check whether you have provided people with the right information and communicated your expectations accurately and clearly before assuming they will deliver.

12 Balanced Outlook: Pessimistic

- Balance identifying problems with focusing on solutions and developing contingency plans. Help others to see ways around problems and picture successful outcomes.

- When making decisions, check your emotional state, such as do you feel annoyed? Pause and reflect on whether this is skewing your perception or if you are acting impulsively and could you be more objective.

- Be aware if you have a tendency to catastrophise or imagine the worst. You are probably right; things will not go perfectly which is not the end of the world or of you. Develop more realistic and balanced thinking, such as positive reframes. (Refer to Chapter 7.1.4)

- There may be times that you use overly negative language when experiencing difficulties, for example; *it's hopeless, pointless, or will never work*. Look to balance or moderate your language with positive messages designed to encourage and motivate, such as; *good idea*, *nice job*, or *well done*.

Over Optimistic

- Elicit views from others in order to get a balance of perceptions, use this information to inform your decision.

- Balance your enthusiasm for an idea with finding out the facts and checking details before finalising a decision.

- When making decisions, check your emotional state such as, do you feel excited? Pause and reflect on whether this is skewing your perception or if you are acting impulsively and could be more objective.

- Continue to use your optimism to engage and motivate others, however, be prepared to look for contradictory evidence and challenge your own judgment in order to ensure the course of action set is still the right one.

13 Emotional Expression: Under Controlled

- Identify what situations cause a strong emotional reaction in you. Notice your feelings early. For example, annoyance before it becomes anger and then rage, and anticipation before it becomes anxiety and then panic.

- If you feel compelled to express a feeling, pause for six seconds and allow time before you do or say anything. Think about your feelings, your possible reactions and their likely consequences.

- If you are prone to emotional outbursts, recognise when this has been inappropriate. When you feel calm, be prepared to make appropriate reparation or an apology.

- Consider doing more physical activity to provide a release from stressful situations.

Over Controlled

- When you are around people who express their feelings with calmness and control, take note of the impact they have on yourself and others. Ask for their advice on the approach they take.

- Find opportunities to safely and gradually express your feelings more often. Starting with feelings and situations you find more comfortable. Record the differences this makes to improving your relationships and achieving your goals.

- Being Over Controlled does not necessarily mean you experience less emotion than other people do. Consider how else you may be releasing your feelings, such as through physical activity. Seek to broaden the effective expression of emotion to other areas of your work.

- Although high levels of emotional expression may not come naturally to you, work is not devoid of feeling. Make a conscious effort to notice and acknowledge the emotions of others and demonstrate your passion, for example, overtly state your commitment and show encouragement.

14 Conflict Handling: Passive

- If you feel uncomfortable about disagreement or asking people to do something for you, prepare what you are going to say first and keep it short and to the point.

- Most people feel uncomfortable giving feedback, yet often the person receiving it is more able to deal with it than we expect. If you tend to avoid addressing issues, don't make excuses and deal with them early.

- Conflict is resolved where there is mutual respect and all parties are not under pressure. Find a conducive environment and an appropriate time to hear the other person's views, and fully state yours.
- Get beneath the presenting disagreement and find common ground, for example, you both want to achieve the same outcome and have different views on how best to achieve this.

Aggressive

- Practice listening to others and reflecting back what you have heard, before giving your opinion.
- If you feel yourself becoming frustrated use techniques to reduce the frustration, for example, breathing deeply, taking a short break or expressing feelings before they become too strong.
- Take care that your personal ambition and drive does not have a detrimental effect on others, for example, being overly competitive, only focusing on tasks and not people or losing sight of the team objectives.
- Identify the cause of your frustration or aggression and find strategies to manage these stressors early.

15 Interdependence: Over Dependent

- Before asking others for advice or direction, pause to consider what your personal view is and what you would do if you were the sole decision maker.
- Do you tend to procrastinate, avoid making decisions and spend time deliberating? Work out which decisions are important to spend time on and which ones you should act upon.
- Be prepared to try activities where there is nobody to provide help but which stretch your comfort zones.
- Prioritise your decisions, allocate set times to consider options and set yourself a deadline for a decision to be made.

Over Independent

- If you have a preference for being an individualistic expert, endeavour to share your expertise and thinking with others. Involve people early in a project; elicit their ideas before deciding the way forward.
- Having your own inner conviction is a good basis for managing others; ensure you convey this to people in a way they can engage with.

- For a piece of work you have, check whether there is someone more appropriate to delegate it to and allocate time to develop and coach them to complete the work.
- Create a team environment where generating ideas and solutions are encouraged. Where ideas are welcomed without criticism, ridicule or risk.

16 Reflective Learning

- Build a clearer picture of your strengths and development areas. Actively seek feedback from your boss and subordinates, undertake a 360 feedback process and ask people for their views.
- Analyse significant personal events soon after they happen. What was the trigger? How did you feel? What thoughts did you have? Was this a one–off or a habit? What attitudes may underlie your behaviour?
- Take the above suggestion one step further and consider what you learnt about yourself from this experience. What might you do differently in a similar situation in the future? How do you feel about yourself right now?
- Record regular reflections on your week, both positives and negatives, and what you choose to take from these experiences. Ensure you build these reflections into useable information to guide your future behaviour.

This chapter has provided an overview of how to develop EI and the EIP scales in particular. Further advice on how to develop each scale is given within the EIP reports. The next chapter discusses how EI and the EIP can be applied in the business context in relation to individual leadership, team working and creating an emotionally intelligent organisation.

Summary points from Chapter Seven

There are several psychological stages to the process of being emotionally intelligent (as described in Chapter 2.3 on the brain). This chapter describes how each of these stages (SAFE-TBO) provide the opportunity for intervening and developing EI. Key suggestions are summarised below for each of the psychological stages.

- **Stimulus:** Much of a person's behaviour is an automatic response to a stimulus (such as events, circumstances and other people). Therefore by changing, removing or creating new stimuli a person can trigger an entirely different set of responses. The emotionally intelligent individual will learn to identify their triggers and how to manage these accordingly.

- **Stimulus:** Some of the most powerful triggers come from a person's social needs such as; for status, consistency, and fairness. Learning to identify and meet these needs can help avoid the threat response (defensive behaviour) and instead activate the reward response (EI behaviour) in oneself and others.

- **Attitudes:** Attitudes tend to be evaluative and categorical, therefore by creating an element of doubt in them leaves the attitude open to question and the opportunity for change.

- **Attitudes:** Even if a person lacks the relevant skills and behaviour, they are more likely to achieve the outcome they want if they hold an appropriate attitude. For example, a leader is more likely to get the best from others by having respect, trust and regard for others rather than from applying clever motivational techniques.

- **Feelings:** Humans have a basic set of emotional needs, such as for security, intimacy and attention. As with all living things, humans also possess a set of innate resources to meet their emotional needs; such as their ability to self-observe, to apply logic and reason, and to empathise. Learning how to apply these innate resources to meet their emotional needs is central to EI development.

- **Feelings:** People often know what they should do, but do not behave this way in practice, because they have only learnt it at an intellectual rather than emotional level. Changing behaviour requires learning through emotional and experiential activity.

- **Feelings:** Emotions provide people with feedback about themselves and others. If ignored, negative feelings will increase, such as frustration growing into anger, which can manifest as ill-health and defensive behaviour. By noticing feelings early, people can learn to listen to their body's feedback and respond to their feelings appropriately.

- **Thinking:** Most irrational or unhelpful thinking is the result of excessive emotion. Too much emotion restricts a person's capacity to think clearly and choose how they behave. Learning how to reduce levels of arousal, by relaxing and managing day to day stress is a vital part of EI.

- **Thinking:** Calming the emotional brain (above) may be complimented by learning how to quieten the rational thinking brain, together they allow for more insightful, creative, intuitive and inspired levels of thinking.

- **Thinking:** One way for an individual to manage their feelings is to manage their thinking. For example, reframing negative experiences more positively, challenging negative assumptions about people or situations and using positive language rather than negative generalisations.

- **Behaviour:** There are two main reasons why people do not achieve their personal development goals. Firstly, they did not want to achieve these goals for themselves and, secondly, their goals were too large. Therefore, when changing a habit it is important that the new behaviour is very specific and of clear benefit to the individual. They will then need to practice this new behaviour for a few minutes every day for a period of weeks, in order that the new behaviour becomes a habit.

- **Outcome:** Imagination is a very powerful human tool for creating a person's own virtual reality. Used effectively people can learn how to become more relaxed, create positive feelings, rehearse difficult situations, increase their confidence and lead themselves to the outcomes they desire. However, if not managed well, a person's imagination can be equally destructive.

- **Communication:** Self Regard is the essence of EI and is largely determined by the communication a person experiences throughout their life. To raise Self Regard a person must learn how to accept Praise but to reject Put-Downs, both from oneself and from others. To raise the Self Regard of others, a person must learn how to show appreciation and value towards others and not to give Put-Downs.

All of the psychological approaches described above give rise to specific actions, methods and techniques for raising EI in each of the sixteen EIP scales. Some practical suggestions for this have been given in this chapter and are also provided in the EIP reports.

● ● ●

Chapter Eight

Applying Emotional Intelligence and the EIP in organisations

Introduction

So far, the focus of Section Three has been on the individual and their personal development. This final chapter examines EI and the EIP from a business context, answering questions like *what evidence is there that EI improves performance? How does EI relate to leadership? What is an emotionally intelligent team? And what makes an emotionally intelligent organisation?* The three main themes to this chapter are the individual (leadership), teams (relationships) and the organisation (climate).

8.1 The business case for Emotional Intelligence

There are three key criteria that may be considered the 'holy grail' for any construct of personal development such as EI. These are:

1 **It can be developed (and sustained):** It is a quality that a person can change, improve and sustain, rather than it being fixed.

2 **It is measurable:** Improvement of this attribute can be measured.

3 **It relates to performance:** It is a desirable quality that can make a positive difference to a person's effectiveness.

Throughout this book the case has been made for the first two criteria; that by using the EIP, Emotional Intelligence is developable, sustainable and measureable. The third criteria, that EI (and the EIP) predicts performance and has a bottom line impact on output and productivity in work, will now be discussed.

There is clearly something missing for employees in today's workplaces; research by Gallup[1] found an astonishing 71% of employees were not engaged in their work, Zenger and Folkman[2] found that 46% of employees report low job satisfaction and commitment, and a survey by Freedman[3] reported that 97% of employees said they could be more productive; 49% of whom said they could be 50% more productive! There is considerable opportunity for increased productivity in the workplace, so how much difference can EI make?

Daniel Goleman[4] in his book *Emotional Intelligence: Why it can matter more than IQ,* argues that IQ contributes to about 20% of life success, while the remaining 80% is, to a large extent, determined by EI. The evidence he presents is mostly anecdotal, yet his explanations caught the interest of executives the world over. Perhaps this represented a tide of opinion from business leaders who are intuitively aware that the key differentiator of high performers is more emotional and relational than cognitive. This has been supported by several studies such as the Forum on Manufacturing and Services[5] which revealed that 70% of customers are lost because of EI related reasons, the Denning Centre for Quality Management[6] found that 50% of time in business is wasted due to a lack of trust, and a study by the Royal Navy[7] showed that EI was a better predictor of overall and leadership performance than IQ and managerial competencies.

A key application of EI has been in leadership development. Schmidt and Hunter[8] indicate that EI becomes increasingly important higher up the organisation. In complex jobs, top performers are 127% more productive than average performers with one third being due to technical differences and two thirds being due to EI related differences. A global study by Johnson & Johnson on 358 of their managers found that high performers were significantly more 'emotionally competent' than other managers.[9] Research by UCLA indicated that only 7% of leadership success is attributed to intellect, the rest is attributed to trust, integrity, authenticity, honesty, creativity, presence and resilience.[10] A pool of senior managers from Siemens Global who were trained in four EI domains; drive, initiative, team-working and leadership delivered an additional $1.5 million profit, double that of the comparison group that had no such training. In a large scale study across industry sectors, EI explained nearly 60% of job performance across all managerial and executive levels.[11] As part of the same study at AT&T, 91% of top performers were high in EI, while only 26% of low performers were high in EI. Egon Zehnder's analysis of 515 senior executives found EI to be a better indicator of future success than either previous experience or IQ.[12]

As suggested by the Zehnder study, organisations are not just interested in how EI relates to leadership performance but what this can deliver by way of actual output and productivity. A number of studies that demonstrate the link between EI and business performance are summarised below.

- *In one multinational consulting firm, partners scoring higher on twenty EI competencies earned 139% more than low EI partners.*[13]
- *L'Oreal sales agents selected on EI outsold sales people selected on the old procedures by $91,000 and had 63% less staff turnover.*[14]
- *Sales people at Met Life who scored higher on 'learned optimism' sold 37% more than the more pessimistic individuals.*[15]

- *Insurance sales agents scoring higher in five key EI competencies had double the policy sales of lower scorers.*[16]

- *American Express introduced 4 days of EI training to all of its incoming financial advisers after finding that trained advisers increased business by 18%.*[17]

- *At Coca-Cola, division leaders who developed their EI competencies outperformed their targets by 15%. Division leaders who did not develop their EI were 15% below their targets.*[18]

- *When Motorola manufacturing implemented stress and EI programmes, 93% of employees increased their productivity.*[19]

- *A meta-analysis on 43 separate studies found significantly strong correlations (r=0.24 to 0.30) between EI and job performance.*[20]

As well as improving performance and productivity, several other benefits of EI have been found, such as; increased retention (in the US Air force recruiters reported a $3million immediate saving),[21] reduced attrition,[16,18] and fewer work related accidents and grievances.[22]

The positive results from EI studies have been replicated by the EIP, showing that EI development is sustainable.[23] A sample of 189 leaders who completed the EIP showed an 18% improvement in their EIP scores six months after completing a 3-day EI development programme. If this improvement in EI transferred directly into productivity, then conservative estimates indicate that an 18% improvement in productivity for senior managers would lead to 150% increase in pre-tax profits.[24] Also, a case study presented at the UK National EI Conference (2006) by Skandia Group found middle managers to have a 20-32% increase in leadership performance following EIP coaching and training over a 3 month period. Further studies on the EIP predictive validity may be found in the technical manual.[25]

8.1.1 The business demand for EI

There has been considerable growth in the field of EI at work since the early 1990's. In no small part, this rising popularity has been due to the writings of Daniel Goleman who has produced several accessible books.[26,27,28] His work became prominent in the business field following two papers in the Harvard Business Review (HBR); *What makes a leader?*[29] and *Leadership that gets results*[30] which rank as the most requested HBR articles to date. His work helped popularise some of the work by academics and researchers in the field including Reuven Bar-On, who produced the EQi (version 1) measure of EI[31] and Mayer, Salovey and Caruso who developed the MSCEIT™ EI measure.[32]

There are other key reasons for the growing popularity of EI within business, such as neurological evidence on the importance of emotions for clear thinking, decision making and effective behaviour (refer to Chapter 2). There has also been an increased acceptance of feelings being significant to performance, engagement and retention in the workplace and greater recognition in society generally, such as emotional literacy being taught in schools, politicians referring to EI, and popular business books on EI. In addition, there has been a large body of academic research and practitioner evidence giving continued support to the importance of EI in workplace performance. Perhaps the main reason for organisations buying into EI is because there is an increased need for emotionally intelligent employees to meet the demands of current day working.[33] Some of these demands upon employees and the relevant EIP scales to help address these demands are described below.

The rate of change: Change is often seen as exponential, led by advances in technology, access to information and increased globalisation. This typically comes with a high human toll as employees are expected to be more adaptable and responsive to changing circumstances. For the 15th year in succession, managers in Roffey Park's annual survey of managers reported managing change as their biggest organisational challenge.[34] What demands does this place upon the EI of managers today? In EI terms this involves them being aware of their automatic and ingrained responses (Self Awareness) and then learning how to move outside of their comfort zones to adapt to a changing world (Flexibility).

A changing economic climate: The health of the economy cascades down to organisations and to individuals. When the economy is buoyant, organisations experience rapid growth and individuals are expected to adapt quickly, take on greater responsibility, manage more resources and deliver to high expectations. During an economic slowdown organisations consolidate and individuals are expected to do more with less, remain competitive with reduced resources and cope with job uncertainty. Those organisations and individuals who cope well with such changes will develop their Emotional Resilience, provide others with emotional support (Connecting with others), be Flexible enough to move outside of their comfort zones and become stronger from the experience (Reflective Learning).

Increased competition: With globalisation, and in times of economic crisis, comes increased competition. To come out on top requires several EI attributes such as; Emotional Resilience (to cope with and persevere after setbacks); Self

Awareness (to draw on creativity and intuition); Connecting with Others (to engage with clients) and Balanced Outlook (to have a positive rather than pessimistic outlook).

Less hierarchy: Organisational structures are constantly being revised and a common trend has been the de-layering of hierarchies. As a consequence, employees are given greater autonomy, independence and accountability and are expected to be more self-managed. This demands greater Self Management in areas such as knowing one's own strengths and weaknesses (Self Awareness), self-motivation (Goal Directedness) and self-confidence (Personal Power).

More team working: In tandem with the previous demand for greater Self Management the demand for Relationship Management has been equally dramatic, such as virtual teams, collaborative working practices, matrix structures and networking sites. Some of the relevant EIP scales here include having Regard for Others, Connecting with Others, trusting others (Trust) and being trusted by others (Authenticity).

A job is not for life: Unlike 50 years ago, very few CEO's or company directors have dedicated their working lives to the same organisation. Such dedication is often seen as a handicap rather than an asset. Today's high flier will not only work in different organisations but different industry sectors. This requires of them the capacity to adapt to new environments and people (Connecting with Others) to continually learn from their experience (Reflective Learning) and to adopt versatile styles of working (Flexibility).

Increased job demand: Despite improved efficiency and speed in operating technology, the demands on the typical employee, such as working hours, information load and job variety, have dramatically increased. In a survey by PriceWaterhouseCoopers,[35] of over 1000 CEO's from 54 countries, 97% said that their employees had to do more work than they would have done previously, but in the same amount of time. The main concern with this has been the rise in stress related problems, such as absenteeism, low morale, illness, increased turnover and underperformance. EI in the workplace is about how people manage their emotional state under challenging conditions to perform effectively, which requires attributes such as: Emotional Resilience, Emotional Expression and Control, and Conflict Handling. EI is also about creating working cultures that engage people and help them to work to their strengths. This may include EI attributes such as Self Regard,

Regard for Others, Self Awareness, Awareness of Others and Reflective Learning.

Just as the increased demand on leaders and employees requires greater EI, so too does the increased demand placed upon organisations to attract and retain the best human capital.

The war for talent: Attracting and retaining the best staff continues to be a challenge; (refer to Mckinsey 'The war for talent')[36] as the opportunity for travel, job change, transferability of skills, career growth and personal development becomes more important to these aspiring leaders. The need for employers to motivate and satisfy employees is ever present. Understanding people's emotional needs (Awareness of Others), building loyalty (Connecting with Others) and creating trusting relationships (Trust) are significant factors to attracting and retaining skilled workers with high potential.

An ageing population: People continue to live longer, retirement age rises and the characteristics of employees change with every generation (often referred to as 'baby boomers' and generations X, Y and Z). Results from research based on the EIP have shown EI to increase with age and that different generations have different strengths and preferences. Employers may wish to embrace these differences, such as drawing upon the experience and wisdom of older employees (Reflective Learning) and supporting the dynamic enthusiasm of younger employees (Flexibility).

Human capital: The UK economy has shifted from being predominantly product based (manufacturing and construction) to being more people led (services and knowledge). The net effect is that human capital is the primary resource for most organisations. Knowing how to maximise human potential (Relationship Management) and sustain performance (Goal Directedness) for ever greater productivity (Personal Power) can be leveraged through a greater understanding of EI in the workplace.

8.2 The emotionally intelligent leader

The importance of effective leadership is well accepted within business. The pervading question is how best to lead with an ever growing number of theories, leadership styles, research studies and books on the subject. Since the early 1990s, EI has become firmly established as a major factor in effective leadership. This section gives a brief overview of EIP for leadership and the links between the EIP, leadership styles and leadership competencies.

'There is no difference between becoming an effective leader and becoming a fully integrated human being' (Warren Bennis).[37] Being a fully integrated human being and an effective leader is, arguably, about developing all parts of EI (the sixteen EIP scales). The integral relevance of EI and JCA's approach to leadership is described below.

The JCA leadership process consists of five parts within a learning cycle (Fig. 8.1)[38] which include: deciding what to do, getting others on board, planning & implementing it and keeping it going; all centred around meeting the customer's needs. In essence, this is what great leaders do. Being able and willing to do this effectively also requires a set of five psychological attributes, one of which is Emotional Intelligence (Table 8.1).

Fig. 8.1 The JCA leadership process

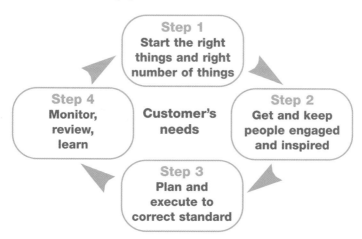

Table 8.1 The five psychological attributes of leadership

Psychological attributes	Description	EIP related scales
Cognitive Intelligence	*Having the ability to effectively and pragmatically problem solve by employing the capacity to analyse and manipulate complex information (Intelligence) and by referencing assimilated facts (Knowledge) and personal experience (Tacit learning).*	**Self Awareness Reflective Leaning (Also refer to EI links with IQ in Chapter 1.3.2)**
Emotional Intelligence	*The ability to build and maintain positive relationships with clients and colleagues (Interpersonal skills) by recognising, accepting and managing attitudes, energy, and behaviour (Personal*	**All EIP scales**

Psychological attributes	Description	EIP related scales
	skills) both in the immediate moment (Flexibility) and in the longer term (Consistency).	
Motivation	*The individual understanding what they want/need to achieve (Focus/Goal orientation) and having the desire, confidence and resilience to pursue goals and objectives in a sustainable manner (Motivation).*	**Self Awareness** **Goal Directedness** **Emotional Resilience** **Personal Power**
Character Trait	*Strong character traits exhibit themselves in terms of how the individual consistently/typically approaches tasks (Task orientation) and their usual approach to dealing with people (People orientation). If people are consistently seen to act in accordance with their character traits and espoused values people see them as predictable, stable, readable and trustworthy (Authenticity).* *(Note - Character traits in-and-of themselves are rarely seen as either inherently right nor wrong and can only be viewed as positive or negative given the context of the role).*	**Authenticity** **(Also refer to EI links with Personality in Chapter 1.3.1)**
Learning Agility	*Allows individuals to progress and keep pace with changing environments. Those with Learning Agility remain curious, and are humble enough to recognise that they can always learn something new or explore new perspectives (Open-mindedness). They are happy to experiment and take risks with new approaches, invest time reflecting on what worked and what didn't, and are willing to commit time and effort to building new habits and skills towards the goal of real long-term sustainable behavioural change (Willingness to change).*	**Reflective Learning** **Flexibility**

8.2.1 The relevance of EIP scales to leadership

Although Emotional Intelligence is one of the five psychological attributes of effective leadership, the EIP scales are also prominent within many of the other leadership attributes. From the perspective of the EIP, a number of scales are of particular importance to emotionally intelligent leadership:

Self Regard: This is the cornerstone to all aspects of EI. It is evident that not all leaders are happy and do not necessarily hold themselves in high self-esteem. In fact the opposite is often the case, where leaders are driven by a conditional sense of being OK, meaning they have unconscious drivers such as; *I am only OK... if I have control, if I am perfect, if I am strong, if I please others, if I work hard...*, etc. These may typically fit with the 'striving for achievement' characteristic of many leaders, but at what cost? One cost may be to relationships and the climate the leader creates, another may be a lack of Flexibility.

Flexibility: If a leader is driven to 'Be Perfect', 'Work Hard', or 'Be Strong' to support their Self Regard, then they run the risk of being rigid and dogmatic rather than responsive and adaptable to the demands of the present situation. Given the changing nature of organisations discussed in the previous section, any inflexibility in a leader may lessen their effectiveness.

Authenticity: If a leader is driven to feel OK by 'Pleasing Others', they may respond by over committing themselves, and not keeping their promises, rather than being guided by their own inner principles. Being led by someone who is inconsistent and unpredictable creates considerable anxiety as it becomes difficult to anticipate how they will respond or what they want. This is particularly problematic when the leader's mood affects how positive or negative they are towards others. Some of the greatest leaders may not be the most charismatic but are greatly trusted by their followers because of their consistency and principles (Ghandi, Nelson Mandela, the Dalai Lama, Steve Jobs and Queen Elizabeth II).

Balanced Outlook: Research on the EIP[23] has shown senior leaders to have less extreme and more balanced EI scores than lower level managers. For example, senior managers are more likely to be realistic and considered than emotionally impulsive or over optimistic. They also tend to score in the middle on the multi-scales than rebound from one extreme to the other, therefore being seen as calm, steady and consistent. It may just be that leaders with more extreme EI scores (possibly charismatic) are the ones that get noticed yet this is neither a typical or necessary aspect of leadership.

Goal Directedness and Personal Power: Goal Directedness is a person knowing what they want and Personal Power is them believing they are able to make this happen. From EIP research, high achievers and strong leaders often score highly on these two scales. The application of these is also dependent on having reasonably high Self Awareness.

Self Awareness: This is necessary in order for the leader to accurately calibrate and not overestimate their capacity to deliver. They should also have high Awareness of Others so as to select the right advisers to balance their own weaker areas.

Reflective Learning: Self Awareness also supports Reflective Learning which is necessary to develop self-knowledge and knowledge of others. With this knowledge the leader can make informed choices on how to manage their own thoughts, feelings and behaviours, how to lead and influence others and how to develop themselves.

Interpersonal Intelligence: All of the above scales relate to Personal Intelligence, but equally important to leadership is *Inter*personal Intelligence; the leader is one half of each and every interaction. Many leadership models emphasise relationships such as Transformational Leadership and Social Exchange Theory. Sustainable leadership requires both personal and interpersonal intelligence, as a leader who lacks Self Management is unlikely to be skilled at or able to sustain Relationship Management.

Regard for Others: Having Regard for Others is the starting point and basis for effective Relationship Management. Holding a positive intent and attitude towards others (not necessarily approving of what they do) will filter out in micro-behaviours and be detected by the other person even if the leader lacks interpersonal skills. Equally, a leader who has slick interpersonal skills but low Regard for Others may leave others feeling cold, despite having said and done all the 'right' things. An exercise first used on an EI leadership programme at Stanford University[10] asks individuals to identify one person who has particularly influenced them - in other words changed what they do (which is a core aspect of being a leader). They are then asked to identify what it was about this person and what they did that made the difference. The usual response is that *this person believed in me,* often, more than they believed in themselves. Effective leaders have high belief in others (Regard for Others) and do so in a supportive way. They also have high Awareness of Others, the next relationship scale.

Awareness of Others: It is important that the leader accurately perceives the correct level of expectation to have of others. Too high expectations can leave people feeling disheartened, too low and people may feel demotivated. Awareness of Others is a vital tool for the leader to know what others need, when they need it and how much of it they need, whether that is through giving the correct level of encouragement, advice, autonomy or direction. Most other skills, habits and behaviours of Relationship Management tend to occur as a natural consequence of having Regard for and Awareness of Others. One of these is Connecting with Others.

Connecting with Others: A survey by Gallup[1] defined twelve questions that best predicted employee engagement; high on the list was that employees felt their boss cared about them. Forming trusting, honest, and caring relationships is a significant attribute of top leaders. Leaders who get the best out of others will often form close bonds and go beyond transactional, business-like communication by sharing themselves, expressing vulnerabilities and creating a closer level of trust.

8.2.2 Emotional Intelligence and leadership styles

Although many aspects of EI are relevant to effective leadership, it will depend on the context as to which style of leadership and therefore which aspects of EI are most appropriate. One model that identified seven leadership styles is based on the original work of David McClelland at Harvard University in the 1970s that was linked to EI by Daniel Goleman.[12] These leadership styles have clear conceptual links with EI and are mapped against the EIP scales below.

Table 8.2 EIP scales relevant to leadership styles

Leadership style	Encapsulating statement	Links to EIP scales	Works well when...
Coercive	*I expect others to do what I say without question.*	Personal Power Goal Directedness Emotional Resilience Conflict Handling	There is a crisis. Dealing with poor performers.
Authoritarian	*I have a clear vision and lead people towards it.*	Self Regard Self Awareness Goal Directedness Flexibility Personal Power Authenticity	Change is needed. Clear vision and objectives are required.
Pace-setting	*I have clear standards and expect my team to meet them.*	Emotional Resilience Goal Directedness Balanced Outlook Interdependence	Good when results are needed quickly.
Affiliative	*I work closely with people to build effective working relations.*	Regard for Others Connecting with Others Trust	Teams or individuals are facing stressful situations.
Democratic	*I like to work as part of a team rather than taking the lead.*	Regard for Others Awareness of Others Trust Interdependence	The team needs to own a project. To get the most out of skilled and valued staff.
Coaching	*I like coaching others, enabling them to perform effectively.*	Regard for Others Awareness of Others Connecting with Others	Employee's skills need developing.

Key to emotionally intelligent leadership is being able to move between these leadership styles as and when appropriate (scale 8; Flexibility), knowing when to use each leadership style (scale 4; Awareness of Others) and knowing how to apply them (scale 16; Reflective Learning). As with all aspects of EI this is more likely if the person has an attitude of high Self Regard and high Regard for Others (I+U+). A leader with high Self Regard and low Regard for Others (I+U-) may overuse and misuse the Coercive, Authoritarian and Pace-setting styles. A leader with low Self Regard and high Regard for Others (I- U+) is more likely to overuse and misuse the Affiliative, Democratic and Coaching styles of leadership.

8.2.3 Emotional Intelligence and leadership competencies

Most organisations define effective leadership behaviour and style with competencies. The relationship between EI and competencies is explained in Chapter 1.3.3; EI is the mechanism that enables people to develop and maintain their behavioural competence. Not surprisingly, therefore, many competencies are closely related to EI and are the backbone to several competency based EI measures.

In a study of 121 worldwide organisations, Goleman[12] found that 67% of competencies deemed to be essential for effective job performance were emotional competencies. He further supported his findings with a study by the Hay Group of 40 companies; showing that 'star performers' were only 27% more likely to have greater strengths in cognitive competencies but were 53% more likely to have greater than average strengths in emotional competencies. In further work by Goleman et al.,[39] a study of 2000 supervisors and middle managers showed that 16 competencies (Table 8.4 column 'b') distinguished the star performers from the average performers and that all but two of these were emotional competencies. This research led to the development of the Hay/McBer Emotional Competency Inventory (ECI 360).

A large scale review of previous research by Higgs and Dulewicz[40] found that job competencies clustered into 12 independent dimensions (Table 8.4 column 'c') which accounted for 72% of the variance in managerial performance. These they termed 'supra competencies' from which they later developed the Emotional Intelligence Questionnaire (EIQ).

The JCA approach to competencies and EI is different to other EI theories (as described in Chapter 1.3.3); rather than defining EI as a set of behavioural competencies, competencies are seen as being dependent on the individual holding emotionally intelligent attitudes. JCA have defined a total of 30 behavioural competencies that cluster into four broad headings shown below (Table 8.3).[41] Table 8.4, column 'a', shows the EIP scales that underpin the JCA competency behaviours.

Table 8.3 The JCA competency framework

ADAPT

Providing Support	Adapting to Challenges
• valuing people	• managing conflict
• acting with integrity	• resilience
• ethics and values	• responding to change
• team working	• flexibility & adaptability

DELIVER

Managing Tasks	Pursuing Goals
• organising & prioritisation	• driving for success
• following procedures	• customer focus
• quality focus	• commercial awareness
• delivering results	• acting with initiative
	• career drive

THINK

Analysing Information	Learning and Creativity
• research & investigation	• thinking strategically
• analysis & judgement	• learning
• written communication	• creativity & innovation

INSPIRE

Shaping Relationships	Providing Leadership
• building relationships	• inspiring others
• communicating & presenting	• directing & guiding
• influencing people	• empowering people
	• developing performance

Table 8.4 Primary relationship between competencies and the EIP scales

EIP scales	JCA Competencies (a)	EI Leadership competencies (b)	Management supra competencies (c)
1 Self Regard	Resilience (Flexibility & adaptability)* (Responding to change)	Self-confidence	Achievement-motivation
2 Regard for Others	Valuing people Customer focus (Inspiring others) (Directing and guiding) (Empowering people) (Developing performance)	Empathy Developing others	Interpersonal sensitivity Managing staff
3 Self Awareness	Resilience relatinships (Ethics and values)	Emotional self-awareness Accurate self-assessment	Resilience and adaptability Analysis and judgement
4 Awareness of Others	Valuing people Building relationships Customer focus Developing performance (Communicating and presenting) (Inspiring others) (Directing and guiding) (Empowering people) (Managing conflict) (Written communication)	Empathy Organisational awareness Developing others	Interpersonal sensitivity Oral communication Managing staff
5 Emotional Resilience	Resilience (Responding to change)	Self-confidence Adaptability	Resilience and adaptability
6 Personal Power	Quality focus Directing and guiding Acting with initiative Delivering results (Communicating and presenting) (Influencing) (Career drive) (Commercial awareness) (Driving for success) (Resilience)	Initiative Self-confidence Inspiration	Assertiveness and decisiveness Energy and initiative
7 Goal Directedness	Organising and prioritisation Strategic thinking Driving for success Delivering results Following procedures (Directing and guiding) (Career drive)	Achievement	Achievement-motivation Planning and organising Strategic perspective Analysis and judgement Business sense

EIP scales	JCA Competencies (a)	EI Leadership competencies (b)	Management supra competencies (c)
	(Quality focus) (Developing performance)		
8 Flexibility	Responding to change Flexibility & adaptability (Learning) (Creativity and innovation)	Adaptability Change catalyst	Resilience and adaptability
9 Connecting with Others	Team working Building relationships (Influencing) (Inspiring others) (Empowering people) (Developing performance) (Written communication)	Empathy Transparency	Interpersonal sensitivity Oral communication
10 Authenticity	Ethics and values Acting with integrity	Transparency	
11 Trust	Inspiring others Empowering people Acting with integrity	Teamwork and collaboration	Managing staff
12 Balanced Outlook	(Researching and investigating) (Analysis and judgement) (Strategic thinking) (Inspiring others) (Resilience)	Optimism	Resilience and adaptability Analysis and judgement
13 Emotional Expression and Control	Communicating and presenting (Inspiring others)	Self-control Emotional self-awareness	
14 Conflict Handling	Managing conflict Influencing (Creativity and innovation)	Conflict management Influence	Managing staff Persuasiveness Assertiveness and decisiveness
15 Interdependence	Team working Building relationships Acting with initiative	Teamwork and collaboration	Managing staff
16 Reflective Learning	Learning (Career drive)	Accurate self-assessment	

* Competencies in brackets have only a secondary relationship to the EIP scale.

There are clear benefits in relating EIP scales to competencies. Competencies are the result of practicing EI, and EI is the practice of managing one's personality. In other words there is a natural relationship between personality, EI and competencies (as described in Chapter 1); EI is what turns human potential (personality) into effective behaviour and performance (competencies). Competencies are effective to the extent that they are supported by complimentary EI attitudes. For example, there is little point in a team leader holding regular team meetings (a competency) if they have little Regard for Others (an EI attitude). It is therefore clearly beneficial to relate the organisational competencies to the EIP scales. By developing the related EIP scale (attitudes and habits) the individual will find it far easier to develop the corresponding behavioural competencies.

8.3 The emotionally intelligent team

So far this chapter has discussed EI in the context of individual leadership. EI is also applied widely in the context of teamwork and for improving relationships. There is clear evidence that EI not only improves performance of the individual, but also that of teams.[42,43] JCA have developed a parallel team measure of EI; the Team EIP, to compliment the Individual EIP instrument. Constructed by the same authors (and updated in 2013),[44] both products share the same EI attitudes, principles and theoretical framework. The table below shows the framework for the Team EIP.

Table 8.5 The Team EIP framework

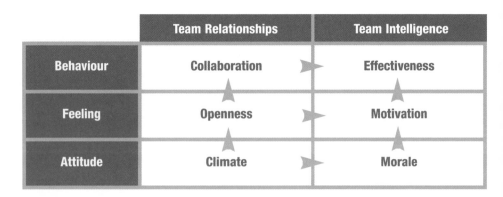

	Team Relationships		Team Intelligence
Behaviour	Collaboration	➤	Effectiveness
Feeling	Openness	➤	Motivation
Attitude	Climate	➤	Morale

As with the individual EIP, the arrows of influence move from the bottom upwards. The Attitude of the team (Climate and Morale) underpins the Feeling within the team (Openess and Motivation) which influences team Behaviour (Collaboration and Effectiveness).

Team EIP, as with the individual EIP framework is made up of two parts, Team Relationships (as opposed to Interpersonal Intelligence for the EIP) and Team Intelligence (as opposed to Personal Intelligence).

- **Team Relationships:** Team members who positively value and respect each other *(Climate)* are more likely to be open and attentive towards one another *(Openness)*, which will lead to strong and effective relationships *(Collaboration)*.

- **Team Intelligence**: A team that is united by a shared belief and confidence *(Morale)* will be more motivated and engaged in whatever it is doing *(Motivation)* thus helping the team to perform well and achieve what it sets out to do *(Effectiveness)*.

Unlike the individual EIP framework, Team Relationships (Interpersonal Intelligence) is on the left and Team Intelligence (Personal Intelligence) is on the right of the framework. This is because it is necessary to have strong relationships between team members first *(Team Relationships)* if the team as a whole is to perform effectively as a unit *(Team Intelligence)*. The influence between each pair of scales is described below.

- **Attitude:** Team members who respect and value one another *(Climate)* are likely to have greater shared belief in the team and what they can achieve *(Morale)*.

- **Feeling:** Team members who are open in their communication and aware of each other's feelings *(Openness)* are likely to have a collective energy and enthusiasm for what they set out to achieve *(Motivation)*.

- **Behaviour:** Team members who have strong relationships and work well together *(Collaboration)* are likely to behave and perform effectively as a team in achieving what they set out to do *(Effectiveness)*.

8.3.1 The Team EIP scales

The six team scales are directly linked to the six parts of the individual EIP framework as shown below:

Table 8.6 Team EIP scale links to the individual EIP framework

The EIP framework	Team EIP scale	Scale definition	Individual EIP corollary
Attitude	1 Climate	*The degree to which team members have positive regard for one another and create an atmosphere of safety within the team.*	Regard for Others
	2 Morale	*The shared belief and confidence this team has in itself, its members, and in what they set out to achieve.*	Self Regard

The EIP framework	Team EIP scale	Scale definition	Individual EIP corollary
Feeling	3 Openness	*How openly team members engage with one another and how aware they are of each other's feelings.*	Awareness of Others
	4 Motivation	*The collective energy and enthusiasm this team has to succeed in what they set out to achieve.*	Self Awareness
Behaviour	5 Collaboration	*The degree to which team members create strong interpersonal relations and work well together.*	Relationship Management
	6 Effectiveness	*How effectively the team behaves and performs in order to achieve what they set out to do.*	Self Management

Scale 1: Climate

Climate is an Attitude scale and reflects the attitude team members have towards one another (and to others outside of the team). Team members who value and respect one another will create a positive climate within the team. The climate of a team reflects *how it feels* to be a member of the team (such as feeling trusted and non-threatened), and therefore underpins all other team scales such as team Morale, Motivation and how effectively team members work together (Openness and Collaboration). A positive climate is created when team members care for each other, do not blame one another, their contributions are properly valued and recognised, they are accepted for who they are, and their individual differences are fully appreciated. An individual's sense of identity and their own value or self-worth will be affected by the responses they receive from others when they express their feelings. If their feelings are accepted, and they are appreciated rather than criticised, then they will tend to feel better about themselves and about those around them, perform better, communicate more openly (Openness), and co-operate more effectively (Collaboration), as described in the other two Team Relationships scales.

Scale 2: Morale

Morale is an Attitude scale that underpins the Team Intelligence scales. A team with high Morale is likely to be motivated and committed (scale 5), perform effectively and achieve what it sets out to do (scale 6). Team Morale consists of three main parts: 1- *Belief in the team*: team members that believe in the team are likely to be proud to be part of the team, work for the good of the team, and have confidence in what the team can achieve; 2- *Confidence in each other*: team members that have confidence in each other are likely to be loyal to one another, make a valuable contribution to the team, and have an active participation within the team; 3- *Shared belief in what the team sets out to achieve*: a defining principle for teamwork is that team members hold shared objectives. Team members that are aligned in this way are more likely to work closely together, make decisions more easily and be committed to the team purpose. For a team to be successful, it is necessary that all members share a common goal rather than each working for their own individual goals or gains. This is not to say that people will not be valued for their individual differences (see scale 1: Climate), nor that disagreements and conflict aren't discussed openly (see scale 3: Openness).

Scale 3: Openness

Openness is a Feeling scale and reflects the level of communication (about feelings) and emotional awareness team members have of one another (and of those outside of the team). Openness is underpinned by the Climate scale, as individuals who feel respected and valued are likely to be more open and engaged within the team. There are several aspects to this scale which include *being open with others* (through skillful expression of emotions, giving and receiving feedback, sharing feelings, vulnerabilities and intuitions, and listening to others), *being aware of others feelings*, and *handling difficult conversations* in a constructive manner. Teams that experience limitations in their communication often do not talk openly enough or listen effectively. The talking and listening that is done may also be limited to certain thoughts and ideas and exclude or avoid talking about feelings, vulnerabilities, intuitions, and off-the-wall ideas. Teams which do discuss these subjects tend to be more cohesive, flexible, creative and perhaps more fun to be part of, as discussed in scale 5: Collaboration.

Scale 4: Motivation

Motivation is a Feeling scale and represents the emotional energy of the team. A team that has an optimistic and positive mindset, where team members are enthusiastic and committed, and they look forward to and are excited about the future, will be high on Motivation. A motivated team is also one where team members know how to raise the energy, they are success oriented rather than problem oriented, they are optimistic rather than pessimistic, they have fun and let themselves get excited, and they celebrate when they have a success. There are several factors that contribute to a team's Motivation such as team members motivating and supporting one another, feeling empowered and responsible, having clarity on their job roles and responsibilities, and feeling that they are treated fairly. Team Motivation is strongly influenced by team Morale (scale 2), as a motivated team will be one where team members have a shared belief in the team and what they aim to achieve.

Scale 5: **Collaboration**

Collaboration is a Behaviour scale and reflects how effectively team members relate to one another and get along with each other (and also with other teams). Team relationships are dependent on creating a positive Climate where team members feel valued and an atmosphere of Openness where individuals listen, communicate and are aware of one another. A collaborative team is one where team members support and encourage one another, are co-operative rather than obstructive, actively connect with each other and deal effectively with any conflict. Teams that score low on this scale tend to be hostile, tactless and emotionally detached from one another, which blocks them from working well as a team. Teams that score high on this scale tend to be friendly, sociable and considerate of others in the team which helps build trusting and supportive relationships. They therefore work well as a cohesive team, with high Morale, Motivation and Effectiveness, as described by the Team Intelligence scales.

Scale 6: **Effectiveness**

Effectiveness is a Behaviour scale and as such reflects how well the team behaves and performs as a cohesive unit to achieve what it sets out to do. This consists of three parts: *team competence* in terms of striving for success, sound judgement, balanced decision making and creating opportunities; *emotional resilience* in terms of coping with setbacks, learning from mistakes, and supporting each other under pressure; and being *solution focussed* by producing creative solutions, adapting and responding to change, and all team members taking responsibility. Team Effectiveness is the net result of all other scales. A team is more likely to be *Effective* if it has a positive *Climate* and *Morale*, team members are *Open* and *Motivated* and they have strong *Collaborative* relationships.

8.3.2 Applying the Team EIP

Unsurprisingly, the EI of a team is largely dependent on the EI of the individuals within it,[45] therefore it is difficult to get effective collaboration and positive results if individual team members are defensive and uncooperative. In particular, the EI of the team leader has a strong impact on the whole team by raising or lowering the emotional atmosphere.[46] However, team EI is more than the sum of its parts, as it is quite possible to have high performing individuals who do not work well when placed together. Many elements of effective emotional functioning in teams come from the norms (patterns of behaviour and attitude) that team members develop with one another rather than the EI of individuals.[47] It is therefore valuable to measure team EI separately from individual EI and provide group interventions alongside individual coaching. It is generally recommended that individuals complete and explore the individual EIP first before doing the Team EIP. This way they can understand how they may be contributing personally to the team's strengths and development areas (as identified by the Team EIP), and they may be more committed to their own self-development. Explanation on how to apply the Team EIP is not within the scope of this book, and requires additional training to using the individual EIP. As with all assessment products, it is important that the user has the appropriate skills for team facilitation, as well as being competent to use the Team EIP instrument.

Team EI not only connects with individual EI, it is also related to the EI of the organisation. In other words, *everything is connected*.[48] In order to develop an emotionally intelligent organisation it is necessary to develop emotionally intelligent individuals and teams, and vice versa. The EIP framework for the individual and the team may be placed together (see below) such that Individual Regard for Others supports team Climate, Awareness of Others encourages Openness, and Relationship Management builds Collaboration.

Table 8.7 The individual and team EIP frameworks combined

	Individual		Team	
	Personal Intelligence	**Interpersonal Intelligence**	**Team Relationships**	**Team Intelligence**
Behaviour	Self Management	Relationship Management	Collaboration	Effectiveness
Feeling	Self Awareness	Awareness of Others	Openness	Motivation
Attitude	Self Regard	Regard for Others	Climate	Morale

In terms of developing the EI of teams, many of the suggestions given in Chapter 7 are entirely relevant. Two suggestions in particular, *Providing opportunity for interaction* and *Making change experiential*, lend themselves well to team events (refer to Chapter 7.4). Also, consider applying the suggestions given below on *How to create an emotionally intelligent organisation*, such as *Creating an atmosphere of openness* within the team, *Encouraging responsibility* across team members and encouraging the team to *Value and appreciate* one another (refer to Chapter 8.4.1).

8.4 The emotionally intelligent organisation

Today, Emotional Intelligence is well established as a model and process for coaching individuals and developing teams. Although, there is far less research and practice on creating Emotional Intelligence within the organisation. This section briefly examines the application of EI in the organisation and how this cascades down to teams and the individual.

Whatever activities it is engaged in, an organisation will be more effective at what it does (more output for less input) if they harness the full potential of all of their employees. Creating an environment and managing employees in a manner which fosters the development and application of their Emotional Intelligence promotes their effectiveness in both Self Management and Relationship Management. It has been estimated that approximately 80% of activities in an organisation involve some collaboration.[49] The impact of improved engagement can be seen at an organisational level in terms of customer loyalty, productivity, profitability, reduced turnover, and improved well-being.[50] JCA see the emotionally intelligent climate and organisation as an integrated and interdependent whole comprising of individuals, teams (relationships) and the organisation.

Table 8.8 The emotionally intelligent organisation

Individual's feel	Relationships are	Organisational climate is
Alive	Energetic	Participative
Self-determined	Adult	Responsible
Self-aware	Honest	Open
Significant	Acknowledged	Recognition
Competent	Cooperative	Rewarding
Likeable	Friendly	Human

Evidence suggests that the organisational climate can significantly promote or inhibit emotionally intelligent behaviour.[51,52] For example, by creating a *participative* organisational environment, relationships and teams are more *energetic* and individuals feel more *alive*.[53] Equally, findings show that coaching individuals to feel more engaged in their work will ripple into their relationships,[54] which in turn will cascade across the organisation.[55,56] Development can work through the individual, in teams and across the organisation; applying all three levels of intervention has by far the greatest and most sustainable impact.

Having one of these levels does not automatically mean the others will coexist. It is possible to have a group of emotionally intelligent individuals who do not form an emotionally intelligent team (the whole is different from the sum of its parts), which is the case when individual team members hold different values and intentions. Also, establishing EI within teams will not necessarily produce an emotionally intelligent organisation, such as when teams compete with each other rather than collaborate.

8.4.1 How to create an emotionally intelligent organisation

Based on research into organisational EI[57] and drawing upon the application of FIRO® theory (The Human Element® programme),[58] JCA have identified four key principles that enable organisations to create a conducive climate for organisational change, team compatibility and individual development:

1 *Adopt positive intentions (attitudes)*
2 *Create an atmosphere of openness*
3 *Encourage responsibility*
4 *Value and appreciate others*

Adopt positive intentions is the first principle as it reflects the Core Attitudes of EI: Self Regard and Regard for Others. The second principle of *Create an open atmosphere* provides the conditions for change to take place. Principle three, *Encourage responsibility,* is the necessary attitude for choosing to make any change. The final principle of *Value and appreciate others* is, in practice, what helps create an EI climate (this is also explained in more detail in Chapter 7.8). These four principles can be used to inform the design of any organisational development intervention.

Principle 1: Adopt positive intentions/attitudes

At the heart of EI is holding positive intentions (attitudes) towards oneself and others. People's attitudes manifest in all aspects of their behaviour. For instance, high Regard for Others will be apparent in a person's actions, mannerisms, body language and voice. Equally, if a person does not respect others, then this will be apparent in their behaviour, even if they have strong interpersonal skills, however much they may try to disguise their feelings.

An organisation can foster positive intentions by stating its values and acting on them, showing respect to everyone, seeking to help and support others and treating people fairly. Holding positive intentions may also be encouraged through the EIP scales of Self Regard, Regard for Others, and the eight EI attitudes (described in Chapter 1.5). During difficult times such as an economic downturn, the natural human response is to move into *survival mode*, which stems from an attitude of conserve, protect, fight and defend (rigidity). A more helpful conscious strategy would be for organisations to adopt a *thrive* attitude of collaboration, openness and opportunity (flexibility). Attitudes tend to be self-fulfilling, so an organisation that promotes positive intentions internally with staff and externally with customers is likely to create the same. Positive intentions are also crucial for helping to motivate people, minimise defensive behaviours and enable people to develop and grow.

Table 8.9 Survive versus Thrive intentions

Survive intentions	Thrive intentions
Protect	Grow
Defend	Learn
Defeat	Connect
Win	Mutual gain
Be right	Understanding

© 1999, Ronald J. Luyet and James W. Tamm, RC Group LLC, from their Radical Collaboration® workshop.

Principle 2: Create an atmosphere of openness
One intention an organisation can choose to adopt is to be open, honest and truthful. This may be promoted through the EIP scales of Authenticity, Emotional Expression and Connecting with Others. A concern people often have with being open is that they may upset people if they said what they really thought. However, encouraging people to go to a deeper level of openness and truthfulness with themselves and others will help them go beyond the level of Blame (level 1) as shown in the example below.

Table 8.10 Levels of openness

	Levels of openness	Example
-1	Unaware	*I don't see anything to discuss*
0	Withholding	*I don't want to tell you*
1	Blame	*You are an idiot*
2	Explanation	*Because you ignore me*
3	My feeling	*You don't like me*
4	My story	*I think you feel I am unlikable*
5	My fear	*I fear I am not likeable*

Copyright © 1994, 2005, 2008 Business Consultants, Inc. Published by The Schutz Company.

An organisation can facilitate an atmosphere of openness by keeping people informed, sharing information, encouraging the expression of feelings, giving constructive feedback and finding solutions to problems rather than seeking who to blame. There are many examples of how a lack of openness and truth has led to the demise of organisations. The Challenger Shuttle disaster (1986) was initially seen to be the result of technical errors but, following a public enquiry, the underlying cause was later traced back to a lack of open communication within the NASA culture. The Enron fraud scandal (2001), the Iraq intelligence dossier (2002) and the 2007 sub-prime mortgage and banking collapse are all examples of how catastrophic failure can be traced back to a lack of openness and truth.

Principle 3: Encourage responsibility

Organisations can do a lot to help people feel more in control and responsible for their working lives, such as giving people choices, including them in decision making and empowering people to act autonomously. A distinguishing feature of the emotionally intelligent organisation is that everyone feels fully accountable. This means that when things go wrong people do not blame individuals but problem solve to improve things. A useful analogy here is to think of the team or organisation as a single united organism like the human body; it would be pointless, for example, for a person to blame their hands for dropping a ball.

One of the EI attitudes underpinning the EIP is that *Everyone is in control of and responsible for their actions*. This is reflected in the EIP scale Personal Power which recommends that people accept they have at least 1% of influence over situations and they take one action each day towards achieving their goals. Organisations that promote these attitudes and behaviours will encourage people to operate at a deeper level of responsibility as shown in the example below.

Table 8.11 Levels of responsibility

	Level of responsibility	Example
-1	Unconscious	*I don't know why I get angry*
0	Chance	*My behaviour is caused by the stars*
1	Genetics	*It's my parent's fault I am like this*
2	Blame	*Other people make me angry*
3	I choose my response	*I can remain calm*
4	I create the situation	*I can choose my environment*
5	Everything is my choice	*I determine my life, my thoughts and my feelings*

Principle 4: **Value and appreciate others**

Showing regard for, belief in, and appreciation towards others is one of the easiest and most powerful ways to raise EI. Evidence suggests that organisations that foster a culture of value will have happier and more productive employees. For example, the Gallup Q12 survey found that people with a best friend at work are seven times more likely to enjoy their jobs, have fewer accidents and be more creative. Also, that close friendships at work boost job satisfaction by 50%.[59] A key attribute of effective leadership is believing in the potential of others (Regard for Others) as, by doing so, people will believe in themselves. Believing in others is consistent with holding the EI attitudes: *However you are and others are, is OK*; and *People have a natural tendency towards growth and health*.

As with openness and responsibility, appreciation may be considered at different levels. The lowest level of appreciation is to ignore people as if they do not exist (levels -1 and 0). One step up from this is to acknowledge people and offer feedback (level 1) although, all too often feedback is used as a way to disguise criticism and blame. More enlightened companies will provide training courses in how to offer 'praise' (levels 2 and 3) which is a conditional form of appreciation; people get recognition on condition they perform well, are productive and add value. The deepest level of appreciation is to show value towards others (level 4 and 5), which is an unconditional form of appreciation, such that even when a person makes a mistake they will still feel valued. It is this that motivates individuals, creates loyalty and builds long-term trusting relationships, which are some of the most valued and sought after human qualities from organisations and employers.

Table 8.12 **Levels of appreciation**[57]

Levels of appreciation	Example	Link to the communication grid*
-1 Not noticing	*Do I know you?*	Put-Down
0 Discounting	*That's your job*	Put-Down
1 Acknowledge	*That's nice **but***	Feedback
2 Generalised	*That was good*	Praise
3 Personalised	*I like what you did because...*	Praise
4 Unconditional	*I like you, e.g. a smile*	Value
5 Unconditional	*In your presence I feel good*	Value

*For further information on applying Principle 4 refer to the 'communication grid' in Chapter 7.8.

8.4.2 Measuring the Emotional Intelligence of an organisation

To measure the EI of an organisation, JCA developed the Leadership Climate Indicator (LCI). The LCI is designed to focus on the behaviour of leaders as a key factor in determining the emotional climate or tone they set within the organisation. The EI of leaders has been found to have a powerful impact on the climate and effectiveness of groups.[60,61,62] The LCI helps leaders build trust in the organisation and cultivate a leadership climate which creates a sustainable culture for performance.

The questionnaire measures the extent to which leaders exhibit positive leadership behaviours (Inspiring and Including) that create a climate of trust in leaders and in which people feel inspired to perform to their potential. It also measures negative leadership behaviours (Controlling and Withdrawing) which erode trust and engagement if used habitually.

There are twelve scales grouped into four clusters or quadrants. The twelve scales are all aspects of EI and closely related to the EIP scales and their associated feelings (the climate) as shown below.

Table 8.13 Leadership Climate Indicator (LCI) scales

Cluster	Description	LCI Scale	EIP related scale	Associated feelings (climate)
Inspiring	When leaders act in this way they generate a positive climate where people feel inspired, motivated and challenged to move out of their comfort zones and perform at their best.	Visioning	Self Awareness Goal Directedness Balanced Outlook Emotional Expression Reflective Learning	**Performance zone.** Core Attitude: I+ U+ Positive, high energy: ● *Happy* ● *Optimistic* ● *Engaged* ● *Creative* ● *Confident* ● *Motivated*
		Stretching	Personal Power Goal Directedness Trust Balanced Outlook Assertiveness	
		Encouraging	Regard for Others Awareness of Others Goal Directedness Connecting with Others Balanced Outlook Emotional Expression & Control	

Cluster	Description	LCI Scale	EIP related scale	Associated feelings (climate)
Including	By acting in this way, leaders generate trust, loyalty and commitment and build emotional capital which can be drawn on to sustain performance and maintain resilience in the face of pressure.	Collaborative	Awareness of Others Flexibility Connecting with Others Trust Interdependence	**Renewal zone** Core Attitude: I+ U+ Positive, low energy: • *Calm* • *Peaceful* • *Relaxed* • *At ease* • *Mellow* • *Committed* • *Secure*
		Trusted	Connecting with Others Authenticity Trust	
		Appreciative	Regard for Others Awareness of Others Emotional Expression	
Controlling	Controlling behaviours can be effective and appropriate for mobilising energy in a short term crisis, but if used habitually they erode trust and instil fear and defensiveness in others. Over time, a controlling style can impede collaboration and innovation and can be toxic leading to burnout and disengagement.	Competitive	Regard for Others (low) Mistrusting Aggressive	**Survival zone** Core Attitude: I+ U- Negative, high energy: • *Anxious* • *Defensive* • *Frustrated* • *Angry* • *Defiant* • *Intimidated*
		Aggressive	Regard for Others (low) Emotional Under Control Aggressive	
		Demanding	Flexibility (low) Mistrusting Over Optimistic	
Withdrawing	When leaders are operating in this quadrant they tend to detach themselves from people and issues. Energy is low and innovation, healthy conflict and connection with others are the victims of leaders who retreat into their comfort zones.	Avoidant	Self Regard (low) Awareness of Others (low) Personal Power (low) Connecting with Others (low) Pessimistic Over Independent	**Burnout zone** Core Attitude: I- U- Negative, low energy: • *Exhausted* • *Depressed* • *Sad* • *Hopeless* • *Empty* • *Fearful*
		Dependent	Self Regard (low) Self Awareness (low) Over Trusting Passive Dependent	
		Rigid	Self Regard (low) Flexibility (low) Emotional Over Control Pessimistic	

The emotional climate is represented by the feelings people experience within the organisation. This may be shown as a 2x2 matrix (adapted from Shwartz's 'energy quadrant'),[63] with feelings being either positive (pleasant) or negative (unpleasant), and as high energy or low energy. This results in four emotional zones:

Table 8.14 The emotions matrix

The Survival zone	The Performance zone
High energy and negative feelings	*High energy and positive feelings*
These feelings provide useful feedback on aspects of dissatisfaction that a person needs to respond to. It is important that they do not spend too much time here or they are likely to drop into the Burnout zone.	Being in this zone leads to very productive results but is not sustainable and will require time in the renewal zone.
The Burnout zone	The Renewal zone
Low energy and negative feelings	*Low energy and positive feelings*
This zone can be very unproductive for individuals. It is important that they recognise these feelings early before disappointment and sadness turn into feelings of hopelessness and despair.	This zone is essential for rest and recovery, and can also facilitate creative and insightful thinking.

Ideally, an organisation and its leaders will create an environment where individuals feel energised and motivated to be in the Performance zone, where they have the opportunity for relaxation and recovery in the Renewal zone, where they are discouraged from being in the Survival zone and where they are supported when they fall into the Burnout zone.

The LCI is completed by employees within the organisation who rate the behaviours of the leadership group. The LCI data provides a rich resource for implementing appropriate organisational development interventions. For example, if the leadership behaviour is Aggressive and Competitive this may create a climate where employees feel anxious and intimidated. This leadership behaviour could be replaced by one that is more Appreciative and Encouraging so as to create a climate where people feel more engaged and motivated.

8.5 An integrated approach to assessing Emotional Intelligence

In this chapter a clear case has been made for applying EI at an individual (leadership), team (relationships) and organisational (climate) level. Although discussed separately, they are all interdependent;[64] creating a more emotionally intelligent climate will support better relationships which will improve individual motivation and leadership. In addition, EI should not be considered in isolation as it forms part of a process for turning personality and potential into effective behaviour and performance. The relationship between all these aspects is represented by the framework shown below. The framework also shows the JCA products that have been developed to help increase effectiveness and performance at the individual, team and organisational levels.

Table 8.15 The JCA development products framework

	Personality +	Emotional Intelligence =	Performance
Individual	Personality Type Profile	EIP	Behaviours 360
Team	Team Personality Type Profile	Team EIP	MI group 360 Profile
Organisation		Leadership Climate Indicator	

Summary points from Chapter Eight

- Emotional Intelligence has been shown to be measurable, developable (and sustainable) and to predict performance, three criteria that are vital ingredients for leadership development.

- There is now a substantial body of research demonstrating the benefit of EI for improving organisational productivity, performance and financial return.

- Many of the demands on organisations such as increased competition, rapid change, an ageing workforce and globalisation provide a compelling case for the need to develop EI attributes in the workplace.

- EI is now firmly established as a central part of leadership performance, having been popularised by Daniel Goleman in the Harvard Business Review, academically researched in leadership journals, recognised by many authoritative writers on leadership such as Warren Bennis, and become a core part to many established leadership competency frameworks.

- Despite extensive research into leadership there has been relatively little work carried out on how to create an emotionally intelligent organisation. To this end, JCA make four key recommendations for the design of organisational development programmes:

  - *Adopt positive intentions (attitudes)*
  - *Create an atmosphere of openness*
  - *Encourage responsibility*
  - *Value and appreciate others*

- Due to the fundamental and underlying nature of the EIP theory, model and scales, it can easily be mapped onto other developmental models used in business. This has been done with the JCA leadership competencies, Team EIP, organisational climate (the Leadership Climate Indicator), personality type theory (Appendix 3), and FIRO® theory (Appendix 4). Providing this link with the EIP gives greater opportunity for supporting individual, team and organisational development.

- JCA have created an assessment framework that maps onto three levels of assessment (individual, team and organisation) and three psychological domains (personality, EI and behaviour). These different facets determine a large part of what constitutes effective business performance, and can be measured by the range of JCA products, one of which is the EIP.

●　　●　　●

Appendix One

Advanced descriptions of the sixteen EIP scales

For the EIP user who wishes to explore the EIP scales in greater detail, a more comprehensive description and analysis of each of the sixteen scales is given below.

Scale 1: Self Regard

'No one can make you feel inferior without your permission'
Eleanor Roosevelt

1 Definition

Self Regard is scale 1 of the EIP questionnaire and is defined as the degree to which an individual values and accepts themselves.

2 Description

Low Self Regard: Low Self Regard may manifest as feelings of self-doubt and insecurity, worrying about shortcomings and putting oneself down. Having a low Self Regard may also distort a person's Self Awareness (scale 3) causing them to interpret experiences negatively, such as exaggerating problems and ignoring positives. Low Self Regard may be driven by certain unconscious negative attitudes such as *I am only OK…. if everybody likes me….if I am perfect…if I am strong and don't show my feelings*. Negative attitudes tend to lead to all manner of rigid behaviours such as insisting on being the centre of attention (or avoiding people altogether) and always wanting to be in charge (or avoiding any responsibility). Someone who has high Self Regard on the other hand will accept themselves unconditionally; warts and all, rather than feeling compelled to behave in a certain way in order to feel OK about themselves. A low score on Self Regard may hinder a person from developing their Emotional Resilience (scale 5), a sense of Personal Power (scale 6) and being Goal Directed (scale 7).

High Self Regard: Self Regard is the basis for developing all aspects of Emotional Intelligence, in particular Self Management. A high score on Self Regard may help an individual to be Emotionally Resilient (scale 5), have a sense of Personal Power (scale 6) and be Goal Directed (scale 7). Having higher Self Regard suggests that, for the most part, a person feels happy with themself and who they have become, and have a strong inner self-belief. The exception to this would be if they are masking a low Self Regard through having a low Regard for Others (scale 2). This may manifest as the individual finding fault in other people, so as to avoid looking at their own shortcomings, being arrogant, and seeing themself as superior or more valuable than others. Assuming this is not the case and they have a high Regard for Others, then their high Self Regard indicates they are happy with and accept themselves, even though there will be aspects of themself they may wish to develop. For example, if they make a mistake they are more likely to see this as useful learning rather than blaming and criticising themselves (or others).

3 Interpretation

Scale 1 forms the cornerstone to JCA's theory of Emotional Intelligence and the EIP framework. It greatly influences all of the EIP scales, forms one half of the Attitude Matrix and is one of the eight attitudes of Emotional Intelligence; *However you are and others are, is OK.* It is, therefore, the first of the sixteen EIP scales.

Unconditional Self Regard: Self Regard is experienced as the feelings an individual has about their self-concept (their identity or being), which may be conscious or unconscious and can be considered in three parts:

- *Their sense of self-significance (or belonging)*
- *Their sense of self-competence (or Personal Power and self-efficacy)*
- *Their sense of self-liking (or self-acceptance and unique value)*

However, most people, the majority of the time, tend to believe (if unconsciously) that *I am only OK if I do 'x',......and if I do not do 'x' then I am Not OK.* In other words, they have conditions as to their self-worth and feeling OK. These conditions vary from person to person depending largely on how adults treated them when they were children.[1]

Conditions of self-worth: Conditions of worth were originally defined by Carl Rogers[2] and are also referred to as 'drivers' as they drive a person's behaviour, although not in a healthy way. Drivers tend to be endlessly pushing a person; often followed by exhaustion and burnout. The most common conditions of self-worth are described below;

Table 1.1 Conditions of self-worth

Title	Definition	Description
1 Be Strong	Don't have, or at least don't express, feelings or needs.	This is perhaps the most common condition of worth in the UK, particularly amongst men. It will inhibit a person's Self Awareness (scale 3; being aware of the body, feelings and needs), which in turn will undermine their Self Management (particularly if combined with a 'Try Hard but don't succeed' driver).
2 Be Perfect	Never be in the wrong and never make a mistake, however small.	This may affect a person's willingness to learn through trial and error (Flexibility; scale 8) or allowing others to do the same (Trust; scale 11), and to express themselves openly and freely without self-criticism (Emotional Expression; scale 13).
3 Please Others	Put others first and keep them happy.	This is more common in women and for people who choose the helping professions. It will impair their Relationship Management despite this being the area of most concern to them. They are likely to be Over Dependent on others (scale 15), tending to be too Passive in asserting themselves (scale 14) and withhold expressing their wants and feelings (Emotional Expression; scale 13), especially if they also have a Be Strong driver.
4 Try Hard ... but don't succeed	In other words, it is the trying that counts, not achievement, and suffering that earns merit.	This is also common for men in the UK. It is likely to impair their Personal Power (scale 6) as they do not allow themselves to experience success and in the long-term will affect their Emotional Resilience (scale 5) as they are unlikely to allow themselves sufficient rest and recovery (which is common to all conditions of self-worth).
5 Hurry Up	Be quick and do lots of things at once; never relax or take your time.	This is likely to make Reflective Learning (scale 16) more difficult and impair their Relationship Management in terms of Connecting with Others (scale 9) and Interdependence (scale 15) if they are too impatient with others.

The basis of self-acceptance: These conditions of worth influence people's behaviour patterns greatly because the experience of feeling Not OK is so unpleasant, people will do whatever is required to avoid these feelings. For example, a boy who is brought up to believe that 'boys must not be scared' will not allow himself (as a boy, or later as a man) to be in touch with his fear. He will suppress it and perhaps convert it into something else; such people sometimes act angrily (and believe themselves to be angry) as a substitute for the fear that they do not allow themselves to feel. A person will only allow themselves to be fully self-aware, if they believe that they are unconditionally OK, valuable and lovable, however they are. Otherwise the realisation that they are not fulfilling their conditions of worth will provoke feelings of not being OK, which may be too painful to accept and be aware of.

The ultimate purpose of Emotional Intelligence is to help individuals to be self-accepting and unconditionally OK (at least most of the time). This is achieved through dismantling the attitudes and beliefs, often acquired in childhood, that cause a person to feel they are Not OK. These attitudes interfere with an individual achieving their innate potential and is neatly illustrated by Timothy Gallwey's 'inner game' book series[3] that introduces the formula:

$$\textit{Performance} = \textit{Potential} - \textit{Interference}$$

That is, people will naturally *Perform* to their *Potential* once their *Interference* factors (drivers and defences) are removed.

Links with other scales: Self Regard and Self Awareness (scale 3) are fundamentally inseparable. Starting from the assumption that *however you are and others are, is OK* (EI attitude No. 1), then to be truly self-aware is to be aware of this attitude, that 'I am OK' and therefore have high Self Regard. Self Awareness is also feedback for developing Self Regard as it enables a person to be aware of what emotional needs are not being met (listed in Table 7.2) such as their needs for intimacy, attention and recognition.

Within the EIP framework, Self Regard is the cornerstone of Self Awareness and Self Awareness is the cornerstone of all the other EIP scales. Self Regard is therefore linked to all of the EI scales and the Self Management scales are ordered by how closely they correlate with Self Regard. Hence, Emotional Resilience (scale 5) is the first of the Self Management scales, followed by Personal Power (scale 6) which is one of the three strands to Self Regard (one's sense of self-competence). Goal Directedness (scale 7) is next as people high in Self Regard are likely to be focused on what they want, and have Flexibility (scale 8) which requires moving outside of one's comfort zones, also influenced by Self Regard. Scale 9 (Connecting with Others) involves allowing oneself to be known by others (and potentially vulnerable) and scale 10 (Authenticity) may involve risking disapproval, being in the minority or being unpopular. All of these scales will require the inner strength of Self Regard for them to be maintained. Further explanation of how Self Regard relates to the EIP scales is given within each of the scale descriptions that follow and in Chapter 5.

The scale that is most closely associated with Self Regard is Regard for Others (scale 2) and the two are best interpreted together using the Attitude Matrix described in Chapter 4.3. For instance, a person who is critical of others (who has low Regard for Others) and claims they are entirely happy may be hiding a low Self Regard. Regard for Others is the next scale to be discussed.

Scale 2: Regard for Others

'If you want others to be happy, practice compassion.
If you want to be happy, practice compassion'
The Dalai Lama

1 Definition

Scale 2, Regard for Others, measures the degree to which an individual accepts and values others as people, as distinct from liking or approving of what they might do. Regard for Others is integrally related to Self Regard and should therefore be considered in relation to the previous scale and the Attitude Matrix described in Chapter 4.3.

Fig. 1.1 The Attitude Matrix

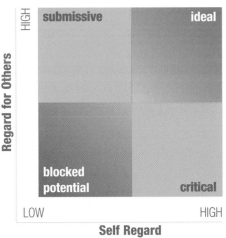

2 Description

Low Regard for Others: This scale underpins all of the Relationship Management scales for Emotional Intelligence. Having a low score on Regard for Others may hinder a person from Connecting with Others (scale 9), building Trust (scale 11), handling conflict (scale 14) and acting interdependently (scale 15). Low Regard for Others suggests a person may be judgmental of others, which is likely to impair their ability to be truly aware of people's differences (scale 4) and therefore to respond appropriately and with choice. Judging others negatively may mean they are less inclined to listen to people, or adapt and respond to people's needs (Flexibility, scale 8), and that they may be critical, unsympathetic and intolerant of others rather than seeking to understand.

High Regard for Others: Having a high Regard for Others will help an individual connect with others (scale 9), build Trust (scale 11), handle conflict (scale 14) and act interdependently (scale 15). Their high Regard for Others also suggests that they tend to be less judgmental of others, which will enhance their ability to be truly aware of people's differences (scale 4) and therefore be more able to respond appropriately to them. By accepting and valuing people as they are they may be more inclined to listen to people, seek to understand, adapt and respond to their needs (Flexibility, scale 8), and be supportive, sympathetic and tolerant.

3 Interpretation

Self Regard: An individual with high Self Regard but low Regard for Others comes from the Critical position (I am OK, you are Not OK) on the Attitude Matrix. A good example of this are bullies who put their own interests first to the detriment of others and will pick on individuals who respond submissively (I am Not OK, you are OK). The Critic is, in fact, masking their own feelings of low Self Regard which becomes apparent when they are stood up to, when often the mask drops and they become Submissive. In effect both the Critic and the Submissive need the same thing, to raise their self-esteem/Self Regard. For further links between Self Regard and Regard for Others refer to Chapter 4.3.

Awareness of Others: High Regard for Others is important because it underpins the right hand pillar of the EIP framework (Interpersonal Intelligence). Directly above Regard for Others is Awareness of Others; if a person has low Regard for Others they will perceive others through this lens, seeing them from a critical perspective. They are also less likely to pay attention to others' feelings and needs if they have less concern for them. People who are low in Regard for Others will tend to be judg-mental, critical, blaming, rejecting, mistrustful and disregarding of others. As a result they will find it difficult to be accurately aware of others and their feelings. It is some-times the case that a person scores high on Awareness of Others because they are hyper-vigilant and suspicious of others (due to a low Regard for Others and being Mistrusting), not because they have an accurate and balanced perception of others. Those who have high Regard for Others will still be accepting and respectful of them even if they dislike, disagree with or disapprove of what the person does or says.

Scale 3: Self Awareness

'Few are those who see with their own eyes and feel with their own hearts'
Albert Einstein

1 Definition

Self Awareness is the degree to which an individual is in touch with their physiology, feelings and intuitions and is the basis to developing Emotional Intelligence.

The EIP framework of Emotional Intelligence shows that the causal arrows for Awareness of Others, Self Management and Relationship Management derive from and depend upon developing Self Awareness. Consequently it is of fundamental importance to understand what Self Awareness is, and what can be done to enhance it. Links between Self Awareness and other EIP scales are given in Chapter 5.1.

Table 1.2 The EIP framework

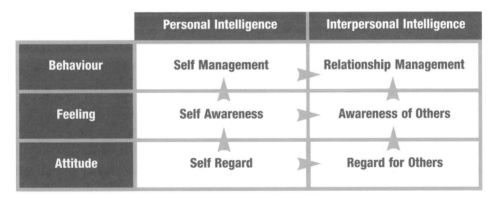

	Personal Intelligence	Interpersonal Intelligence
Behaviour	Self Management	Relationship Management
Feeling	Self Awareness	Awareness of Others
Attitude	Self Regard	Regard for Others

2 Description

Low Self Awareness: Low Self Awareness suggests that the individual is less in touch with their feelings, wants, needs and intuitions, which is likely to have a knock-on effect on most other aspects of their EI. If an individual tends not to notice their feelings of frustration, they are likely to grow into feelings of anger. If they do not notice how they feel under stress then they are less likely to learn what causes them stress and how to manage it effectively. And, if they don't notice feelings of joy they may not learn to appreciate and enjoy the moment. One reason people stop paying attention to how they feel is because they do not like how they feel about themselves. If this is the case, then they may have also scored low on scale 1; Self Regard. The risk here is that they may negatively distort their feelings, such as, interpreting feelings of 'expectation' as 'anxiety' or if they have a low

Regard for Others (scale 2) they may negatively distort their feelings towards others, such as interpreting feelings of 'fear' as 'anger'.

Scoring low on Self Awareness provides an ideal opportunity to improve an individual's EI more generally, as increasing this single scale will help them to develop many other parts of their EI. For example, it is difficult to be aware of others' feelings (scale 4) if they do not notice their own feelings, and it is difficult to be goal directed (scale 7) if they are not in touch with what they want and like.

High Self Awareness: This suggests that the individual is likely to be closely in touch with their feelings, wants, needs and intuitions, which will have a positive knock-on effect on other aspects of their EI. For example, if they tend to notice when they feel frustrated then they will be more able to intervene and prevent the feeling escalating into anger. If they notice how they feel under stress they are more likely to learn what causes them stress and how to manage this effectively. Or, if they recognise feelings of joy they will be better able to know what they enjoy doing and what gives them satisfaction in life. It may be worth checking that their Self Regard score (scale 1) is also relatively high. Sometimes people with low Self Regard are acutely self-aware of personal imperfection, resulting in a negatively biased self-perception.

3 Interpretation

Bodily awareness: Feelings are experienced in the body rather than the brain and they are mediated largely through hormones rather than neurons (refer to Chapter 2.1 for more information on this). Different sources of feelings include: physiological (such as hunger, thirst and nausea), emotional (such as anger, fear and joy), and intuitive (such as gut feeling or inner knowing). An important element of Self Awareness is paying attention to the body's physical needs such as the need for rest, recuperation, nutrition and exercise. The body may be likened to the workforce of an organisation, if the workforce is not looked after then it will become demotivated, underperform and go on strike (illness and depression), much like the human body.

Intuition: Intuition is an aspect of Self Awareness, that people perceive through feedback from their body, such as their 'gut feelings', rather than through cognitive thinking. Some people may be considered as naturally more intuitive than others, although intuition is something that everyone can develop with practice. Intuition is based on bodily awareness, so it is of the moment, transitory and ever changing. Being intuitive involves self-monitoring to detect any changes that occur in the body that then inform a person's thinking and decision making (refer to Appendix 2 for neuroscientific evidence on this). This monitoring process does not require constant conscious effort, although, for those low in Self Awareness, it may be needed initially. People are more likely to detect the quieter neurological and physical signals of intuition when they are relaxed and their brain is less active and noisy. Regularly checking in with oneself and one's feelings will become more automatic and habitual with practice.

Self Knowledge: Self Knowledge is what a person knows about themselves (cognitively) based on Self Awareness (feeling experiences). For example, over time a person may start to notice that whenever they feel hungry their thinking deteriorates and they become irritable more easily. This is their Self Knowledge which has been acquired through reflecting upon (Reflective Learning; scale 16) their past experiences (Self Awareness). Having formed this piece of Self Knowledge they will know to eat something when they feel hungry, before their thinking deteriorates.

Self Regard: As explained previously, Self Awareness is highly dependent on Self Regard; if an individual is secure in their 'OKness' they can afford to be aware of whatever they are feeling without their value being threatened. However, if their 'OKness' is dependent on them being and feeling a certain way (a conditional self-worth) then they will judge the acceptability of what they feel which will impair their level of Self Awareness.

Scale 4: Awareness of Others

'The greatest gift you can give another is the purity of your attention'
Richard Moss

1 Definition

Awareness of Others is the degree to which a person is in touch with the feelings of others. This scale is fundamental to developing relationship aspects of Emotional Intelligence.

2 Description

Low Awareness of Others: If a person is less inclined to understand, empathise and intuit others feelings or to notice what people need and want, then they will be less able to adapt or respond appropriately to them. For example, Conflict Handling (scale 14) depends on being aware of others' feelings and reactions, and Interdependence (scale 15) involves recognising others needs and preferences. There are several possible reasons for a person being less aware of others; they may be inwardly focused and less interested in people, they may find it difficult to empathise, they may not be very observant of people, they may have lower Regard for Others (scale 2) and not value others feelings greatly, or they may believe that people are all the same or at least the same as them, so wrongly assume that they know how others are feeling. Underlying many of these reasons is an often unconscious attitude of; *I already know about people,* or *I don't need or want to know about others,* rather than being open to finding out.

High Awareness of Others: A person with a high Awareness of Others is likely to understand, notice, empathise and intuit what people feel, want and need which will help them to adapt and respond appropriately to others. This may help them develop Conflict Handling (scale 14) which depends on being aware of others' feelings and reactions, and Interdependence (scale 15), which involves recognising the needs and preferences of others. Underlying their Awareness of Others may be an attitude that *people are different*, and an appreciation of individual differences, which may be reflected by a higher score in Regard for Others (scale 2). If on the other hand their Regard for Others is low, their Awareness of Others may be negatively distorted. They may be hyper-vigilant of others because they assume people cannot be trusted. Equally, if their Regard for Others is high but their Self Regard (scale 1) is low, they may have an overly positive perception/Awareness of Others in relation to themselves.

244

3 Interpretation

Perceiving others: There are a number of different ways of becoming aware of the feelings of others.

A It may be a conscious cognitive process; *I notice that this person is tense and tapping their fingers on the table and I therefore think that this person is feeling irritable or angry.*

B It may be an unconscious cognitive or intuitive process; *I don't know why, but I sense this person is annoyed about something.*

C It may be the cognitive consequence of the feeling process of empathy: *I notice that I feel irritable, but that this is really somebody else's irritation, and so I am aware of what the other person is feeling.*

Developing Awareness of Others is likely to require developing Self Awareness too. Lane and Schwartz[4] found these two functions of the brain to be closely related anatomically and to be almost indistinguishable early in a child's development.

Empathy: A person's ability to empathise with others in order to feel what they are feeling is hardwired within the limbic system of the brain. The evolutionary purpose of this is to help people predict how others are likely to behave and if they are a potential threat. There is a growing body of research into what is sometimes termed 'the social brain', showing how emotionally connected people are. People have the capacity to pick up what others may be thinking and feeling from minute variations in their behaviour, such as their tone of voice and facial movements, much of which is only detected at an unconscious intuitive level. Psychologist Paul Ekman,[5] has catalogued over 10,000 different facial expressions revealing that from birth babies have an instinctive tendency to read their mother's face and to detect meaning in voices. It has also been established that empathy fires off the same neuronal patterns as the person being empathised with, such as wincing at someone else's pain. These so-called 'mirror neurons'[6] that reproduce emotions might also explain why emotions are contagious; such as laughing when others laugh and sharing emotions at a music concert. A similar set of neurons known as 'oscillator neurons' help people to coordinate themselves with others, such as when getting into rapport, connecting with others and being in physical harmony (for example, an orchestra or dance group).

People vary in the degree to which they naturally experience empathy. One group that illustrate being at the low end of the empathy spectrum are individuals with Alexithymia (from the Greek meaning 'lack of words for emotions'). Although they may not easily develop empathy they can learn techniques or cognitive rules for developing their Relationship Management skills, such as 'when other people laugh, then laugh along', or 'when someone looks at their watch it may be time to end the conversation'. But these learnt rules are often poor substitutes for reading how people are feeling. For the majority of people being more attentive to and aware of people's feelings is something that can be improved with practice. Some specific suggestions for this are given in Chapter 7.4.

Relationship Management: Awareness of Others sits on the Interpersonal Intelligence side of the EIP framework and has a strong link with Relationship Management. An individual who lacks understanding and an Awareness of Others' feelings will be less able to adapt or respond appropriately to them. For example, when making a presentation it is necessary to notice the energy of the audience; if the energy is low (such as people yawning, looking downward or slumping in their chairs) to take appropriate action by either taking a break or doing an activity.

The Relationship Management scales of the EIP are heavily dependent on developing Awareness of Others. Trust (scale 11), for example, requires accurately reading others to know whether to trust them, Conflict Handling (scale 14) depends on being aware of the feeling states and reactions of others, and Interdependence (scale 15) requires responsiveness to the feelings and needs of others.

Knowledge of Others: The link between Awareness of Others and Relationship Management is Reflective Learning (scale 16), as shown on the complete EIP framework (refer to Appendix 1, scale 16). Through reflecting on past experiences with other people (Awareness of Others) a person forms their Knowledge of Others which informs how they choose to behave with others in the future (Relationship Management). For example, a line manager may notice that one of his reports has become unusually quiet, they look more serious, they don't have so much eye contact with them and their communication towards them is more abrupt (Awareness of Others). From past experience they recognise this behaviour is often when the individual is feeling unhappy towards them as a line manager (Knowledge of Others). The line manager may decide to check out their assumptions and have an informal chat with them over lunch. They may then find out that the individual is actually feeling annoyed with them because they had asked them to do several tasks that were not within their job description.

Defensive behaviours: Low Awareness of Others can often be tracked back to low Regard for Others. If a person does not value others or see them as significant then they are unlikely to pay much attention to them and may choose to ignore them. Low Awareness of Others combined with low Regard for Others can result in a variety of defensive behaviours (described in Chapter 4.3). The Critic who is blaming of others will tend to have a negative perception of people, assuming others to be at fault. The Victim also makes negative assumptions about others, assuming that people unfairly judge and pick on them. The Helper assumes that others are incapable of helping themselves, and the Demander assumes that people do not like them unless they are receiving constant reassurance. The common thread in all of these defences is a negative assumption about other people, based on their own low Regard for Others. Making assumptions about others is a judgment and when people judge others this can reduce their capacity to accurately perceive and be aware of others.

Suspending judgment: A fundamental skill for improving Awareness of Others is to listen to others. Listening at a deeper level involves suspending judgment and keeping an open mind. Conversation is often predicated on the pattern; *you tell me your story, then I will tell you mine,* which is an exchange of information rather than paying close attention to the other person. Deeper listening involves using all of one's senses to detect the other person's feelings and the meaning behind their words. This also requires being Aware of Others in the moment, not being distracted by inner thoughts or planning what to say next. Sometimes people get hampered by their own stories of other people, such as; *I think you feel this about me.* These inner stories create an automatic block to being openly aware of others. The first step, therefore, to developing Awareness of Others is for the individual to develop their Self Awareness (scale 3) and to notice how their own feelings towards people may be interfering with their perception of others.

People are different: Appreciating that *people are different* is the fourth of the EI attitudes. This principle is clearly tied in with Awareness of Others; if a person's attitude is that *all people are the same* then there would be no need for them to think about other people because they would automatically assume that others feel the same way as they do in that same situation (a phenomenon known to psychologists as 'projection'). For Awareness of Others, as with all EIP scales, it is useful to explore what underlying attitudes may be influencing a person's feelings, thoughts and behaviours.

Scale 5: Emotional Resilience

'It is not whether you get knocked down; it is whether you get back up'
Vince Lombardi

1 Definition
This is defined as the degree to which a person is able to pick themselves up and bounce back when things go badly for them.

2 Description
Low Emotional Resilience: Inevitably in life people will experience disappointment and setbacks; a low score suggests they may find this particularly difficult to cope with, becoming despondent and stressed. This does not mean that they have more problems than most people but that they cope less well with life's challenges. They may tend to become overly anxious, catastrophise problems, assume problems are unsolvable, be unforgiving towards themselves (perhaps perfectionist), feel they have little control over events in their life (check this with their Personal Power score; scale 6) and tend to anticipate the worst (check this with their Pessimism score; scale 12). If prolonged, low Emotional Resilience may affect their physical health and vice versa; if they are living an unhealthy lifestyle they will tend to have fewer inner resources to cope with adversity and setbacks.

High Emotional Resilience: A high score suggests that the individual is particularly effective at applying their inner resources to cope with life's demands. They are more likely to learn from failure than let it get them down, anticipate success rather than failure (check this with their Balanced Outlook score; scale 12), remain calm in a crisis, think through problems rationally, look for and find solutions to challenges, be more forgiving towards themselves and keep problems in perspective rather than ruminate over things they have little control over. They may also take care of themselves physically through exercise and nutrition which will support their recovery, particularly in times of stress and adversity. Check that their high score is genuine and not a 'Be Strong' driver masking low Emotional Resilience. This may be indicated by lower Self Regard and Self Awareness (if they are distorting or ignoring feelings of vulnerability or weakness).

3 Interpretation
Core Attitudes: Emotional Resilience is clearly related to Self Regard. To hold on to self-worth and confidence in the face of disappointment or rejection, a person

needs to believe 'I am OK' (high Self Regard; scale 1) and to remain hopeful in a world filled with other people they need to believe 'You are OK' too (high Regard for Others; scale 2). The Self Management scales are ordered according to their correlation with Self Regard, therefore Emotional Resilience is at the top of the list. How easily a person picks themself up when things go wrong will be determined by how positive they feel about themselves. But if their Self Regard is low or highly conditional then they will take knocks hard and find it difficult to recover.

Stress: A closely related area to Emotional Resilience is stress. This is sometimes experienced as a rather confusing concept because the external and the internal sources of stress are not adequately distinguished. What is perceived as stressful by one person may be perceived as exciting or fun by another. One piece of research has shown librarians to suffer more stress than fire fighters.[7] Much depends on the demands placed upon a person and how well these are met by an individual's resources for coping, as to how much stress a person experiences. The greatest demands are likely to be those that the individual places upon themselves. For example, the conditions of worth, described under scale 1, (*I am only OK if....I please others, be strong,* etc.) put significant self-imposed demands upon the individual. If the individual feels they 'must' meet certain conditions in order to feel OK about themselves then this is inherently stressful. Combining conditions of worth can be particularly stressful such as to Be Perfect and Hurry Up; will compel a person to do everything just right and very quickly, which will inevitably put them under considerable pressure. This would be compounded by a Be Strong driver, meaning they ignore their feelings of stress, and further still by a Try Hard driver so they resist the need to rest, driving their body to exhaustion and ill-health.

One antidote to this happening is to develop Self Awareness (scale 3) in order to pay greater attention to the body's feedback and learn how to manage feelings of stress. Another important scale that supports Emotional Resilience is Connecting with Others (scale 9). Human beings are social animals and gain considerable benefit from sharing problems and receiving emotional support from others.

Scale 6: Personal Power

'Between stimulus and response there is a space, in that space is our power to choose our response'
Victor Frankl

1 Definition

Personal Power is defined as the degree to which a person believes that they are in charge of and take sole responsibility for their outcomes, rather than viewing themselves as the victim of circumstances and/or of other people.

2 Description

Low Personal Power: This suggests that the individual may currently not believe that they have much influence or control over their circumstances. There are a number of possible reasons for this. They may have low Self Regard (scale 1) and feel despondent about themself and their general self-worth which may be affecting the confidence they have in their skills, abilities and effectiveness to make things happen. Alternatively, they may have much higher Regard for Others (scale 2) than they do for themselves which may cause them to feel they have little control over their circumstance and that they are dependent on other people (scale 15). It could be that they have low Self Regard and low Regard for Others and feel generally helpless and nothing or nobody can make a difference. Alternatively, they may hold the belief that their life and future is determined by factors other than themselves, such as fate, God, luck, other people and chance. In all these cases beliefs tend to be self-fulfilling, so if they believe they can or they believe they can't then this will probably be true for them. The consequences of having low Personal Power tend to mean that they will externalise most events by blaming others for failures, not acknowledging their own successes, avoiding responsibility, using phrases like; *I couldn't help it,* and *they made me*, and generally feeling disempowered.

High Personal Power: This suggests that the individual has a strong sense of self determination and responsibility for what happens in their life and for creating their future. It is therefore important that they have a clear view of what they want (Goal Directedness, scale 7) so as to channel their energy in the appropriate direction. As Personal Power is often associated with having confidence in one's skills and abilities to create effective outcomes they may also have a high Self Regard (scale 1), although the two scales are different. If their Self Regard is low they may expect a lot from themselves but be overly self-critical and demanding at the same time (possibly holding a Be Perfect condition of self-worth – refer to scale 1). If their Regard for Others is low they should be cautious that their high Personal Power doesn't spill over into being Over Optimistic (scale 12) about what they can achieve, or Over Independent (scale 15) believing that they have to go it alone.

3 Interpretation

Locus of control: Personal Power is closely related to the concept of 'locus of control', meaning the individual has the largest effect on their own outcomes (internal locus of control); not anyone else and not the situation or the environment. As with the other aspects of EI, what is being tapped into here is an attitude; even when being constrained by others or blocked by circumstances, it is important for the individual to recognise what power they still have. There is a self-fulfilling prophecy to Personal Power which is highly correlated with effective performance and more generally to life outcomes. In a moving book by Victor Frankl, he describes how people retained some degree of Personal Power despite the conditions of being imprisoned in a Nazi concentration camp:

'We who lived in concentration camps can remember the men who walked through the huts comforting others, giving away their last piece of bread. They may have been few in number, but they offer sufficient proof that everything can be taken from a man but one thing: the last human freedoms – to choose one's attitude in any given set of circumstances, to choose one's own way... in the final analysis it became clear that the sort of person the prisoner became was the result of an inner decision, and not the result of camp influences alone.' - Man's Search for Meaning[8]

Frankl also describes how he felt the need to survive in order to tell the rest of the world of these atrocities, a strong demonstration of the next EIP scale: Goal Directedness.

Choice: The concept of choice will often arise when discussing the Personal Power scale on the EIP. The extent to which an individual believes they have choice and control over their behaviour will greatly influence their EI development as it is one of the EI attitudes; *Everyone is in control of and responsible for their actions*. People are fully entitled to disagree with this and any of the EI attitudes, but by adopting this attitude and assuming it to be true a person is more likely to feel in control of their life and become more self-responsible and emotionally intelligent in how they live their life. It may, of course, be the case that a person chooses not to be responsible for themselves, which is itself a choice.

Choice is not an all or nothing concept and may be practiced and developed at different levels. Consider the five levels of responsibility described previously in Chapter 8.4 and Table 8.11.

Level 1: *The lowest level of responsibility is to explain everything as being down to chance or fate and entirely absolving oneself from any choice or control.*

Level 2: *Is to attribute circumstances and behaviour to unchangeable factors such as one's upbringing and their genes, which may often be used as an excuse.*

Level 3: *A level up from this is to attribute outcomes to other people, such as when blaming others for one's behaviour or not accepting praise and recognition.*

Level 4: *Is when a person believes they can choose how they respond to events, such as coping well with adversity or standing up for oneself.*

Level 5: *The highest level of Personal Power, and therefore EI, is when a person believes they can choose and create the stimulus (their circumstances and their environment) as well as choosing how they respond to this. For example, being positive and friendly towards others (stimulus) is likely to be reciprocated with a positive and friendly response (which is also a stimulus).*

Self Regard and Personal Power: Personal Power relates closely to one of the key three strands of Self Regard; one's sense of self-competence and self-efficacy. However, it is entirely possible to score high on one of these scales and not the other, an individual may see themselves as very capable at influencing people or at playing ball games (high Personal Power) yet still feel awful about themselves as a human being (low Self Regard). Alternatively they may feel incompetent at a particular task (low Personal Power) without letting this undermine their Self Regard. Remember that true Self Regard is unconditional and therefore is not dependent upon having high scores on any of the other EIP scales.

'If you are not sure where you are going, you'll probably end up somewhere else'

Lewis Carroll, *Alice in Wonderland*

1 Definition

Goal Directedness is defined as the degree to which the individual relates their behaviour to long-term goals.

2 Description

Low Goal Directedness: There are a number of reasons for a person not being goal directed. They may be unaware of what they actually want and would benefit from developing their Self Awareness (scale 3). They may be easily distracted from their goals, tending to be impulsive or constantly seeking something new and exciting to do. Their attention may be directed towards the present or on the past rather than thinking or planning ahead. Also, they may focus more on meeting the needs of others at the cost of meeting their own needs. This is especially so if their Regard for Others (scale 2) is higher than their Self Regard (scale 1). The risk in all of these cases is that they do not create the future they want.

High Goal Directedness: This suggests that the individual knows what they want and are not easily distracted from staying focused on it. Knowing what a person wants is one key ingredient to general happiness; another is being able to make this happen (see scale 6; Personal Power). They may also want to check that their Goal Directedness is balanced by high Flexibility (scale 8) in order to avoid the risk of not knowing when to change their goals or to cut their losses. At the extreme this may appear as being 'driven' where a person feels compelled to achieve their goals at almost any cost (if their Regard for Others (scale 2) is low, the cost may be to those around them). Their high Goal Directedness will also be a useful attribute in helping them take action on their own personal development.

3 Interpretation

Self Regard: Goal Directedness is pretty strongly correlated with scale 1; in order to set goals and to align behaviour towards them, whatever the temptations or distractions, the individual needs to believe that they, and what they want matter. One of the tricky things about Goal Directedness is that while the scale measures a single variable there are two key factors which affect the level of a person's Goal

Directedness; knowing what they want and not being easily distracted from achieving these goals.

Knowing what they want: In order to remain focused on what they want, people need first to know what it is that they want. Most people will see this as a non-issue; of course people know what they want, almost by definition. But actually there are some people who are much less clear than others about what it is that they want from life. Sometimes this is because they don't really have an interest in anything, so it is hard for them to know what they want and what they should aim for. Goal Directedness is an important element in helping children develop. Giving children choices and allowing them to make decisions for themselves, rather than being Over Dependent (scale 15) on others is likely to lead to higher Goal Directedness as an adult.

Some people do not know what they want because they have been taught to ignore their own feelings for what they want, like and need (their Self Awareness, scale 3). This may be because of expectations placed upon them as children such as to please others (the message being: your feelings, wants and needs are not as important as other peoples). Or, they may have experienced that when they do make an effort to get their wants and needs met, they are unsuccessful, such as being told; *'I want' doesn't get,* or not being given much attention, or never being rewarded for making an effort as a child.

Not being distracted: Even if a person does know what they want, their Goal Directedness may still be limited if they allow themselves to be easily distracted. Those who allow themselves to be distracted by other people tend to hold the Submissive attitude (low Self Regard, high Regard for Others); their needs are less important than other people's, or perhaps other people are more powerful than them and therefore will elbow them aside. An example of this would be when someone drops whatever they are doing immediately when asked to do something by others.

People may also be distracted from achieving their life goals not by other people but by *themselves*. For instance, they may find time to watch hours of television but never get around to completing their qualifications or doing exercise. To counter this they need to become consciously aware of what they are doing, of the choices they are making and what are likely to be the long-term consequences of their choices. This may be done by checking in with themselves at regular intervals; *will this help me towards where I want to go? Will I be glad later that I have spent time and energy doing this now?* And to then adapt their behaviour according to the answers.

Impulse control: One particular kind of self-distraction which is quite difficult to deal with is impulse control, such as eating chocolate bars when aiming to lose weight or losing one's temper when trying to remain calm. It may seem to those who have poor impulse control that they have no choice in the matter, that they 'can't help it', but they can. Remember the EI attitude; *Everyone is in control of and responsible for their actions*. If a person is regularly subject to such impulsive 'emotional hijacks', then they need to reflect on the pattern or their feelings and behaviour and the long-term consequences this has for them (Reflective Learning, scale 16). They may also want to develop their Personal Power (scale 6) to choose more carefully how they manage their feelings and behaviour.

In an interesting experiment, Mischel[9] observed how well children as young as 4 years of age could resist the temptation of eating a marshmallow in order to secure a further marshmallow later on. The children were followed up into adulthood and there was a remarkably strong correlation between children who had more marshmallows and their success later in life (as measured by their SAT scores, earnings and happiness questionnaires). One conclusion from this was that learning to defer gratification to achieve longer term goals is a vital emotional skill to develop early in life. Much of learning, education and self-development requires some deferring of gratification and rewards hard work, long-term investment and early 'sacrifice'. This attitude and behaviour is inherently difficult for children to develop, who are naturally opportunistic and live in the present moment. However, attitudes can be acquired and with emotional maturity comes a greater capacity for foresight and aligning one's behaviour to longer term goals.

Goal driven: There is a balance to be struck between impulse control (building for the future) and living for the present. Some people have deferred gratification as a condition of their self-worth; *I am only OK if… I try hard*. These are often individuals who are high achievers but will be constantly striving for more, unable to enjoy the present and relax. Deferring gratification to this extent may mean they have an 'until'/'once' script such as; *I will enjoy myself 'once' I pass my school exams, I can't stop worrying 'until' I get a job, I can't be happy 'until' I am promoted, I can switch off 'once' the kids leave home, I can't relax 'until' I have saved enough money, I will take it easy 'once' I retire…* Their goals may not even be their own but the expectations that others (their parents, their family, their employers) have of them. Goal Directedness is not about being goal *driven* and should be balanced with the next scale of Flexibility.

'A ship in harbour is safe, but that is not what ships are made for'
John A. Shedd

1 Definition

Flexibility is the degree to which the individual feels free to adapt their thinking and their behaviour to changing situations. It is closely related to EI attitude No. 7; *Change is possible.*

2 Description

Low Flexibility: This suggests the individual may be unwilling to move outside of their comfort zones and try new ways of doing things. One reason for this could be they have a fear of failure and therefore avoid the risk of change, or they may assume that if they try something new they are bound to fail (scale 12; Pessimism), which may be driven by a low Self Regard (scale 1). This can lead to fairly rigid ways of behaving, unwillingness to experiment and a lack of adaptation to changing circumstances, which in turn may inhibit creative thinking and learning from new experience. Another possibility is that they do not believe they can change the way they are, and that they have deeply ingrained habits of behaviour they are unaware of (scale 3; Self Awareness). Also, if their Regard for Others (scale 2) is low they may be unwilling to adapt to what others want.

High Flexibility: This suggests that the individual is willing to move outside of their comfort zones and try new ways of doing things which may be driven by a high Self Regard (scale 1) and an optimistic attitude towards change (scale 12; Balanced Outlook). This is good news as it is likely to help them to think creatively, to experiment, learn from experience, adapt to others, respond to changing circumstances and to change their behavioural habits. It may be worth checking that their Goal Directedness (scale 7) is also high, otherwise they may lack direction and not see things through. Also, some people are 'rigidly flexible', in that they find it difficult to stick with one course of action. Remember, Flexibility is about the *capacity* to change not the frequency of change.

3 Interpretation

Flexibility and Goal Directedness: This scale follows on from and provides necessary balance to Goal Directedness. As with all linear scales, a person cannot have too much Flexibility, rather they may have insufficient Goal Directedness. An individual who has a high capacity to flex but lacks Goal Directedness is likely to change direction constantly and not see things through. Equally, a person who is highly Goal Directed but lacks Flexibility is unlikely to shift their approach or position regardless of how futile the direction chosen may prove to be.

Rigid Flexibility: Some people are surprised that Flexibility is a linear, 'more is better' scale, rather than a multi, 'you can have too much of a good thing' scale. The crucial point in this respect is the definition. Flexibility refers not to the degree to which a person adapts, but to the degree to which they feel free to adapt; so that they can easily adapt when necessary and appropriate but also can stick to their guns when that is what is needed. Having the capacity to flex is not the same as doing it. Some people, for example, are rigidly flexible in that they insist on always doing things differently and avoid any repetition or routine. In effect this is actually being inflexible, as true Flexibility involves adapting appropriately to the circumstances, rather than insisting on change when change is not required. In order to adapt appropriately, people need to be aware of themselves and of others. If, for example, an individual begins to realise through their increased Self Awareness (scale 3) that they constantly change the way they behave because they get easily bored or they don't want people to get to know the real them, then they will begin to understand that their behaviour is likely to be maladaptive and ineffective. This may be because it is determined by their own internal fears, rather than by their inner principles (Authenticity; scale 10) or the external needs of the situation.

Rigidity: The opposite of Flexibility is rigidity. People who are rigid, who stick to the same patterns of behaviour, thinking or feeling, usually do this out of fear. They tend to stick with what they know, because they fear the unknown. Adapting behaviour appropriately often requires moving outside of one's comfort zones. If a person has low Self Regard they may resist trying out new behaviours as this may expose them to failure and humiliation (as shown by Fig. 1.2). Someone with higher Self Regard, on the other hand, will tend to build fewer boundaries around their behaviour because they have a more stable inner core. This allows them to experience failure as useful learning and as conditional feedback (about their behaviour rather than about their whole being) rather than causing them to feel terrible about themselves. Consequently they will be far more willing to experiment, learn through trial and error and try new things out, so helping them to learn and develop more quickly (as shown by Fig. 1.3).

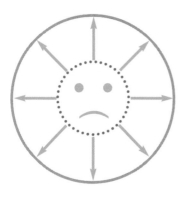
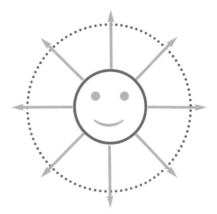

Fig. 1.2 Rigid boundaries

Low Self Regard

Fig. 1.3 Flexible boundaries

High Self Regard

Core Attitudes: It is not just Self Regard that has an influence on a person's Flexibility; so too does their Regard for Others (scale 2). Having low Regard for Others is likely to reduce a person's willingness to flex and adapt themselves to the needs of others. If they assume that they are right and that others are wrong then they may be less aware of the needs of others and less reasonable and flexible in compromising or cooperating with the wants of others.

Habits: One way to develop Flexibility is through changing habits of behaviour (as explained in Chapter 7.6). Habits are unconscious and automatic responses people apply to a given situation, implying therefore a degree of inflexibility and lack of conscious choice. A barrier to people changing their habits is if they do not believe they can change (EI attitude No. 7; *Change is possible*) and so they see no point in attempting to do so.

Scale 9: Connecting with Others

'Honesty and transparency make you vulnerable. Be honest and transparent anyway'
Mother Teresa of Calcutta

1 Definition

This scale measures the extent to, and the ease with which, an individual makes significant connections with other people.

2 Description

Low Connecting with Others: One reason for scoring low may be that the individual needs to develop some basic interpersonal skills, such as making small talk, listening to people, asking open questions or remembering people's names. More underlying reasons could stem from a low Self Regard (scale 1) such as they are shy and retiring, they lack confidence with people and they avoid initiating contact due to a fear of being ignored or rejected. Building connections with people requires investing time and energy into relationships, listening without judgment, being prepared to express feelings and vulnerabilities and having Regard for Others (scale 2). If a person is guarded and does not give much away in how they present themselves, others may find them to be detached or superficial which could prevent them from forming close connections and trusting relationships with people (scale 11; Trust).

High Connecting with Others: A high score suggests that they invest time and energy into maintaining and developing their relationships, they are open in sharing their thoughts, values and ideas, and are prepared to express their feelings and vulnerabilities. It is this willingness to take down their guard, to be spontaneous, to listen and show others appreciation that will help them build close and trusting relationships (see scale 11). This may have several benefits such as building networks with people at work, giving and receiving help in times of trouble (supporting their Emotional Resilience; scale 5) and generally enhancing the quality and depth of their relationships.

3 Interpretation

Openness and connectedness: This scale measures two things, personal openness (the depth of relationships) and personal connectedness (the breadth of relationships), rather than one. Each is the inevitable consequence of the other.

People connect with others not just by spending time together, but above all by sharing their feelings and their vulnerabilities. This scale is similar to Emotional Expression (scale 13) but also includes sharing thoughts and demonstrating connection through behaviour.

Self Awareness and openness: Being open with others about feelings is closely dependent on Self Awareness (scale 3). If a person is not self-aware they may not have much to be open about, or their openness may lack depth and feeling. Once a person becomes aware they can choose whether to share their thoughts and feelings or withhold them. One reason people avoid being open is because they fear that what they say may upset someone or cause conflict. This is often because people's first level of awareness and openness is to blame or finger point; *what I honestly think is…you are an idiot.* Explaining why they think this; *because you ignore me,* and how they feel; *which upsets me,* is a deeper and more constructive level of openness and awareness. They could be more open still by explaining their own 'inner story'; *I think you don't like me,* which may reflect their underlying attitude; *people don't like me* and the feeling they have towards themselves *I fear I am not likeable.* This example represents different levels of Self Awareness and openness, moving from a knee jerk response of criticising others to explaining their behaviour, then their thinking, then their attitude and finally their feelings towards themselves. Openness with others begins by being open with oneself which involves peeling off layers of awareness to reveal deeper levels of self-insight.

Levels of appreciation: Just as there are levels of Self Awareness and openness, there are also levels of Awareness of Others (scale 4) and the expression of this through deeper levels of appreciation. This is explained in Chapter 8.4 and Table 8.12 as the difference between expressing praise for what a person does and expressing value, which is about them as a person. Showing appreciation is one of the most powerful ways of building a strong, close and trusting connection with others.

Scale links: Connecting with Others is a critical resource for developing EI in other areas such as Self Regard, Regard for Others, Awareness of Others, Emotional Resilience, Trust, Emotional Expression, Conflict Handling and Interdependence. The act of communicating with others, and listening acceptingly and non-judgmentally, creates the opportunity to understand others, to be known by others and for relationships to improve.

260

As with all EIP scales, Connecting with Others depends on the attitudes of Self Regard and Regard for Others. The 'Ideal' position on the Attitude Matrix (I+U+) is required for making good connections with others. People respond to being valued and respected, so Regard for Others (U+) is obviously required. But also, there is a risk involved in opening up to others and in order to take that risk a person needs to be sure of their own value no matter what, so Self Regard (I+) is required too.

Risk being open: Building relationships can take time and involves the risk of being ignored and rejected, but the risk of not doing so or waiting for others to be open first is far greater in the long run. An important element to openness is being spontaneous, natural and uninhibited. Close relationships form when people let down their guard and have fun together ('child to child' in Transactional Analysis (TA) terms).

Some people find it difficult to develop their connection with others because they lack some basic interpersonal skills, such as how to introduce themselves, when to listen and talk, and how to show an interest in what a person is saying. Helping people learn these basic skills can make a profound difference to their relationships and hence their well-being.

A person's capacity for making connections with others impacts on the quality of their work performance; it enables them to network effectively, to build alliances and to give and receive help. It also affects their whole life experience, since it will largely determine the quality of their relationships. Also, as can be seen in the next scale; Authenticity, being known (by being open) is a prerequisite for being trusted, which in turn is an essential element of effective leadership and team membership.

Scale 10: Authenticity

'That you may retain your self-respect, it is better to displease the people by doing what you know is right, than to temporarily please them by doing what you know is wrong'
William J.H. Boetcker

1 Definition

Scale 10, Authenticity, is defined as the degree to which an individual invites the trust of others by being principled, reliable, consistent and known.

2 Description

Low Authenticity: One reason others may not risk trusting a person is if they are difficult to get to know, difficult to read and a 'closed book', in which case they may want to develop the previous scale of Connecting with Others. Another reason people may not trust others is if, in the past, they have found them to be unreliable, unpredictable and not keep their promises (low on Authenticity). One explanation for this would be if they are trying to please others by agreeing to do things that they are unable to deliver on, which may be because their Regard for Others (scale 2) is higher than their Self Regard (scale 1). A more negative interpretation would be that they lack inner guiding principles and integrity which may manifest as inconsistent behaviour, such as betraying confidences, manipulating people and saying things they do not believe.

High Authenticity: A high score suggests that the individual 'walks their talk' (they do what they say they will do and do not do what they say they will not), keeps their promises, behaves the same when on their own as when observed by others and that they are predictable in that they can be relied upon. They are likely to have largely resolved their inner conflicts and have integrity so that their behaviour is congruent with their beliefs and values. People will therefore tend to see them as authentic which will help them to collaborate and build trusting relationships. Note that this scale reflects whether the individual is trusted by others and as such it is useful to get other people's feedback to validate their own self-perception.

3 Interpretation

Being trustworthy and knowable: Authenticity involves two steps, firstly being authentic and secondly being known to be so, which requires Connecting with Others (scale 9). If a person does not connect with others then they will not be known to be trustworthy and so will not be trusted. Therefore a person may not be trusted for two reasons: either because they are not known by others, or because they are known to be untrustworthy through experience.

Core Attitudes: To be truly trustworthy and authentic requires both high Self Regard and high Regard for Others (I+U+). People who do not value others are less inclined to keep their promises to others and so will let others down. People with low Self Regard will tend to make promises they cannot keep, therefore being seen as untrustworthy and not authentic.

Authentic people tend to keep their promises, they have integrity and can be relied upon to behave consistently whether on their own or with others. The TA (Transactional Analysis) corollary of being emotionally intelligent is being an Integrated Adult (the 'Integrated' bit meaning integration between Parent, Adult and Child 'ego states').

Inconsistency: People who score high on all three parts of any multi-scale (a less common but possible result) may be indicative of low Authenticity. One reason for this profile is that the person wants to be liked, so they are constantly changing their behaviour to the environment rather than checking if it is consistent with their inner principles. Another possible explanation is if they are manipulative or inconsistent, such as being friendly one moment and aggressive the next. Inconsistency and unpredictability tends to make other people feel very uncomfortable; in a work setting people would rather work with a consistently firm or demanding boss than with one who is inconsistent and difficult to read. There is a clear neurological explanation for this; the limbic (emotional) brain is there to keep a person safe by anticipating what will happen next. If someone is difficult to read, the limbic brain panics and prepares for a possible threat.

A person can learn to detect whether their behaviour fits their inner principles by listening to their intuition. A part of the brain called the basal ganglia acts as an 'ethical rudder' providing intuitive feedback as to whether an action feels right and is in line with their guiding principles.

Scale 11: Trust

'You may be deceived if you trust too much, but you will live in torment if you don't trust enough'

Frank H. Crane

1 Definition

Scale 11, Trust, is the tendency for a person to trust others. It measures the balance between being Mistrustful (too little trust), Carefully Trusting (the right amount of trust) and Over Trusting (too much trust). This is the first multi-scale on the EIP questionnaire. As with all multi-scales, a person can have too much Trust as well as too little of it.

2 Description

Mistrusting: Mistrusting is often the result of an avoidance of being Over Trusting rather than from choosing to be Mistrusting. For example, a police officer may be more inclined to be Mistrusting than risk being Over Trusting. There is also a self-fulfilling bias in all aspects of Trust; if a person expects the best from others or expects to be let down by people then they will tend to notice and look for evidence that supports their (usually unconscious) expectation.

Mistrust can also stem from not being able to anticipate how people are going to behave in terms of whether they are consistent and knowable (see scale 10; Authenticity). What an individual does not know about another person they tend to create their own stories for, which can lead to exaggeration, unfounded fear and mistrust.

Carefully Trusting: The ideal Trust profile is to score high on Carefully Trusting and low on both Mistrusting and Over Trusting. A person with this profile would be inclined towards trusting others, but at the same time would be wary of evidence and intuition that they should or should not trust a particular person about a particular matter.

Over Trusting: This profile indicates a tendency to be too trusting of people and an avoidance of being Mistrusting. It is often seen in counsellors and coaches who are keen to develop trust and rapport with people so may ignore indications of untrustworthiness. Consequently they may 'tread on eggshells', agree unconditionally with clients views and fear to challenge their clients for risk of being seen as Mistrusting.

People sometimes assume that more Trust is always better and many other measures of EI treat this scale (and most other multi-scales) as linear. Holding a more trusting view towards others in most circumstances is likely to be reciprocated but it is important to balance this with the consequences. For example, a person may be far more willing to risk trusting someone to look after their shopping bag than to look after their children, or more willing to lend them £5 than lend them their credit card.

Over Trusting to Mistrusting: It is possible for a person to score high on both Over Trusting and Mistrusting but low on Carefully Trusting. This combination appears contradictory, being both over and under trusting, but is explainable. A person who is Over Trusting is likely to be let down by others and then may swing to the other extreme of not trusting people, before gradually returning to their home position of Over Trusting people and so their pattern of behaviour continues.

Another explanation for the apparent contradiction of scoring high on both Mistrusting and Over Trusting is that a person's level of trust is situationally determined. Some people can be Mistrusting of others in personal and relationship matters (perhaps because they have in the past been hurt by someone they loved), while at the same time tending to be Over Trusting in another part of their life such as in business and financial matters.

3 Interpretation

Patterns of trust: If a person has a pattern of experiences that are often repeated, such as being let down by people, then it may indicate an underlying attitude held by the individual such as, *people always let me down*. They may reaffirm this attitude through their own behaviour, by giving others too much responsibility, idealising someone or expecting too much from people (Over Trusting). Sooner or later the other person will not live up to their unrealistic expectations, so confirming their belief; that *people will always let them down*. Ironically, their mistrust of others is predicated by their Over Trusting behaviour. By recognising this and being more Carefully Trusting the individual will reduce both their Mistrusting and Over Trusting scale scores.

Core Attitudes: Trust is clearly linked with the Attitude Matrix. Coming from the Critical position (I+ U-; high Self Regard and low Regard for Others) an individual is more likely to be Mistrusting. From the Submissive position (I- U+; low Self Regard and high Regard for Others) they are likely to be Over Trusting. From the

Ideal position (I+ U+; high Self Regard and high Regard for Others) they are likely to be Carefully Trusting, and from the Blocked Potential position (I- U-; low Self Regard and low Regard for Others) to rebound between Over Trusting and Mistrusting.

Using intuition: One way to develop better judgment on how much to Trust others is to improve both Self Awareness and Awareness of Others. Awareness of Others allows a person to read people more accurately and to know when and to what degree they may be trusted and depended upon. For instance, it is important for line managers to get the right balance of Trust, as Over Trusting their reports may lead them to fail and become disheartened, and Mistrusting may disengage them. Self Awareness reinforces Awareness of Others by giving a person greater access to their intuition which provides deeper insight on how they feel about others. This intuitive feeling of Trust is hardwired into deeper parts of the brain because of the evolutionary necessity to instantly ascertain whether someone is safe or a threat, friend or foe, and trustworthy or not. This is partly why Trust is so important to human relationships, if broken, it activates the primitive survival threat response; to move against others (fight), move away from others (flight) or no movement/disengage (freeze).

Trust is also related to the next scale, Balanced Outlook. People who are Over Optimistic and assume the best in others tend also to be Over Trusting, but when they are let down they may rebound to feeling disappointed (Pessimistic) and Mistrusting.

Scale 12: Balanced Outlook

'A pessimist sees the difficulty in every opportunity; an optimist sees the opportunity in every difficulty'

Sir Winston Churchill

1 Definition

Balanced Outlook is defined as how well the individual manages to balance optimism with realism. It is concerned with a person's general outlook on the world and where they stand in terms of being Pessimistic, Realistic and Over Optimistic. All the multi-scales are also Relationship Management scales; although it could be argued that Balanced Outlook is more to do with Self Management than Relationship Management. This scale has therefore been included in the Self Management calculation for the Behaviour Matrix reports described in Chapter 4.5.

2 Description

Pessimistic: Balanced Outlook tends to be a self-fulfilling attitude; if a person expects the worst then this is more likely to happen as the individual will not be alert to potential opportunities. Those who are Pessimistic anticipate failure and are unconsciously drawn to making this happen, which will undermine their level of commitment, motivation, morale and enthusiasm towards tasks and life in general. For suggestions on how to create positive and realistic outcomes refer to Chapter 7.7.

Realistically Optimistic: The middle position is titled Realistically Optimistic; it is important to have a generally hopeful outlook and expectation, but not to ignore reality in the face of clear evidence. Even if a person thinks everything is going to go well, they still need an alternative plan in case it doesn't. As Oliver Cromwell said before a battle; *Trust in God and keep your powder dry.*

Over Optimistic: Unlike other EI measures that claim that more Optimism is always better, Balanced Outlook is a multi-scale where the ideal is to be Realistically Optimistic; neither Pessimistic nor Over Optimistic. Being Over Optimistic (seeing the world through rose tinted spectacles) suggests that the individual is too ready to believe what they want to believe, without checking whether this is justified, which may prevent them from dealing effectively with the world as it actually is. The risk being that they ignore potential problems, repeat the same mistakes, make too many unrealistic assumptions and have poor judgement and decision making. Those who are Over Optimistic may also lack Flexibility (scale 8) by not learning from their mistakes and being unwilling to accept or adapt to changing reality.

Over Optimistic to Pessimistic: One explanation for being both Over Optimistic and Pessimistic, is that the individual may rebound from expecting everything to turn out well (Over Optimistic) to feeling disappointed and pessimistic when things don't work out as they had hoped. The trick is to be Realistically Optimistic and to find the right balance of checking their hopes against reality but remaining positive at the same time.

3 Interpretation

Core Attitudes: Balanced Outlook has an interesting link with the Attitude Matrix (Self Regard and Regard for Others). People who hold a Critical attitude; 'I am OK' (I+) 'You are Not OK' (U-) may be Over Optimistic about themselves and Pessimistic towards others and consequently may ignore cautionary advice from others. Correspondingly, someone who holds a Submissive attitude; 'I am Not OK' (I-) 'You are OK' (U+) may be more Pessimistic about themselves and Over Optimistic towards others, so seek reassurance from others. In other words it depends on who is responsible for the outcomes as to their level of optimism or pessimism. Someone who is in the Blocked Potential position; 'I am Not OK' (I-) 'You are Not OK' (U-) is likely to be pessimistic about both themselves and others. People can also swing from being Over Optimistic to Pessimistic, as their unrealistic assumption that things are going to work out well (Over Optimistic) is often followed by surprise and disappointment when it doesn't (Pessimistic).

Attributional style: How a person attributes success and failure is indicative of their Outlook. A useful summary of this being the three P's of attribution; Personal, Permanent and Pervasive. The pessimist will tend to attribute failure internally (Personal), generalise the problem (Pervasive) and assume it will remain the same (Permanent) and do the reverse for success; *I got lucky* (not Personal*); it was a one-off* (not Pervasive); *and it won't last* (not Permanent). For the Over Optimistic person the opposite applies; their perception of failure is; *it is someone else's fault* (not Personal*); it's not that important anyway* (not Pervasive); and *tomorrow is another day* (not Permanent). And for success; *I alone made this happen* (Personal); *I am better than others* (Pervasive); and *everything will always be fine* (Permanent). The skill is to be optimistic but at the same time not to ignore reality, which, as with all EI scales, requires accurate Self Awareness (scale 3).

Emotional Expression and Control

'No man is free who is not master of himself'
Epictetus

1 Definition

Emotional Expression and Control is the degree to which an individual is emotionally controlled, that is, they achieve appropriate balance in the expression and control of their emotions.

2 Description

Emotional Under Control: Those who are emotionally under-controlled may need to learn how to express their feelings; in the words of Aristotle's Nicomachean Ethics,[10] *Anyone can become angry—that is easy, but to be angry with the right person, to the right degree, at the right time, for the right purpose, and in the right way—this is not easy.* Underpinning this is EI attitude No. 5; that *feelings and behaviour are separate.* A young child may automatically and without hindrance express all of their emotions, such as having a tantrum, sulking, laughter and unbridled excitement, but part of emotional maturity is learning how to manage the expression of feelings. Another EI attitude that is particularly relevant to this scale is EI attitude No. 3; *no one else can control our feelings.* Others may greatly influence how a person feels but this does not mean they have *control* over their emotions. For those people who do allow others to dictate how they feel, they are likely to be vulnerable, easily manipulated, dependent on others (scale 15), have low Personal Power (scale 6) and find it more difficult to manage their own behaviour and relationships. For suggestions on how to manage emotions refer to Chapter 7.4.

Free and in Charge: 'Free and in charge' means that the individual feels free to express their emotions but is also in charge of when and how they do this. Their low score on Emotional Under Control indicates that they can separate their behaviour from their feelings so as to be emotionally mature and even-tempered. Their low score on Emotional Over Control indicates they tend not to suppress their feelings, so they are able to show people warmth and be emotionally responsive when appropriate to do so. Having this balance on Emotional Expression and Control will help bring maturity to their behaviour and closeness in their relationships.

Emotional Over Control: Most people have certain emotions which they are less comfortable in expressing than other feelings. For example, boys who are brought up with a Be Strong driver may inhibit any expression of perceived weakness like crying, fear or love, and girls with a Please Others driver may hide their feelings of anger, frustration and dislike. There may be certain feelings that are less socially acceptable within a culture or less demonstrated within a family which become the individual's normal way of showing or hiding emotions. The problem occurs when the individual does not find constructive ways to release their emotions so they are expressed inappropriately, such as through passive-aggressive behaviour, stress and ill-health. Being emotionally over controlled can also impair a person's relationships as they may be less able to connect with others (scale 9) and be less known and trusted by others (Authenticity; scale 10).

The emotional rebound: This scale provides a classic example of how people can swing from one extreme to the other on a multi-scale (the 'tuning fork' profile). People who tend to bottle up their feelings (Emotional Over Control) are sooner or later likely to explode emotionally (Emotional Under Control); rather like keeping the lid on top of a kettle that eventually goes bang! Many people who have this characteristic recognise that they are under-controlled, especially as the results can be greatly damaging to their relationships, but they are less aware that the cause comes from over-controlling their emotions. Instead of trying harder to keep their emotions under wraps, which will only delay the explosion and make it worse later, they should learn to notice their feelings sooner and let them out before they become overwhelming. As with all aspects of EI, the key to managing this process is to develop Self Awareness (scale 3) and to recognise their feeling patterns so that they are able to detect the early signs of emotions within their body.

3 Interpretation

Core Attitudes: Emotional Expression and Control, as with all EIP scales, is underpinned by the Core Attitudes of Self Regard and Regard for Others. An individual who comes from the Submissive position (I–U+) may believe that their thoughts and feelings are less important than other people's or that other people will not want to hear what they have to say. They may therefore hold themselves back and be emotionally over-controlled. On the other hand, someone coming from the Critical position (I+U-) will be less concerned with other people's feelings and believe that how they feel and what they think is more important and so be under-controlled in how they express their emotions. Sometimes being emotionally under-controlled may appear to come from the Submissive position but is actually coming from a Blocked Potential position (I-U-). When people are highly sensitive, become easily upset and catastrophise about their problems (low Self Regard; I-) they are often highly self-absorbed rather than attentive to the needs of others (*my problems matter more than yours*) and they do not take responsibility for their problems, tending instead to blame others and their circumstances (low Regard for Others; U-).

Cultural differences: A further point to remember about this scale is that people's behavioural response may not accurately reflect their underlying emotional experience, that is, behavioural expression should be considered in context of the person's background. The Italian culture is renowned for being emotionally expressive, children may display pain differently from adults, men may be less inclined to cry and people differ in how they display certain emotions.

Emotional labour: A popular area of emotional research in the workplace focuses on emotional labour, which is when an employee must alter their emotional expression in order to meet the display rules of an organisation.[11] When the required behaviour is congruent with their emotions this is known as surface acting. When the required behaviour is incongruent with their emotions this is known as deep acting (such as being polite to a customer when feeling annoyed with them). Having emotional control is a useful short term solution but in the long-term may lead to burnout.[12] The emotionally intelligent individual will be Authentic (scale 10) so that their attitudes are congruent with the emotions and behavior they express.

Scale 14: Conflict Handling

'Hear one side and you will be in the dark. Hear both and all will be clear'
Thomas C. Haliburton

1 Definition

This scale measures how well conflict is handled; how assertive a person is. Conflict is an inevitable part of life since *people are different* and want different things (EI attitude No. 4). Handling conflict is therefore essential to maintaining relationships, dealing with confrontation, collaborating effectively, working creatively and being productive. Where the problem arises with conflict is how the person deals with it, or fails to deal with it effectively; it is not the existence of conflict that is problematic in itself.

2 Description

Passive: A high score on Passive suggests that the individual may avoid conflict, be overly accommodating and less inclined to assert themselves or to stand up for what they want. If their Self Regard (scale 1) is lower than their Regard for Others (scale 2) they may tend to put their own needs second, not express their needs, put up with things that are not right for them and agree to things that they do not want. It is also worth considering whether they suppress their feelings too much (Emotional Over Control; scale 13) and whether they know what they want (Goal Directedness; scale 7) as it is impossible to assert oneself if they don't know what they want.

Assertive: 'Assertive' suggests that the individual stands up for what they want without undermining others, balances the needs of others with their own, focuses on the task without ignoring people and creates mutually beneficial outcomes from confrontation. Their lower scores on Passive and Aggressive also indicate that they are not likely to back down or avoid conflict but at the same time they do not tend to become aggressive or hostile towards people.

Aggressive: A high score on Aggressive suggests that the individual may be overly assertive, competitive to the expense of others, hostile, demanding and perhaps dismiss the needs of others. One explanation for this is that their Regard for Others (scale 2) is lower than their Self Regard (scale 1), in which case they may be seen as a bully. Aggressive behaviour often masks a fear of not feeling in control, of losing out, or of feeling threatened. If they also have a tendency to feel angry, frustrated and to be impatient this may adversely affect their physical health.

Passive and Aggressive: One reason for being high on both scales could be a tendency to rebound from being Passive (bottling up frustration) to Aggressive (being unable to contain feelings of anger). Learning to be more Assertive than Passive will help prevent feelings of anger from building up. Another explanation for this score is if the individual is passively aggressive as described below.

3 Interpretation

Core Attitudes: The correlation between Conflict Handling and the Core Attitudes are very clear. Passivity is the expression of the I-U+ attitude: (low Self Regard, high Regard for Others); *You are more significant and powerful than me so I will not challenge you.* Aggressive is the expression of the I+U- attitude (high Self Regard, low Regard for Others); *I am more important than you so my wishes take priority over yours.* The emotionally intelligent position is in the middle; Assertive, I+U+ (high Self Regard and high Regard for Others); *Both of us matter as do our interests.* These Conflict Handling attitudes also map onto the Harvard model of negotiation. Assertive, (I+U+) is 'I Win You Win'; Passive, (I-U+), is 'I Lose You Win'; Aggressive, (I+U-), is 'I Win You Lose'; and Passive Aggressive, (I-U-), is 'I Lose You Lose'. This seems quite helpful in explaining why anyone would approach a conflict or negotiation situation with a 'Lose Win' or 'Lose Lose' orientation; because their Self Regard is low.

Passively Aggressive: People who fall into the Blocked position (low Self Regard and low Regard for Others; I- U-) are likely to be passively aggressive. Because they have low Self Regard, their resulting conflict behavior will be passive as they do not have enough self-belief or self-confidence to stand up for themselves. Because they do not value others any more than they value themselves (U- as well as I-) they resign themselves to their passivity which can be reflected, albeit subtly, in the ways they express their aggression towards others. For example, agreeing to do something but then not doing it, not completing tasks, being unwell at crucial times, criticising people behind their back and undermining agreed decisions after a meeting. What makes passively aggressive behaviour more difficult to identify is that it may not be expressed overtly and is normally done in a way that can be denied.

Assertiveness Skills: Assertiveness is a set of skilled behaviours that can be learnt, although assertiveness training often fails because it is not backed up by a corresponding change in the person's attitude. If an individual has a low Self Regard then they are likely to return sooner or later to their Passive behaviour. Another reason why assertiveness training does not always work is because it has not been sufficiently rehearsed and embedded at an experiential and emotional level. At the moment a person is required to be assertive, they are likely to be feeling a degree of anxiety as they are in a potential conflict situation. Anxiety makes it more difficult to think clearly and so the person will fall back on their automated response. Rehearsing and practicing a very specific automated response to a conflict situation is usually more effective therefore than teaching people multiple or complex strategies. For example, when someone asks, *can you do x for me?*, instead of instantly saying *yes* and dropping everything else they are doing, ideally they could recite a rehearsed phrase such as; *can you give me a moment to check my schedule*? This will give them time to compose themselves and think through what they want to do.

Aggressive Behaviour: It is worth mentioning a few issues about anger, as this emotional state leads to aggressive behaviour and can be highly destructive to a person's health and their relationships. Anger is an addictive emotion as it can get people's immediate needs met such as 'winning' an argument, putting someone down or taking control. However, any benefits are usually heavily outweighed by the negative consequences of excessive anger. Anger is driven by more primitive emotional centres of the brain that inhibit the brain's higher functions which block a person's ability to think rationally (described in Chapter 2.3 as an 'emotional hijack'). Also, the negative physiological effects of anger are numerous; it is the only emotion that reduces the pumping efficiency of the heart, it increases Cortisol production depleting the immune system, and the higher arousal it creates puts great strain on the body. Chronic anger causes hypertension, increased cholesterol, damaged arteries, increased illness, leads to heart disease and slows recovery. Despite being as common as anxiety, anger is given far less prominence and is culturally less recognised. Anger that turns into uncontrolled rage is a clear example of poor Emotional Intelligence, as it is associated with low Self Awareness (scale 3), low Emotional Resilience (scale 5), Emotional Under Control (scale 13) and poor Conflict Handling (scale 14). Developing each of these scales, starting with Self Awareness is at the root of reducing chronic anger and aggressive behaviour.

It should be noted, as with all emotions, anger is an adaptive survival response and serves an important purpose. Anger helps raise adrenalin to prepare to fight. It also creates the energy and desire to rectify an injustice and challenge unfairness, which is what drives much political reform and changes in society.

Scale 15: Interdependence

'Don't walk behind me, I may not lead. Don't walk in front of me, I may not follow. Just walk beside me and be my friend'
Albert Camus

1 Definition

Interdependence is the last of the Relationship Management scales and measures how well an individual manages to balance taking themselves and others into account.

2 Description

Over Dependent: Scoring high on Over Dependent suggests that the individual prefers to work with other people, to have others around them for support and to avoid independent activities. This may be because they are very extraverted and avoid working independently or that they have a low Self Regard (scale 1) so lack the confidence to act independently, and higher Regard for Others (scale 2) so assume that others know better than they do. The effect of this could be that they avoid making decisions independently, ask people for help before thinking of a solution for themselves, seek regular reassurance and guidance from others, avoid too much responsibility, and find it difficult to work on their own. They may typically score lower on Personal Power (scale 6) and be more Passive (scale 14).

Interdependent: The ideal profile pattern is to score relatively higher on the middle scale, Interdependence, than the other two extremes. This suggests that they are equally comfortable and flexible at including others or working independently when appropriate. By not being Over Dependent on others they are more likely to take the lead and responsibility when necessary, and be willing to make decisions for themselves. By not being Over Independent they are more likely to listen and communicate with people and be prepared to follow others when required. Having the capacity to work interdependently is necessary for effective team working, collaboration, building partnerships and effective relationships.

Over Independent: Over Independent suggests that the individual prefers to work on their own, to do things in their own way and have less collaboration or teamwork activity. This may be because they are a more introverted person preferring to work alone, that they have low Regard for Others (scale 2) and see less value in what other people can contribute, or that they are Mistrusting (scale 11) so choose not to rely on others. The potential effects of being Over Independent are that they do not form close collaborative partnerships (scale 9), are less aware of others (scale 4), do not benefit from other people's contributions, miss out on opportunities to learn from others and the benefits of team working, and people may feel excluded by them.

Dependent and Over Independent: The least desirable profile pattern is to be higher on both Dependent and Over Independent, but lower on Interdependence. This suggests that they may be quite changeable depending upon the context. When they feel less confident they may be very dependent on others and when they no longer need their support they may detach or drop them, leaving people feeling confused by their inconsistent behaviour towards them. In the long run this could jeopardise their relationships, as people may be cautious about offering them their support and feel rejected by them, which could make friendships, collaboration and teamwork difficult to sustain.

3 Interpretation

Core Attitudes: Interdependence requires both Self Regard (to work well independently) and Regard for Others (to work well with others). People who are Over Dependent may be coming from a Core Attitude of low Self Regard and high Regard for Others (I-U+). They may lack a degree of confidence to make their own decisions and to act independently. Over independence is effectively the reverse of the above. It tends to reflect a Core Attitude of (I+U-) high Self Regard and low Regard for Others.

Link to Transactional Analysis (TA): In terms of TA, someone who is Over Dependent may be coming from their Adaptive child, seeking constant reassurance and guidance, rather than using their Adult ego state to think for themselves. Interdependent relationships are where all three ego states (Parent, Adult and Child) interact effectively between people. Being Over Independent relates more to the Controlling Parent ego state and an unwillingness to meet others at an Adult to Adult level. For more information on this and TA refer to Stewart.[1]

Friend or foe? People naturally collaborate and group with people they know (who are familiar and similar) and move away from people they don't. This is because the brain automatically classifies people as friend or foe and will classify people they don't know as foe (a potential threat) until proven otherwise. Perceiving someone as a foe reduces empathy, raises the threat response and makes it more difficult to trust them. It is therefore important to interact openly with others so as to activate their 'friend' response. Interaction also releases oxytocin, a neurochemical that draws people closer and creates a sense of trust and safety in the other person.[13] A study by Gallup[14] showed companies that encourage collaboration through informal contact such as at the water dispenser had greater productivity. Interaction and openness can easily be encouraged by organisations through practices such as networking, mentoring, social events and informal meetings.

Personality type: Interdependence may be influenced to some degree by a person's personality type preference for introversion (leaning towards Over Independence) and extraversion (leaning towards Over Dependence). However personality preference is not the same as EI and by developing knowledge of one's personality type an individual can learn to manage their behaviour to be appropriate to the situation (Interdependence). This is a central part to the definition of EI; *the practice of managing one's personality to be both personally and interpersonally effective.* Interdependence serves as a useful example of the relationship between EI and personality type which exists for all of the EIP scales, as explained in Appendix 3.

Scale 16: Reflective Learning

'Hindsight is good, foresight is better, but insight is the best of all'
Unknown

1 Definition

Reflective Learning is the degree to which Emotional Intelligence is enhanced by the individual reflecting on what they and others feel, think and do. They may then notice the outcomes of their feelings, thoughts and behaviour, and alter their patterns accordingly. Unlike the other scales, Reflective Learning is not an aspect of Emotional Intelligence itself, but is a vital prerequisite for developing Emotional Intelligence.

2 Description

Low Reflective Learning: Being low on this scale suggests that the individual rarely reflects upon their experiences consciously and/or intuitively, and that they may not have any formal approach for raising their own self knowledge or for their personal development. The risk here is that they may tend to make the same mistakes or repeat patterns without learning from past experiences and adjusting their behaviour accordingly. Some reasons for this include: their attention is focused very much on the future or the present rather than reflecting on the past, they have little interest in personal development, or they have never learnt how to go about developing themselves or their relationships. This single scale is important because it provides a process for developing all other EIP scales.

High Reflective Learning: Having a high score on this scale suggests that they have a regular habit of reflecting upon their experiences consciously and/or intuitively, and that they put their learning into action to improve their personal and interpersonal effectiveness. This may mean that they know themselves well, what motivates them, how they can change their behaviour, what triggers specific feelings for them and how they can manage their emotional state. In order to make best use of this practice they should check that their Self Awareness (scale 3) is also high, as their awareness of experiences provides the feedback necessary for later reflection.

3 Interpretation

Reflective Learning: Reflective leaning is an important part of the EIP framework as it enables the Feeling level (Awareness) to convert to the Behaviour level (Management) as shown in the complete EIP framework opposite:

278

Table 1.3 The complete EIP framework

	Personal Intelligence		Interpersonal Intelligence	
Behaviour	Self Management	➤	Relationship Management	▲
Knowledge	Self Knowledge	▲ ➤	Knowledge of Others	▲
Thinking	Self Reflection	▲ ➤	Reflecting on Others	▲
Feeling	Self Awareness	▲ ➤	Awareness of Others	▲
Attitude	Self Regard	▲ ➤	Regard for Others	▲

Self Awareness Vs. Self Knowledge: Not only do people need awareness in the moment for its own sake, but they also need to adopt the practice of reflecting on their experience to convert their Self Awareness over time (a succession of moments) into Self Knowledge, and their Awareness of Others over time into knowledge of how other individuals and people in general work. It is only by being aware in the moment that a person has the feedback and information necessary to form their knowledge. The practice of Reflective Learning is part of a continuous process of learning and developing; an individual becomes aware of their next experience, reflects upon it and evaluates it in relation to their existing Self Knowledge. This then helps them to either reinforce or update their Self Knowledge. In essence, Reflective Learning is the 'How to' part of the EI definition; which involves *thinking about feeling to guide one's behaviour*. Another set of everyday descriptors used in the English language that relate to the EIP framework levels are shown below.

Table 1.4 Other descriptors of the EIP framework levels

Descriptor	Definition	Link to the EIP framework
Foresight	*Making use of previous experiential learning to antic-ipate and choose future behaviour and responses.*	Self and Relationship Management
Insight	*Understanding why they feel, think and behave as they do.*	Self Knowledge
Hindsight	*Reflecting upon and understanding past experiences.*	Reflective Learning
Midsight	*Being aware of experiences in the moment.*	Self Awareness
No-sight	*Being unaware of feelings, thoughts and behaviours.*	

Core Attitudes: As with all the EIP scales, Reflective Learning is greatly influenced by the Core Attitudes. For a person to observe and evaluate their experience dispassionately they need to come from an I+U+ position (high Self Regard, high Regard for Others). If they believe they are Not OK this negative self-judgment will limit the accuracy and the subtlety of their perception and will interfere with their learning of how they work (and to a lesser extent others). Similarly, if a person believes that others are Not OK then that will interfere with their learning of how other people work (and to a lesser extent oneself).

Conscious learning: People practice Reflective Learning in their own different ways. Some will do it consciously and formally, others will do it intuitively and *en passant*, some will do it regularly and others will do it at irregular intervals. If, however, an individual is seeking to develop a habit of Reflective Learning then there is a great deal to be said for doing it both formally and regularly. After all, advanced EI only comes about from a person first being aware of what they want to change (conscious incompetence) and then practicing what they want to do instead (conscious competence) until it becomes a refined and automatic habit (unconscious competence). The more a person practices Reflective Learning, the more likely they are to behave with emotional intelligence, and the more emotionally intelligent they are, the more likely they are to practice Reflective Learning.

Managing Personality: If EI is about managing one's personality, it is Reflective Learning that allows a person to learn when their personality works for them and when it doesn't through bringing unconscious patterns (attitudes and habits) into conscious awareness. Doing this reflects the middle part of the EI definition of *how* to be emotionally intelligent; *the habitual practice of thinking about feeling and feeling about thinking to guide one's behaviour.* This is the process by which the individual reflects upon their moments of experience (Self Awareness and Awareness of Others) to make choices about their behaviour that are more personally and interpersonally effective.

Appendix Two

An historical overview of Emotional Intelligence

Emotional Intelligence today may be seen as a blend of different psychological paradigms including the cognitive, humanistic and behavioural that combine the different elements of EI; thinking, feeling and behaviour. This appendix examines in brief some of the key historical theories, evidence and explanations for emotions and Emotional Intelligence.

1 Theories of emotion

The origins of the word *emotion* can be traced back to 1579, when it was adapted from the French word *émouvoir*, which means *to stir up*. The earliest theories of emotion date back to the Ancient Chinese and Greeks (approx. 200 BC - 300 AD), although the Stoics viewed emotions such as mood, fear and impulse to be self-centred and unreliable and that wise people admitted no emotion. Many philosophers have written about emotions. Hippocrates[1] popularised the study of emotions with his description of the four humours: sanguine (warm and outgoing), phlegmatic (laid back and unemotional), choleric (aggressive and impulsive) and melancholic (sad and despondent). Aristotle,[2] in his book *Rhetoric*, gives a thorough account of emotions and how they affect moral actions and choices, and differentiates between voluntary and involuntary responses to emotions. In his publication *The Passions of the Soul*, Rene Descartes (1637)[3] asserts that there are six passions from which all others are derived. He defines passions as *the perception, feeling or emotion which refer to the soul itself* and regards every emotion as being caused by a defined physical state (a view shared later by William James).[4] In the late 18th century the European Romantic Movement emphasised the importance of emotions, empathy and intuitive thought as providing insight unobtainable by logic, mostly through art, music and literature. This was partly a reaction to the Industrial Revolution and against the scientific rationalisation of nature. The 1960s saw the arrival of the humanistic movement, in part too as a rebellion against the forces of rationalism in the US and Europe. It may also be that EI was in part a reaction to the growth of capitalism in western society during the 1980s. Humanistic psychology has been defined as *the human need to feel good about oneself, experience one's emotions directly, and grow emotionally* (Herman, 1992).[5] The EIP and EI attitudes are grounded in work from humanistic psychology which includes influential psychologists such as Eric Berne, Abraham Maslow, Fritz Perls, Carl Rogers and Will Schutz.

The evolution of emotion: In 1872, Charles Darwin[6] published *The expression of the emotions in man and animals* to support his theory of evolution and natural selection. He argued that emotions evolved and were adapted over time providing a consistent emotional *language* across many species. A key piece of his evidence was observing the consistency across humans in their facial expression of emotions. This has been positively supported 100 years later by the work of Paul Ekman (1977)[7] who mapped the subjective and physiological emotional experiences of people to distinct facial expressions. Ekman has also found that certain emotions are universally recognised (even in cultures with no media influence). He proposed that there are six basic emotions: anger, disgust, fear, happiness, sadness and surprise.

Along similar lines, Robert Plutchick (1980)[8] defined eight basic emotions that were based on survival adaptations from as far back as the Cambrian era 600 million years ago. For example, sadness and grief are the response to a loss of something pleasurable, and surprise is the brief freezing response to a new stimulus (a possible threat). Plutchick placed the basic emotions into positive and negative pairings: joy versus sadness; anger versus fear; trust versus distrust; and surprise versus anticipation. From this he derived an *emotions wheel* where the basic emotions could be combined and modified through cultural conditioning, to form complex emotions. Anger and disgust combining to form contempt.

In contrast to Plutchick's theory, Nesse (1990)[9] and others have proposed that emotions were selected for in early Hominids when the human lineage diverged from the great ape, 5-8 million years ago, as an adaptation response to survival problems. For example, the emotions of desire and love were required to find a mate, and compassion in order to protect offspring.

Douglas Watt (2004)[10] offers a useful framework of evolution for understanding emotion and cognition. He argues that *emotion is an evolutionary extension of homeostasis, and likewise that cognition is an extension of emotion*. In other words evolution keeps what works and builds upon it, such that emotions are at the service of homeostasis and cognition is at the service of emotion. This suggests there is a pecking order of priority: homeostasis, emotion, cognition (which has parallels with Paul MacLean's[11] triune brain theory of evolution), reptilian (homeostasis), mammalian (emotion), and primate (cognition), as described in Chapter 2.1.

Evolutionary theories of emotion are largely consistent with the EIP basis for Emotional Intelligence, inferring that emotions stem from primitive parts of the brain based initially on a survival response and that complex emotions are more culturally defined than the basic emotions. Evolutionary theory tends to describe emotions as being relatively fixed and automated, while EI (and the EIP) emphasise how individuals can alter their emotional state and choose how they respond to their emotions, as explained by the later neuroscientific research on emotions.

2 The neuroscience of emotion

Research into the neural circuitry and anatomical foundations of emotion has lent considerable weight to explaining EI. This has often centred on the debate over whether emotions originate in the body and/or the brain.

One of the earliest of these theories was by William James who published *What is an emotion?* (1884)[4] and physiologist Carl Lange who independently developed a somatic feedback theory on emotion (1885)[12] which later became known as the James-Lange theory. They proposed that people perceive events and have bodily feelings (such as a change in heart rate, blood pressure, tight stomach and sweaty palms) which they then label as physical sensation/emotion. For instance, when witnessing an external stimuli such as a grizzly bear, the individual experiences trembling in the body, which they interpret as fear. In other words the person's emotional reaction depends on how they interpret their physical reaction. The James-Lange theory was directly challenged by Walter Cannon[13] and Philip Bard[14] in the 1920s. Cannon argued that physiological responses were too slow for the rapid and intense experience of emotions. He also demonstrated that physiological stimulation of the hypothalamus in the brain caused physiological changes in the body. From this, Cannon proposed, in his influential book *Wisdom of the body,* that the physiological and conscious cognitive experience of emotions must occur simultaneously. Bard's research on animals found that physiological information needed to pass through the thalamus in the brain before being available for any further processing. In an experiment by Bard, he kept cats alive and healthy after having their sympathetic nervous systems severed and found that the cats still displayed full emotional responses, such as rage in a response to a barking dog.

Whether emotions originate in the brain or the body continues to be debated today, although current research would suggest that they originate in both. Elmer Green (1977)[15] who pioneered biofeedback for treatment of disease states that *every change in the physiological state is accompanied by an appropriate change in the mental emotional state, conscious or unconscious, and conversely, every change in the mental emotional state, conscious or unconscious, is accompanied by an appropriate change in the physiological state.* In her book, *Molecules of emotion,* Candace Pert (1997)[16] gives a coherent biochemical rationale for emotions originating in both the brain and the body in the form of peptides/neuropeptides and their receptors. She explains how peptides and neuropeptides flow freely in the circulatory system, acting as *information messenger molecules* which will reach all organs and tissues of the body and brain, leading to complex physiological and neurological reactions eventually culminating in emotional responses that influence actions and decision making. She refutes the Newtonian and Cartesian models of the body being a mechanistic clock-like organism, and describes the body as *the unconscious mind... with an intelligence in the form of information (peptides) running all the system (body-mind) and creating behaviour.* Her view of the body and emotions being *intelligent* is also supported by the neurological perspective discussed next, which provides strong foundations for the concept of Emotional Intelligence.

One of the most significant pieces of neurological research in recent times that has supported the concept of Emotional Intelligence is the Somatic Marker Hypothesis by Antonio Damasio (1994).[17] In economic theory there is an assumption that decision making is devoid of emotion and is based purely on cost-benefit analysis. However, social environments are complex and unpredictable, requiring very rapid judgements based on large amounts of information, or what may be termed hunches, intuition and gut feeling. The Somatic Marker Hypothesis is that cognitive decision making is influenced and simplified by the individuals emotional/physiological state (somatic markers) that direct them towards making more advantageous decisions. Somatic markers may be conscious or unconscious and are reinforced by past outcomes. For example, a person may feel happy and motivated to pursue a behaviour or anxious and uncertain to avoid a course of action depending on their previous experiences in similar situations.

Damasio studied patients with lesions to the brain in a region called the ventromedial prefrontal cortex (VMPFC).* He observed that these patients would make decisions against their own interests and were unable to learn to make wiser decisions based on previous mistakes. To test his observation, Damasio adapted a decision making game called the Iowa Gambling Task,[18] where participants would select from one of four decks of cards and learn to anticipate high risk card decks from low risk decks. The high risk decks would give greater rewards but also higher penalties and overall gave lower profits than the other card decks. Participants with damage to their VMPFC continued to make disadvantageous decisions even when made aware of the consequences of their actions. A different region of the brain also involved in emotional

---

* Historical evidence has shown that frontal lobe damage is associated with impaired emotional expression, decision making and social functioning. A classic example is of Phineas Gage,[33] a dynamite worker who suffered an iron bar through his head, damaging his frontal lobes. He survived with normal intellect but it affected aspects of his personality, leading to him becoming irresponsible, untrustworthy and impatient.

decision making is the amygdala, the fight-flight survival mechanism. Patients with damage to the amygdala were found to pursue more harmful and risky behaviour, while those with VMPFC damage, despite making disadvantageous decisions, did not engage in activity that would be immediately harmful to themselves. These findings provide evidence that emotions (and where they are processed) play an important role to informing sound judgement and decision making.

Another important finding from Damasio's research was that normal participants showed greater physiological anxiety (as measured by galvanic skin conductance response) just prior to picking up their card, which was absent in the VMPFC patients. In other words their emotional response preceded their cognitive response, suggesting that thinking and decision making is largely influenced by feeling, one of the key propositions from the EIP model of Emotional Intelligence.

Several other neurological studies have confirmed the importance of emotions in informing thinking and decision making (Zeelenberg, 2008).[19] An intriguing piece of research by Tuan Pham (2012)[20] found that individuals who trust their feelings make more accurate predictions of future events than individuals who have lower trust in their feelings. This *Emotional Oracle Effect* was found across a variety of prediction domains, including the 2008 US Democratic presidential nomination, movie box-office success, the winner of *American Idol*, the stock market, college football, and even the weather!

In another example, V.S. Ramachandran (1998)[21] describes patients with Capgras syndrome who are unable to connect to their emotional memories. Such that, they would recognise a close friend but have no emotional memory of them so consider them to be an imposter. This illustrates the dependence on emotions for accurate perception and decision making.

Other research has supported the view that emotions precede conscious aware-ness. Benjamin Libet (1985)[22] showed that the emotional trigger to act (an *action potential*) takes place 0.3 seconds before a person becomes aware of the desire to act. Joseph LeDoux (1996)[23] found that information is fast-tracked to the amygdala (central to emotions) up to half a second before it reaches the neocortex, suggesting that emotional memories, impressions and evaluations are made prior to the indi-vidual being conscious of them.

The main point to emerge from this neuroscientific research is that emotions are a form of intelligence and wisdom in that they provide sophisticated and instant feedback on how to respond, behave and make decisions based on the wealth of accumulated emotional experience. This would be consistent with evolutionary theory; that emotions may have evolved to help people make better decisions.

Cognitive theories of emotion: An area of research that lends support for the brain-body integration of emotions, and in that respect for EI, are cognitive theories of emotional processing.

An interesting experiment by Stanley Schachter (1962)[24] demonstrated the importance of cognitive appraisal (thinking) for interpreting a physiological experience as an emotion. Subjects were injected with epinephrine to induce physiological arousal but in the absence of an actual emotion-evoking stimulus were unable to interpret their arousal as an experienced emotion. However, when presented with a stimulus (in the form of another person displaying an emotion such as anger or amusement) the subjects were observed to express related emotions. They called this the *two factor theory of emotion*, arguing that the experience of emotions requires both a physiological and cognitive input. This research galvanised several cognitive theories of emotion. Some of the most influential of these include: Affect theory of emotion (Silvan Tomkins,1962);[25] Judgement theory of emotions (Robert Solomon, 1977);[26] *Mind and Body: Psychology of Emotion and Stress (*George Mandler, 1984);[27] *Cognitive appraisal theories on emotions* (Ira Roseman,1984);[28] and *Intentionality of emotions* (Richard Lazarus, 1991).[29]

More recently, *Perceptual theory* (Peter Goldie, 2004)[30] has claimed that cognition is unnecessary for interpreting emotion. It suggests that emotions are themselves *perception* in that they represent a response to a situation, they have meaning and are about something. Emotions, rather like other senses such as vision or touch, provide information about the relationship between the individual and their world. Describing emotions as *perceptions that have meaning*, supports the view that emotions are a form of intelligence within the body.

As well as the evolutionary, biological and cognitive theories of emotion there is also an important social perspective that has clear relevance to EI. Emotions have a strong social and interpersonal component, James Averill (1980)[31] proposes that an emotional response is governed by social norms and expectations, and Brian Parkinson (1996)[32] proposes that emotions typically occur in particular social settings and have specific interpersonal functions, such as to trust others or to withdraw from people. This social aspect of emotions is discussed in the next section on Social Intelligence.

3 Social Intelligence

Emotional Intelligence has its origins in the concept of Social Intelligence, although the two concepts are often used interchangeably or together. Howard Gardner (1983)[34] separates out *Intrapersonal* (emotional) from *Interpersonal* (social) intelligences, Carolyn Saarni (1990)[35] describes *Emotional Competence* as including both emotional and social skills, and Reuven Bar-On (2000)[36] refers to the construct of EI as *Emotional-Social Intelligence*.

Social Intelligence originates from the work of Edward Thorndike who published *Social Intelligence* in 1920,[37] describing socially competent behaviour as *the ability to understand and manage men and women, boys and girls, and to act wisely in human relations*. Hunt (1928)[38] defined Social Intelligence as *the ability to deal with other people*, and Wedeck (1947)[39] characterises it as *the ability to judge correctly, the feelings moods and motivations of others*. The first instrument designed to measure socially intelligent behaviour in young children was produced by Edgar Doll in 1935.[40] Social Intelligence also has historical roots in personality theory and social psychology, such as George Kelly's *personal construct theory* (1955)[41] proposing that individuals form cognitive expectations, called *personal constructs,* to interpret and understand the social world in which they live. Personal constructs are the anticipation of events that influence how the individual will behave and may be likened to attitudes and pattern matching described in the EIP (refer to Chapter 2.3).

Social Intelligence also draws heavily on human need theories (Atkinson, 1981; McClelland, 1992; and Murray, 1938)[42,43,44] asserting that behind much social behaviour are emotional drivers/needs, such as for affiliation, status, achievement, autonomy and intimacy. These emotional drivers/needs include the human emotional needs described in Chapter 1.1 that lie behind the EIP model.

One other important element to Social Intelligence are theories of interpersonal behaviour and group dynamics. Two pioneers in this field were Kurt Lewin (1947)[45] and Will Schutz (1958).[46] Schutz's FIRO® theory was a primary influence in developing the EIP model and is described in Appendix 4. Lewin is considered to be the father of modern social psychology and he established the National Training Laboratory as a way to develop social and emotional learning. Both Lewin and Schutz recognised the importance of experiential group encounter for personal growth, and the development of Emotional and Social Intelligence is much influenced by the principles laid down by their work.

Social Competence: A similar concept to Social Intelligence is Social Competence, which has its origins in terms such as social skills (Combs, 1977)[47] and Social Learning (Bandura, 1977).[48] Keith Topping (2000)[49] defines Social Competence as *the ability to integrate thinking, feeling and behaviour to achieve social tasks and outcomes*. By this definition people may be good at different elements of Social Competence, some people may be good at thinking and knowing what they should do, but be less good at dealing with the emotions of a social situation. Others may have learnt a set of effective social skills but be less able to adapt them to unfamiliar situations. This fits with the principle of the EIP six-part framework; that EI is multifaceted. In addition, the definition of Social Competence is similar to part-two of the EIP definition of EI: *the habitual practice of thinking about feeling and feeling about thinking to guide one's behaviour.*

Practical Intelligence: Social Intelligence falls into the camp of what are termed non-cognitive or non-intellective intelligences. Another non-cognitive intelligence is Sternberg's (1985)[50] theory of Successful Intelligence which can be identified by three key abilities: analytic, creative and practical intelligence. Hedlund & Sternberg (2000)[51] give the following explanation of practical intelligence in relation to EI: *The ability to acquire knowledge, whether it pertains to managing oneself, managing others, or managing tasks, can be characterised appropriately as an aspect of intelligence. The decision to call this aspect of intelligence social, emotional or practical intelligence will depend on one's perspective and one's purpose.*

Alexithymia: At around the same time as there being an interest in exploring Social Intelligence, researchers began to examine the pathological end to this spectrum; the *inability* of individuals to recognise, understand and describe emotions. This was later given the label of Alexithymia by Peter Sifneos (1973)[52] from the Greek meaning *lack of words for emotions* and is characterised by:

- *Difficulty identifying and distinguishing between feelings*
- *Difficulty describing feelings to others*
- *Constricted imagination*
- *An externally oriented cognitive style*

Alexithymia is an aspect of personality originally identified by Ruesch (1948)[53] and Maclean (1949)[54] who observed patients with an inability to verbalise feelings despite sometimes displaying extreme emotions. Alexithymia has been partly attributed to early environmental influences, especially variations in their care-givers capacity to form attachment (Schore, 1994).[55] A similar construct to Alexithymia is Affective Orientation, described as *the degree to which people are aware of their emotions, perceive them as important, and actively consider their affective responses in making judgements and interacting with others* (Booth-Butterfield, 1994).[56] Affective Orientation may be seen as a spectrum, from the very low end being Alexithymia to the high end representing EI.

Psychological Mindedness: Two concepts that closely parallel Alexithymia (or the opposite end of it) are Psychological Mindedness (Appelbaum, 1973)[57] and Emotional Awareness (Lane & Schwartz, 1987).[58] Appelbaum defined Psychological Mindedness as *a person's ability to see relationships among thoughts, feelings and actions, with the goal of learning the meanings and causes of his experiences and behaviours.* Conte (1996)[59] extended the concept beyond self-focus, to include *both self-understanding and an interest in the motivation and behaviour of others*, and identified four broad abilities:

- *Access to one's feelings*
- *Willingness to talk about one's feelings and interpersonal problems*
- *Capacity for behavioural change*
- *An interest in other people's behaviour*

Emotional Awareness is defined by Lane & Schwartz (1987)[58] as *the ability to recognise and describe emotions in oneself and others*, and they describe five levels of Emotional Awareness (which share structural characteristics with Piaget's (1950)[60] stages of cognitive development):

- *Physical sensation*
- *Action tendencies*
- *Single emotions*
- *Blends of emotion*
- *Blends of blends of emotional experiences*

There are many overlaps between EI, Psychological Mindedness and Emotional Awareness in terms of awareness of one's thoughts, feelings and behaviours and those of others. However, EI is invariably defined as a positive attribute, while Psychological Mindedness may also exacerbate negative responses such as anxiety, feelings of loneliness, disappointment in others and lower self-esteem (Farber, 1989,[61] and Feningstein, 1984).[62] That is, too much Emotional Awareness can make a person *wiser but sadder*. This is one of the criticisms also levelled at insight based therapy which requires a reasonable level of self-awareness (Piper, 1998).[63] One reason for this may be that Psychological Mindedness focuses on awareness of feelings (the middle level of the EIP framework) and less so on putting this into action (the top level of the EIP framework) which is a primary recommendation for developing EI.

Emotional Creativity: One other concept that came out prior to Goleman's popularisation of EI was Emotional Creativity. James Averill and Elma Nunley, in their book

Voyages of the Heart (1992),[64] describe Emotional Creativity as a *constructionist* view of emotions. This they contrast with the *rationalist* view of emotion (emotions as primitive responses that must be controlled) and the *romanticist* view of emotion of 'letting it all hang out'.

They describe emotions as a construction analogous to language. Language has biological roots (as do emotions), but specific languages are a product of evolution (as are emotions) and within a language there is considerable opportunity for creativity such as for poetry and literature (as there is for learning to facilitate emotions creatively).

They describe three levels of emotional creativity using the acronym ART:

- **Acquisition:** *This includes the emotional maturity to experience, name and differentiate emotions.*
- **Refinement:** *A more sophisticated mastery of emotions to achieve the end, such as charisma to influence people.*
- **Transformation:** *The expression of emotions that goes beyond the ordinary, as may be done symbolically in poetry, art and music.*

Emotional Literacy: A closely related concept to Emotional Intelligence is Emotional Literacy. Claude Steiner, a TA therapist, published the first paper on Emotional Literacy in 1974.[65] In his book *Achieving Emotional Literacy* (1997),[66] Steiner describes Emotional Literacy as being made up of *the ability to understand your emotions, the ability to listen to others and empathise with their emotions, and the ability to express emotions productively. To be emotionally literate is to be able to handle emotions in a way that improves your personal power and improves the quality of life around you. Emotional literacy improves relationships, creates loving possibilities between people, makes cooperative work possible, and facilitates the feeling of community.* According to Steiner, Emotional Literacy is about learning to understanding your feelings and those of others, so as to facilitate relationships and deal skilfully with emotionally challenging situations. This is done by the individual looking at themselves rather than the external social context.

Emotional Literacy has its roots in counselling and has been applied widely in educational contexts with children, helping them to identify and articulate their feelings. There is perhaps little to distinguish EI from Emotional Literacy other than EI being applied more widely in the workplace.

4 EI in the workplace

Psychologists and managers have been examining the social and emotional aspects of work since the Hawthorne experiments conducted by Elton Mayo in the 1930s.[67] One of these studies, known as the *Hawthorne effect,* found that workers increased productivity when they perceived they were being watched. Such experiments led to greater emphasis being placed on the social and emotional needs of workers. Post WW2 Kurt Lewin began developing programmes for leaders to better manage human relations in the workplace. These include the National Training Laboratories and, in the 1960s, 't' groups which focused on raising individuals self-awareness and interpersonal sensitivity. In the 1980s there was an expansion of leadership and personal development programmes, in areas such as stress management, self-motivation, team building, conflict handling and leadership styles. This was followed in the 1990s by the emergence of EI and a growing popularity of executive coaching.

One of the earliest references to the term Emotional Intelligence was in 1966 by Barbara Leuner,[68] exploring the social roles of women, and later by Wayne Payne in 1985[69] who put forward the first model of EI in his doctoral thesis. In 1990 Peter Salovey and John Mayer[70] describe an *abilities based approach* to EI in a published journal. It was not until 1995 when Daniel Goleman published *Emotional Intelligence; why it can matter more than IQ,*[71] that EI managed to capture the interest of the popular business world. Goleman's book was seen as an egalitarian rebuttal to the Herrnstein and Murray book *The Bell Curve* (1994)[72] that argued the importance of IQ for understanding social class in society. IQ was seen by many as hard, elitist and difficult to develop, while EI (or EQ) was seen to be 'kind', something that all people could develop and as relevant to work performance. In the same year EI was on the cover of *Time* magazine (Gibbs, 1995)[73] and EQ was selected as one of the most useful new words or phrases of 1995 by the American Dialect Society. The growth of interest, research and publications in EI since this time has not relented and has led to the production of several established EI theories and measurement instruments.

In the *Encyclopaedia of Applied Psychology* (2004),[74] Spielberger suggests that there are three major conceptual models of EI. An abilities model (Salovey and Mayer, 1990),[70] a social and emotional competencies model (Bar-On, 1997),[75] and a competency skills model (Goleman, 1998).[76] Two other models that may be added to these are the personality trait model of EI (Petrides & Furnham, 2000)[77] and the attitude based EIP model of EI (Maddocks & Sparrow, 1998).[78] An important distinction between all of these models is whether they are measured objectively (the *abilities model*) or subjectively (*self-perception/self-report*). Self-perception measures of EI typically cluster a broad array of EI related attributes, known as the *mixed model*.

The abilities model of EI: Intelligence tests date back to 1905, when Alfred Binet[79] developed the first IQ tests which included *judgement* as an integral part to using intelligence. David Wechsler (1939)[80] produced the WAIS (Wechsler Adult Intelligence Scale), one of the most recognised measures of intelligence, which included the subscales of comprehension and picture arrangement which appear to measure aspects of Social Intelligence. In subsequent years Wechsler described the non-intellective factors of intelligent behaviour and argued that models of intelligence would not be complete until these factors were adequately described (1943).[81] Within Wechsler's definition of intelligence he includes *the capacity of the individual to act purposefully* (1958),[82] further reinforcing that there was a social aspect to intelligence. This led psychologists to focus their attention on the purpose of interpersonal behaviour (Zirkel, 2000)[83] and influenced the likes of Salovey and Mayer (1990)[70] in their original *abilities based approach* to EI called the MEIS (Multi-factorial Emotional Intelligence Survey), which was later updated in 1997 to the MSCEIT™[84] (Mayer Salovey, Carusso Emotional Intelligence Test). This measures four EI abilities:

1 *Perceiving emotions*
2 *Using emotions*
3 *Understanding emotions*
4 *Managing emotions*

A discussion of the relationship between the EIP model of EI and intelligence is given in Chapter 1.3.2.

Mixed models of EI: The mixed models of EI consist largely of self-report competency based measures of EI. One of the earliest proponents of emotional competence was Carolyn Saarni (1990)[35] who describes emotional competence as including eight interrelated emotional and social skills:

- *Awareness of one's own emotional state*
- *Skill in discerning the emotions of others*
- *Skill in using the vocabulary of emotion*
- *Capacity for empathic and sympathetic involvement towards others*
- *Skill in understanding that inner emotional state need not correlate to outer expression*
- *Skill at adaptive coping to aversive or distressing emotions*
- *Awareness of the structure or nature of relationships*
- *Capacity for emotional self-efficacy*

One of the most recognised EI competency models was developed by Reuven Bar-On (1985)[85] who refers to the construct of Emotional Intelligence as Emotional and Social Intelligence. He defines it as *a cross-section of interrelated emotional and social competencies, skills and facilitators that determine how effectively we understand and express ourselves, understand others and relate with them, and cope with daily demands*.

Bar-On coined the term Emotional Quotient (EQ) and developed one of the first measures of EI, the Emotional Quotient Inventory (EQ-i). Originally designed as an experimental instrument to examine emotionally and socially competent behaviour (Bar-On, 1985),[85] the EQ-i assesses five broad subtypes of EI:

1 *Intrapersonal intelligence*
2 *Interpersonal intelligence*
3 *Adaptability*
4 *Stress management*
5 *General mood*

Another well-established model of EI is by Daniel Goleman who proposed five EI constructs:

1 *Self-awareness*
2 *Self-regulation*
3 *Social skill*
4 *Empathy*
5 *Motivation*

Goleman's contention was that individuals are born with general EI which determines their potential for developing EI competencies, as measured by the Emotional Competency Inventory (ECI, 1999)[86] and the Emotional and Social Competency Inventory (ESCI, 2007).[87] The ECI is based on Boyatzis' set of competencies from the Self Assessment Questionnaire (1994)[88] and Goleman's 25 EI competencies (1998),[76] and was later rewritten to become the Hay/McBer ESCI. The ESCI competencies have been linked to underpinning needs, personality factors and physiological states. For example, need for power drives teamwork, need for affiliation drives empathy (Burruss, 1981)[89] collaboration drives influence (McClelland, 1985),[90] extraversion drives building bonds and communication, and agreeableness drives social awareness. However, this was a post hoc rationalisation and it is noticeable that these EI competency measures do not have a set of underpinning principles behind the development of their scales. Unlike the EIP that has eight EI attitudes which forms the basis of the EIP scales.

Other models of EI: In contrast to the competency models of EI, Konstantin Petrides (2000)[77] proposes a conceptual model of *trait personality* EI. She describes trait EI as *a constellation of emotional self-perceptions located at the lower levels of personality.* Petrides and Furnham (2000)[77] developed the Trait Emotional Intelligence Questionnaire (TEIQ) that measures a person's self-perception of their emotional abilities. The EIP also falls within the mixed model approach to EI, but has its roots in attitudes rather than competencies, personality or abilities. These differences are fully explained in Chapter 1.3.

Criticisms of EI measures: A number of criticisms have been levelled at the concept of EI and EI measures. Perhaps the most significant of these is that EI is not an aspect of intelligence. Hans Eysenck (2000)[91] criticised the lack of scientific basis for the assumptions made by Daniel Goleman that EI is a form of intelligence. There have been several other eminent psychologists who have raised concerns about the theoretical foundations of EI. Edwin Locke (2005)[92] said it is not another form of intelligence, but *is* intelligence. Frank Landy (2005)[93] claimed the few predictive validity studies for EI have shown little incremental validity beyond abstract intelligence or personality measures. In critical reviews of EI it has been described as *an elusive construct* (Zeidner et al, 2001)[94] and as an *intangible myth* (Matthews et al, 2003).[95] Despite these challenges to the concept of EI being a separate form of intelligence, other psychologists have found it useful to differentiate EI from other forms of intelligence (Thorndike,[37] Salovey and Mayer[70] and Wechsler[81]) and evidence has been presented in this appendix for emotions being a form of intelligence (Pert,[16] Damasio[17] and LeDoux[23]).

A second key criticism of EI is that it is simply an aspect of personality. Mayer (1995)[96] suggests that terms used in EI such as motivation, emotion, cognition and consciousness may be seen as the biological functions of personality. Hedlund (2000)[51] questions Goleman's description of EI as an attempt to capture almost everything but IQ. Given the varying definitions of EI, there is the danger of EI expanding into all areas of personality and it not being differentiated. Many EI attributes may be found in personality measures, such as the California Psychological Inventory (Gough, 1986)[97] which includes scales of interpersonal effectiveness, self-acceptance, self-control, flexibility and empathy. EI may also be seen to overlap with other personality types and qualities, such as the *hardy personality*; overcoming hardship and contributing to society (Kobasa, 1979),[98] the *Constructive thinker*; learning and changing for the better and lending a helping hand to people (Epstein, 1998),[99] *Ego strength;* the ability to function rationally and to self-regulate (Block,

1980),[100] and *Self-actualisation*; reaching one's full potential (Goldstein, 1934).[101]

Many EI attributes are correlated with the so-called 'big 5' personality character-istics. In particular *Openness to experience* has been found to correlate with EI (Schutte, 1998),[102] *Awareness of feelings* (McCrae & Costa, 1991),[103] *Emotional attention* (Salovey, 1995)[104] and *aspects of Emotional vulnerability* (McCrae & Costa, 1991).[103] Extraversion, Conscientiousness and Agreeableness correlate with lower emotional stress (Trull, 1994).[105] Neuroticism correlates with self-dissatisfaction. Extraversion correlates with stimulus seeking and low Agreeableness. Compulsiveness correlates with lack of concern for others. Conscientiousness correlates with impulse control (Schroeder, 1992).[106] And the most established of the 'big 5' personality questionnaires; the NEO-PI-R, includes items on empathy and awareness of feelings (Mayer, 2000).[107] The EIP also shows EI to correlate positively with Openness, Conscientiousness, Extraversion, Agreeableness, and negatively with Neuroticism (refer to the EIP technical manual for specific scale correlations).[78]

The 'criticism' of EI being an aspect of personality is legitimate in that personality may include a person's cognition, affect, behaviour and attitude which are all aspects of EI. However, the EIP draws specific distinctions between EI and person-ality temperament (see Chapter 1.3.1) and even defines EI as *the practice of managing one's personality*. It is therefore expected that the EIP will correlate to an extent with personality, but correlation does not mean they are the same thing!

One other criticism of EI measures is that they are mostly self-report and that people who are low on EI may be less self-aware and therefore less able to accu-rately assess their own EI. Davis (1997)[108] found no correlation between individual's estimates of their empathy and their scores on objective tests of empathy. In addi-tion, Paulhus (1998)[109] found that self-report measures of intellect correlate quite modestly (0.2 to 0.3) with psychometric tests of mental ability. A person's self-perception is also influenced by their mood; happy people are more likely to say they understand their feelings, and unhappy people report being confused by them (Mayer, 1988).[110] These observations about self-report measures do raise some concerns, although despite this, self-report personality questionnaires have demon-strated reasonable validity and have stood the test of time (Morgeson, 2007).[111] Furthermore, good questionnaire design will attempt to mitigate against subjective bias and validate the scale constructs. Also of importance is how the questionnaire is being applied; the EIP is designed purely for self-development, so avoids the issues of faking, an inherent problem for selection tests (Morgeson, 2007).[111] One other way to minimise error is to check the accuracy of an individual's self-percep-tion (through discussing their item responses and scale scores) which is a key part of the self-development process when using the EIP (as explained in Chapter 6.2). It should be remembered, as with all self-report measures, that the EIP is only one source of feedback and should be considered alongside all other available findings such as 360 reporting, personal experience and observations during the coaching process.

5 The future of EI

This appendix has reviewed the history of Emotional Intelligence starting with the earliest theories on emotion and their evolution which tended to see emotions as a mechanistic and adaptive response to survival. Since then psychologists have long been interested in how people learn to manage their emotions and their relationships which has given rise to several concepts that are similar to EI, as summarised below.

Table 2.1 Key theories relating to EI

Concept	Key theorists	Date
Social Intelligence	Edward Thorndike	1920[37]
Non-Cognitive Intelligence	David Wechsler	1943[81]
Psychological Mindedness	Stephen Appelbaum	1973[57]
Alexithymia (Affective Orientation)	Peter Sifneos	1973[52]
Emotional Literacy	Claude Steiner	1974[65]
Social Competence/Social Learning/Social Skills	Albert Bandura	1977[48]
Practical Intelligence	Robert Sternberg	1985[50]
Emotional Awareness	Richard Lane & Barry Schwartz	1987[58]
Emotional Competence	Carolyn Saarni	1990[35]
Emotional Creativity	James Averill	1992[64]

These approaches all promote the view that people can develop an *intelligent use of their emotions*. However, it is only in the last thirty years, through advances in neuroscience and body-mind research, that emotions have also been considered to be *a form of intelligence*. This is a contentious issue, and has produced considerable debate about the concept of EI and its measurement.

Despite these debates, EI has proven to be a very useful and popular concept and has been part of a shift in western society towards a more *emotional society* (De Kesel, 2010).[112] For now, EI is still on the ascendancy, but it is fields outside of EI that are likely to influence the future of this concept, in particular the fields of medical research (including neuroscience), technology and psychological well-being.

Neuroscience has become one of the fastest growth areas in medical and psychological research. For example, there are currently two global projects to map the entire brain: the European Human Brain Project (HBP)[113] and the American BRAIN[114] Initiative launched in 2013 by president Obama, who compared its significance to that of putting man on the moon. Such initiatives should also be balanced with caution, as brain research has tended to overstate its findings. In 2011 a comprehensive analysis of 730 neuroscience papers found very low sample sizes rendered 80% of their results to be highly unreliable (Button, 2011).[115] Another advancing area in medical science is DNA and stem cell research where, for example, scientists have recently been able to grow human brain cells and create a *mini brain* roughly at the developmental level of a nine-week old foetus (Lancaster, 2013).[116] The long-term implications of such research on EI are difficult to know, but may provide more insight to profound questions, such as *how intelligent are emotions and what is human consciousness?*

Technology and human factors have always developed hand in hand and this is likely to be the same for EI. For example, there are currently several new mobile phone *app's* for monitoring an individual's level of emotional arousal. This will no doubt be extended to include biofeedback on other emotional states (sad, happy, afraid, etc.) which may be used in helping individuals better understand their feelings. Related to this is the future of the internet which has been dubbed *the internet of everything* (Evans, 2012)[117] whereby anything from household appliances to the food people buy will be chipped to give people live feedback on their status. This could eventually be applied to monitoring a person's emotional state, habits and relationships, providing instant feedback for those choosing to develop their EI. Technology has also greatly influenced how people communicate through social media and remote virtual communication. People are having to adapt to these changes and there are likely to be many further advances in virtual forms of communication that will help retain the vital aspects of emotional connection, such as through instant feedback, 3-dimensional imagery and even virtual tactile contact.

Ironically the advances being made in medical science and technology are perhaps contributing to a reduction in *psychological well-being*. For example, the trend for ever greater dependence on medication rather than developing physical and emotional resilience; greater dependence on technology rather than encouraging human responsibility; and substituting essential human emotional needs for short term materialistic gratification. However, for those who choose to take the emotionally intelligent option, there are plenty of promising opportunities: creating more emotionally intelligent organisations that help individuals achieve their potential within a supportive climate; encouraging an emotionally intelligent lifestyle that maintains well-being in all aspects of a person's life rather than 'fixing' them when they are sick; better understanding of the brain-body system that will provide practical and immediate ways to enhance emotional well-being; and smarter mechanisms that provide in-the-moment emotional, physical and cognitive feedback to help individuals become more self-aware, identify issues early, track their EI development, maintain their well-being, and achieve higher performance.

Appendix Three

Emotional Intelligence and Personality Type

As explained in Chapter 1, Emotional Intelligence and personality are closely related concepts, with EI being defined as *the practice of managing one's personality to be both personally and interpersonally effective.*

One of the most commonly used models of personality for personal development is Jungian type theory (1921)[1] (as measured by the MBTI® and the JCA Personality Type Profile). Appendix 3 examines the relationship between the EIP and Jungian type theory and how both models of assessment may be used in combination. It is assumed that the reader has knowledge of type theory.

In practice a coach will often make use of both the EIP and a type instrument for client coaching. This will usually involve the coach using a type measure to explore the client's behavioural preferences and then using the EIP to explore how effectively they are applying their personality preferences and how these may be developed through EI. Consider the following example:

An ESFP client reported a specific concern that she lacked assertiveness and she didn't want to upset others or risk confrontation. The EIP identified three particularly low scores: Personal Power (the degree to which a person is in charge of and takes responsibility for their outcomes in life), Goal Directedness (the degree to which a person relates his/her own behaviour to long-term goals) and Self Awareness (the degree to which a person is in touch with their body, feelings and intuitions).

From this profile, specific objectives and strategies were identified to improve her assertiveness including:

- Self Awareness; learning her patterns of feeling and behaviour, such as when she says 'yes' but feels and wants to say 'no'.
- Goal Directedness; developing impulse control, knowing what she wants, having clear intentions, and not being distracted from them.
- Personal Power; learning how to ask for what she wants.

The client also used two of her high scoring scales as a resource:

- Flexibility; trying out different approaches and giving it a go.
- Connecting with Others; seeking the support of others to meet her objectives.

Type and the EIP models are closely linked yet retain fundamental differences, which is what makes them so valuable when applied in combination. Type theory provides a model for understanding an individual's personality disposition and the EIP how best an individual may learn to use, manage and develop this.

The next part to this appendix presents a theoretical rationale for how the EIP framework and Jungian type theory are related and may be used in combination.

Theoretical links between the EIP and Jungian type

In broad terms, there are some obvious similarities between the EIP framework and Jungian type theory:

Introversion type preference (focusing attention and energy on the inner world of ideas and experience) relates to Personal Intelligence (the left side of the EIP framework). Extraversion type preference (focusing attention and energy on the outer world of people and activity) relates to Interpersonal Intelligence (the right side of the EIP framework).

The Perceiving functions (Sensing and Intuition types) are related to the middle layer of the EIP framework (Self Awareness and Awareness of Others) as they are about how a person perceives and takes information in. The Judging functions (Thinking and Feeling types) are related to the top level of the EIP framework (Self Management and Relationship Management) as they are about how a person decides and acts upon their perceptions.

Having made these conceptual links, it is possible to assign the eight Jungian preferences within the EIP framework as illustrated below. For example, Introverted Sensing (The Introverted attitude and the Perceiving function) would reside bottom left, under the Self Awareness part of the EIP framework.

Table 3.1 The Jungian type preferences mapped onto the EIP framework

	Personal Introversion	Interpersonal Extraversion
Behaviour	**Self Management**	**Relationship Management**
Judging Functions	Introverted Thinking	Extraverted Thinking
	Introverted Feeling	Extraverted Feeling
Feeling	**Self Awareness**	**Awareness of Others**
Perceiving Functions	Introverted Sensing	Extraverted Sensing
	Introverted Intuition	Extraverted Intuition

Note that the direct parallel between EI and type does not extend to the EIP Attitude scales of Self Regard and Regard for Others. These attitudes will have similar influence on personality type (influencing the manifestation of type behaviour positively or negatively) as they do on the EIP scales. Jungian type dynamics theory describes a hierarchy of preference between the functions. It follows, based on the links made with the EIP, that this pecking order of preferences may also apply to the corresponding parts of the EIP framework, not so much as preferences but as EI strengths. An INFP, for example, would have the following order of type preferences:

Table 3.2 Example hierarchy of type preferences and EIP strengths

	INFP preferences	Related EIP area
Dominant	Introverted Feeling	Self Management
Auxiliary	Extraverted Intuition	Awareness of Others
Tertiary	Introverted Sensing	Self Awareness
Inferior	Extraverted Thinking	Relationship Management

Based on this rationale, it seems likely that an INFP would also find the EIP Self Management scales to be preferable (and probably easier and more natural to develop) than the EIP Relationship Management scales. Knowing this may be particularly useful to a coach as they may decide to look at scales the client may find 'easier' to develop before tackling potentially more 'difficult' EIP scales.

The table below shows the dynamic order and link to EI for each of the personality types. For example I - - J types would have dominant Introverted Sensing or Introverted Intuition which correspond with the Self Awareness part of the EIP framework.

Table 3.3
Theoretical links between type preferences and the EIP framework

Type		Dominant	Auxiliary	Tertiary	Inferior
I - - J	EIP	SA	RM	SM	AO
	Jungian	Si/Ni	Te/Fe	Ti/Fi	Se/Ne
I - - P	EIP	SM	AO	SA	RM
	Jungian	Ti/Fi	Se/Ne	Si/Ni	Te/Fe
E - - P	EIP	AO	SM	RM	SA
	Jungian	Se/Ne	Ti/Fi	Te/Fe	Si/Ni
E - - J	EIP	RM	SA	AO	SM
	Jungian	Te/Fe	Si/Ni	Se/Ne	Ti/Fi

Key:
SA	Self Awareness	Si	Introverted Sensing	Ti	Introverted Thinking
AO	Awareness of Others	Se	Extraverted Sensing	Te	Extraverted Thinking
SM	Self Management	Ni	Introverted Intuition	Fi	Introverted Feeling
RM	Relationship Management	Ne	Extraverted Intuition	Fe	Extraverted Feeling

Incidentally, we can see from this analysis that the dominant and auxiliary of each type link to both the Awareness and Management parts as well as to Personal and Interpersonal parts of the EIP framework. Similar to type theory, it is important for EI development that a person does not get 'locked' into their Management without Awareness (Judgement without Perception in type terms) or Awareness without Management (Perception without Judgement in type terms).

When coaching with the EIP and type it is often the case that clients have more difficulty in developing their tertiary and inferior functions. For example, an individual with an ESFJ preference would have an inferior Introverted Thinking which relates to the EIP scales of Self Management. They may therefore benefit from developing the following EIP Self Management scales:

- *Goal Directedness: for self-motivation*
- *Emotional Resilience: for managing stress and related emotions*
- *Personal Power: to build their inner-confidence*

By extrapolating this theoretical link between EIP and Jungian type, it is possible to draw an informed view on which EIP scales may be used to develop each of the sixteen types as defined by Isabel Briggs Myers and Katherine Cook Briggs.[2] The table below is not definitive, as a case could be made for every EIP scale with every type. The table provides three EIP scale 'strengths' that an individual reporting the type preference may find more comfortable and natural to develop, and three EIP scale 'development areas' that the individual may find more challenging but neces-sary for their self-development.

Table 3.4

Potential EIP strengths and development areas for the type preferences

Type preference	More likely EIP strength scales	More likely EIP development scales
ISTJ	Self Awareness Goal Directedness Authenticity	Awareness of Others Flexibility Emotional Expression
ISFJ	Self Awareness Goal Directedness Authenticity	Emotional Resilience Flexibility Conflict Handling
INFJ	Self Awareness Goal Directedness Reflective Learning	Personal Power Balanced Outlook Conflict Handling

Type preference	More likely EIP strength scales	More likely EIP development scales
INTJ	Personal Power Goal Directedness Authenticity	Awareness of Others Connecting with Others Interdependence
ISTP	Emotional Resilience Flexibility Balanced Outlook	Awareness of Others Connecting with Others Interdependence
ISFP	Awareness of Others Connecting with Others Reflective Learning	Personal Power Emotional Expression Conflict Handling
INFP	Awareness of Others Connecting with Others Reflective Learning	Personal Power Emotional Expression Conflict Handling
INTP	Emotional Resilience Personal Power Goal Directedness	Awareness of Others Connecting with Others Interdependence
ESTP	Emotional Resilience Personal Power Flexibility	Goal Directedness Authenticity Reflective Learning
ESFP	Awareness of Others Flexibility Connecting with Others	Goal Directedness Emotional Control Conflict Handling
ENFP	Awareness of Others Flexibility Interdependence	Goal Directedness Authenticity Balanced Outlook
ENTP	Personal Power Flexibility Conflict Handling	Self Awareness Goal Directedness Authenticity
ESTJ	Emotional Resilience Personal Power Authenticity	Flexibility Connecting with Others Trust
ESFJ	Awareness of Others Connecting with Others Interdependence	Emotional Resilience Flexibility Conflict Handling
ENFJ	Awareness of Others Goal Directedness Interdependence	Emotional Resilience Trust Conflict Handling
ENTJ	Emotional Resilience Personal Power Goal Directedness	Flexibility Connecting with Others Trust

Appendix Four

Emotional Intelligence and FIRO® theory

One of the theoretical models that assisted in the creation of the EIP and Team EIP was Will Schutz's FIRO® theory (Fundamental Interpersonal Relations Orientation), designed as a means of improving relationships and team working.[1]

The premise to FIRO® theory is that people orientate themselves towards others along three dimensions of behaviour; Inclusion (I), Control (C) and Openness (O), which all have links to Emotional Intelligence. Used together, the EIP and FIRO® are complimentary for both individual and team development. A person who has difficulty in situations that require high levels of *Inclusion* (such as socialising) may wish to develop their EI in areas such as Regard for Others, Awareness of Others and Interdependence. A person who wants to be less *Controlling* of others (such as following rather than leading) may develop their Flexibility and Assertiveness (to be less aggressive), and a person who tends to be overly *Open* (such as too informal at work) may choose to develop their Emotional Control and Goal Directedness.

The table below shows which EIP scales may be developed to help individuals operate at both the low or high end of the Inclusion (I), Control (C) and Openness (O) dimensions.

Table 4.1 Links between the EIP and FIRO® scales

	EIP scales that help lower I,C,O behaviours	EIP scales that help raise I,C,O behaviours
Inclusion (I)	Self Regard Self Awareness Interdependence (less Dependent)	Regard for Others Awareness of Others Interdependence (less Over Independent)
Control (C)	Flexibility Assertiveness (less Aggressive)	Personal Power Goal Directedness Assertiveness (less Passive)
Openness (O)	Emotional Resilience Trust (less Over Trusting) Less Emotionally Under Controlled	Connecting with Others Trust (less Mistrusting) Less Emotionaly Over Controlled

Each of these three FIRO® dimensions (I,C,O) can be explored at different levels of depth from Behaviour (B), to Feelings (F), to the Self Concept (S) paralleling the three levels of the EIP framework (Table 4.2). In both models, Behaviours are under-pinned by Feelings which are derived from Attitudes (the Self-Concept).

Table 4.2 Links between the EIP framework and FIRO® theory

EIP theory	FIRO® theory			
Behaviour	Behaviour	Inclusion	Control	Openness
Feeling	Feelings	Significance	Competence	Likability
Attitude	Self-Concept	Aliveness	Self-Determination	Self-Awareness
		Self-Significance	Self-Competence	Self-Like

The three FIRO® dimensions (I,C,O) and three levels (B,F,S) are also examined in terms of four interpersonal dynamics (What I DO, what I WANT to do, what I GET from others and what I WANT to GET from others). These too can be linked to the EIP framework. What I DO (top row) links to Personal Intelligence. What I GET (bottom row) links to Interpersonal Intelligence.

Table 4.3
Links between the EIP and the interpersonal dynamics of FIRO® theory

EIP	FIRO®		
		See	Want
Personal Intelligence	Do	What I see myself Do	What I want to Do
Interpersonal Intelligence	Get	What I see myself Get	What I want to Get

What differentiates FIRO® from the EIP and most other self-report questionnaires is that it looks at the dynamics of interpersonal relationships. Instead of only asking what a person *does*, it asks the individual what they *want* (which may be compared with what they *do*) and also asks them what they *get* (how others behave towards them). This type of information is extremely useful when exploring relationships. For example, how compatible would two people be if one person often takes control and the other person does not want to be controlled? FIRO Elements® (the names given to the revised questionnaires) provide a global picture of the breadth and depth of human relationships. Having close links with FIRO® theory, the EIP may be used to provide specific feedback to explain why individuals behave and feel as they do and to give recommendations for their personal development.

Schutz applied his FIRO® theory through a programme called The Human Element®.[2] This has been successfully delivered within global organisations to help with individual development, improving relationships and creating a positive organisational climate. JCA have applied FIRO® theory and The Human Element® within their own EI programmes to help develop EI within organisations as described in Chapter 8.4.

This Appendix was adapted from a previous publication (Maddocks, 2008).[3]
Reprinted with kind permission from Business Consultants, Inc. Published by The Schutz Company. © 2008

References

Chapter One

1 Griffin, J. & Tyrrell, I. (2004). *The Human Givens. A new approach to emotional health and clear thinking.* East Sussex: Human Givens Publishing.

2 HSE Statistics. (2011). http://www.hse.gov.uk/statistics/causdis/stress/index.htm.

3 Seligman, M.E.P. In J. Buie (1988). 'Me' decades generate depression: individualism erodes commitment to others. *American Psychological Association Monitor.* Oct., 18.

4 Freedman, J. (2008). *Workplace issues report.* Six seconds.

5 Leuner, B. (1966). Emotional intelligence and emancipation: A psychodynamic study of women. *Prax Kinderpsychol Kinderpsychiat.* Aug.-Sep., 15 (6), 196-203.

6 Goleman, D. (1996). *Emotional intelligence: why it can matter more than IQ.* New York: Bantam Books.

7 Goleman, D. (1998). *Working with emotional intelligence.* New York: Bantam Books.

8 Goleman, D. (2006). *Social Intelligence: The new science of human relationships.* New York: Random House.

3 Descartes, R. (1637). transl. Veitch, J. (1924). *Discours de la méthode (Discourse on the Method).* An introduction to the *Essais*, which include the *Dioptrique*, the *Météores* and the *Géométrie*.

10 Darwin, C. (1872/1965). *The expression of the emotions in man and animals.* Chicago: University of Chicago Press.

11 Wechsler, D. (1943). Nonintellective factors in general intelligence. *Journal of Abnormal Social Psychology*, 38, 100-104.

12 Gardner, H. (1983). *Frames of mind.* New York: Basic Books.

13 Salovey, P. & Mayer, J.D. (1990). Emotional intelligence. *Imagination, Cognition, and Personality*, 9, 185-211.

14 Damasio, A.R. (1994). *Descartes' error: Emotion, reason and the human brain.* New York: Grosset/Putnam.

15 LeDoux, J. (1996). *The emotional brain: The mysterious underpinnings of emotional life.* New York: Simon and Schuster.

16 Grinder, J. & Bandler, R. (1975). *The Structure of Magic Vol 1*; A Book about Language & Therapy. Science and Behavioural books Inc.

17 Wolff, S. (1997/2005). *ECI Technical Manual.* Hay Group. Center for Research and Innovation.

18 Bar-On, R. (1997). *The Emotional Quotient Inventory.* Toronto, Canada: Multi-Health Systems.

19 Maddocks, J. & Sparrow, T. (1998). *The Individual Effectiveness Questionnaire.* JCA Occupational Psychologists.

20 Murphy, K. & Dzieweczynski, J. (2005). Why don't measures of broad dimensions of personality perform better as predictors of job performance, *Human Performance*, 18, 343-357.

21 Costa, P.C. & McCrae, R.R. (1997). *Longitudinal study of adult personality.* In R. Hogan, J. Johnson & S. Briggs (Eds.), *Handbook of personality psychology*, 269-290. San Diego: Academic Press.

22 Sherman, S. & Freas, A. (2004). The Wild West of Executive Coaching. *Harvard Business Review*, Nov., 82 (11), 82-89.

23 O'Boyle, E., Humphrey, R., Pollack, J., Hawyer, T. & Story, P. (2011). The relations between emotional intelligence and job performance: A meta-analysis. *Journal of Organisation Behaviour*, 32, 788-818.

24 Joseph, D.L. & Newman, D.A. (2010). Emotional intelligence: An integrative meta-analysis and cascading model. *Journal of Applied Psychology*, 95, 54-78.

25 Lenaghan, J.A., Buda, R. & Eisner, A.B. (2007). An examination of the role of emotional intelligence

in work and family conflict. *Journal of Managerial Issues*, 19, 76-94.

26 Rode, J.C., Mooney, C.H., Arthaud-Day, M.L., Near, J.P., Baldwin, T.T., Rubin, R.S. & Bommer, W.H. (2007). Emotional intelligence and individual performance: evidence of direct and moderated effects. *Journal of Organizational Behavior*, 28, 399-421.

27 Anderson, N., Bertua, C. & Salgado, J. (2005). The predictive validity of cognitive ability test: A UK meta-analysis. *Journal of Occupational and Organizational Psychology*, 78 (3), 387-409.

28 Thompson, H. (2010). *The stress effect. Why smart leaders make dumb decisions.* San Francisco: Jossey-Bass.

29 Feist, G.J. & Barron, F. (1996). *Emotional intelligence and academic intelligence in career and life success.* Paper presented at the Annual Convention of the American Psychological Society. San Francisco.

30 Duckwoth, A.L. & Seligman, M.E.P. (2005). Self–discipline out does IQ in predicting academic performance of adolescents. *Psychological Science*, 16 (12), 939-44. (http://pss.sagepub.com/content/16/12/939.long).

31 Jenkins, D. & Maddocks, J. (2005). *Prison officers, emotional labour and the intelligent management of emotions.* SDR, BPS conference. In J. Maddocks, The EIP Technical manual. (2013).

32 Bar-On, R. (2000). Emotional and social intelligence: Insights from the Emotional Quotient Inventory (EQ-i). In R. Bar-On and J.D.A. Parker (Eds.), *Handbook of emotional intelligence.* San Francisco: Jossey-Bass.

33 Steiner, C. (1974). *Scripts People Live.* Grove Press, NY. Also see 2003 *Emotional Literacy; Intelligence With a Heart.* Fawnskin, California: Personhood Press.

34 Saarni, C. (1990). Emotional competence: How emotions and relationships become integrated. In R.A. Thompson (Ed.), *Socioemotional development. Nebraska symposium on motivation*, 36, 115-182. Lincoln, NE: University of Nebraska Press.

35 Averill, J.R. & Thomas-Knowles, C. (1991). Emotional creativity. In K.T. Strongman (Ed.), *International review of studies on emotion*, 1, 269-299). London: Wiley.

36 Thorndike, E.L. (1920). Intelligence and its use. *Harper's Magazine*, 140, 227-235.

37 Bandura, A. (1977). *Social Learning Theory.* New York: General Learning Press.

38 Gallwey, W.T. (1986). *The inner game of tennis.* London: Pan.

Chapter Two

1 MacLean, P.D. (1973). *A triune concept of brain and behaviour.* Toronto: University of Toronto Press.

2 LeDoux, J. (1996). *The emotional brain: The mysterious underpinnings of emotional life.* New York: Simon and Schuster.

3 Rose, K.D. (2006). *The Beginning of the Age of Mammals.* Baltimore: Johns Hopkins University Press.

4 Griffin, J. (1997). *The origin of dreams.* The Therapist Limited. East Sussex: Human Givens Publishing.

5 Dunbar, R. (1998). The social brain hypothesis. *Evolutionary Anthropology*, 6, 178-190.

6 Damasio, A.R., Tranel, D. & Damasio, H. (1991). Somatic markers and the guidance of behaviour: theory and preliminary testing. In H.S. Levin, H.M. Eisenberg & A.L. Benton (Eds.), *Frontal lobe function and dysfunction*, 217-229, New York: Oxford University Press.

7 Damasio, A. (1991). *Somatic Markers and the Guidance of Behavior.* New York: Oxford University Press.

8 Griffin, J. (1999). Autism: a sea change. *The New Therapist,* 6, 4, 10-16.

9 Amaral, D.G., Price, J. L., Pitkanen, A. & Carmichael, S.T. (1992). Anatomical organisation of the primate amygdaloid complex. In J.P. Aggleton, (Ed.) *The amygdala: Neurobiological aspects of emotion, memory, and mental dysfunction*, New York: Wiley-Liss.

10 Forgas, J. (1995). Mood and judgment: The affect infusion model (AIM). *Psychological Bulletin*, Jan., 117 (1), 39-66.

11 LeDoux, J. (1996). *The emotional brain: The mysterious underpinnings of emotional life.* New York: Simon and Schuster.

12 Libet, B. (1985). Unconscious cerebral initiative and the role of conscious will in voluntary action. *Behavioural and Brain Sciences*, 8, 529-566.

13 Damasio, A.R. (1994). *Descartes' error: Emotion, reason and the human brain.* New York: Grosset/Putnam.

14 Goleman, D. (1996). *Emotional intelligence: why it can matter more than IQ.* New York: Bantam Books.

15 Cunningham, W.A. & Brosch, T. (2012). Motivational salience: Amygdala tuning from traits, values and goals. *Current Directions in Psychological Science,* 21 (1), 54-59.

16 Caruso, D.R. & Salovey, P. (2004). *The emotionally intelligent manager.* San Francisco: Jossey-Bass.

17 Makino, S., Gold, P.W. & Schulkin, J. (1994). Corticosterone effects on corticosteropin-releasing hormone mRNA in the central nucleus of the amygdala and the parvocellular region of the paraventricular nucleus of the hypothalamus. *Brain Research*, 640, 105-12.

18 McEwen, B.S. (1992). Paradoxical effects of adrenal steroids on the brain: Protection verses degeneration. *Biological Psychiatry*, 31, 177-99.

19 O'Keefe, J. & Nadel, L. (1978). *The hippocampus as a cognitive map.* Oxford: Clarendon Press.

20 Ekman, P. (1992). Facial expressions of emotion: New findings, new questions. *Psychological Science*, 3, 34-38.

21 Griffin, J. & Tyrell, I. (2001). *The Human Givens*. East Sussex: Human Given Publishing.

22 Jouvet, M. (1965). Paradoxical sleep – a study of its nature and mechanisms. *Prog Brain Research*, 18, 20-57.

23 Booth-Kewley, S. & Friedman, H.S. (1987). Psychological predictors of heart disease: a quantitative review. *Psychol Bull.* May, 101 (3), 343-362.

24 McEwen, B. & Stellar, E. (1993). Stress and the individual: mechanisms leading to disease. *Arch Intern Med*, 153, 2093-101.

25 Plutchik, R. (1980). *Emotion, a psychoevolutionary synthesis.* New York: Harper & Row.

26 Lövheim, H.A. (2012). A new three-dimensional model for emotions and monoamine neurotransmitters. *Medical Hypotheses*, 78 (2), 341-348.

27 Tomkins, S. (1962). *Affect Imagery Consciousness: The Positive Affects*. New York: Springer.

28 Pert, C. (1997). *Molecules of emotion. The science behind mind-body medicine.* New York: Touchsone.

29 Armour, J.A. (2008). Potential clinical relevance of the 'little brain' on the mammalian heart. *Experimental Physiology*, 93 (2), 165-176.

30 Berne, M. & Levy, M. (1988). *Physiology. International Edition* (2nd edn.). Toronto: Mosby.

31 Childre, D. & Martin, H. (2000). *The HeartMath Solution*. San Francisco: Harper.

32 McCraty, R., Atkinson, M., Tomasion, D. & Tiller, W.A. (1998). The electricity of touch: Detection and measurement of cardiac energy exchange between people. In *An Overview of Research Conducted by the Institute of HeartMath*. (Online: www.heartmath.org).

Chapter Three

1   Maddocks, J. (1997). *The Maps Indicator, Users manual*. JCA Occupational Psychologists.

2   Lapierre, R. (1934). Attitudes vs. actions. *Social Forces*, 13, 230-237.

3   Festinger, L. (1962). *A theory of cognitive dissonance.* London: Tavistock Publications.

4   Eagly, A. & Chaiken, S. (1993). *The psychology of attitudes.* Fort Worth, TX: Harcourt Brace.

5 Huczynski, A. & Buchanan, D. (2001). *Organizational behaviour: An introductory text.* Harlow: Financial Times Prentice Hall.

6 Makin, P. & Cox, C. (2004). *Changing behaviour at work: A practical guide.* London: Routledge.

7 Damasio, A.R. (1994). *Descartes' error: Emotion, reason and the human brain.* New York: Grosset/Putnam.

8 LeDoux, J. (1996). *The emotional brain: The mysterious underpinnings of emotional life.* New York: Simon and Schuster.

9 Lane, R.D. & McRae, K. (2004). Neural substrates of conscious emotional experience: A cognitive-neuroscientific perspective. In M. Beauregard (Ed.). *Consciousness, emotional self-regulation and the brain*, 87-122. Amsterdam: Benjamins.

10 Schutz, W. (1958). *FIRO, a three-dimensional theory of interpersonal behaviour.* WSA, New York: Holt, Reinhart & Winston.

11 Berne, E. (1964). *Games people play.* New York: Grove Press.

12 Griffin, J. & Tyrell, I. (2001). *The Human Givens.* East Sussex: Human Given Publishing.

13 Maddocks, J. & Sparrow, T. (1998). *The Individual Effectiveness Questionnaire.* JCA Occupational Psychologists.

14 Perls, F. (1969). *Gestalt therapy verbatim.* Moab, UT: Real People Press.

15 Grinder, J. & Bandler, R. (1979). *Frogs into princes: Neuro linguistic programming.* Moab, UT: Real People Press.

16 Cattell, R.B. (1946). *The description and measurement of personality.* New York: World Book.

17 Kline, P. (2000). *Handbook of psychological Testing* (2nd edn.). London: Routledge.

18 Jung, C.G. (1921). *Psychological Types.* Princeton, New Jersey: Princeton University Press.

19 Maddocks, J. (2013). *The Emotional Intelligence Profile (EIP) technical manual.* JCA Occupational Psychologists.

Chapter Four

1 Ernst, F.H., Jr. (1971). The OK corral: The grid for get-on-with. *Transactional Analysis Journal*, 1 (4), 33-42.

Chapter Five

1 Maddocks, J. (2013). *The Emotional Intelligence Profile (EIP) technical manual.* JCA Occupational Psychologists.

Chapter Six

1 Burch, N. (1970). *Learning a New Skill is Easier Said than Done.* Gordon Training International, 198.

2 Maltz, M. (1960). *Psycho-Cybernetics: A New Way to Get More Living out of Life.* Englewood Cliffs, NJ: Prentice-Hall.

3 Lally, P., Jaarsveld, C., Potts, H. & Wardle, J. (2010) How are habits formed: Modelling habit formation in the real world. *European Journal of Social Psychology*, October, 40 (6) 998-1009.

4 Festinger, L. (1962). *A theory of cognitive dissonance.* London: Tavistock Publications.

5 Csikszentihalyi, M. (1990). *Flow: The psychology of optimal experience.* New York: Harper & Row.

6 Prochaska, J.O. & DiClemente, C.C. (1983). Stages and processes of self-change of smoking: Toward an integrative model of change. *J Consult Clin Psychol.* Jun, 51 (3), 390-5.

Chapter Seven

1 Rintzler, A. & Brown, D. (2002). *Fast Start Learning* delivered by Resource Associates Corporation. PA: Reading.

2 Pavlov, I.P, transl., ed. Anrep., G.V. (1927). *Conditioned reflexes: An investigation of the physiological activity of the cerebral cortex*. London: Oxford University Press.

3 Grinder, J. & Bandler, R. (1979). *Frogs into princes: Neurolinguistic programming*. Moab, UT: Real People Press.

4 Libet, B. (1985). Unconscious cerebral initiative and the role of conscious will in voluntary action. *Behavioural and Brain Sciences*, 8, 529-566.

5 Baumeister, R., Bratslavsky, E. & Finkenauer, C. (2001). Bad is stronger than good. *Review of General Psychology*, 5, (4).

6 Childre, D. & Martin, H. (2000). *The HeartMath Solution*. San Francisco: Harper.

7 Eisenberger, N. & Lieberman, M. (2009). *The pains and pleasures of social life*. Science, 323, (5916), 890-891.

8 Maslow, A.H. (1943). *A theory of human motivation*. *Psychological Review*, 50 (4), 370-396.

9 Rock, D. (2008). SCARF: A brain-based model for collaborating with and influencing others. *NeuroLeadership Journal*, Dec., 1 (1).

10 Langer, E. & Rodin, J. (1977). The effects of choice and enhanced personal responsibility for the aged: A field experiment in an institutional setting. *Journal of Personality and Social Psychology*, 191-198.

11 Festinger, L. (1962). *A theory of cognitive dissonance.* London: Tavistock Publications.

12 Greenberger, D. & Pandensky, C. (1995). *Mind over mood: Change how you feel by changing the way you think*. New York: Guildford Press.

13 Kahneman, D. & Tversky, A. (1979). Prospect theory: An analysis of decisions under risk. *Econometrica*. 47 (2), 263-29.

14 Maddocks, J. (2011). *A decade of emotional intelligence*. JCA Occupational Psychologists.

15 Cousins, N. (1976). Anatomy of an illness as perceived by the patient. *N Engl J Med*, 295 (26), 1458-63.

16 Grinder, J. & Bandler, R. (1979). *Frogs into princes: Neuro linguistic programming*. Moab, UT: Real People Press.

17 Griffin, J. (2005). 'PTSD: Why some techniques for treating it work so fast'. The *Human Givens Journal*. 12 (3).

18 Callahan, R. (2001). *Tapping the healer within*. Chicago: III Contemporary Books.

19 Shapiro, F. (2001). *EMDR: Eye Movement Desenstization of Reprocessing: Basic principles, protocols and procedures* (2nd edn.) New York: Guildford Press.

20 Ruden, R.A. (2011). *When the Past Is Always Present: Emotional Traumatization, Causes, and Cures*. New York: Routledge, Psychosocial Stress Series.

21 Thompson, H. (2010). *The stress effect. Why smart leaders make dumb decisions*. San Francisco: Jossey-Bass.

22 Griffin, J. (1997). *The origin of dreams*. The Therapist Limited. East Sussex: Human Givens.

23 Feinstein, J., Duff, M. & Tranel, D. (2010). Sustained experience of emotion after loss of memory in patients with amnesia. *Proceedings of the National Academy of Sciences of the United States of America*. April 27, 107 (17), 7674-7679.

24 Berlin, H.A. (2011). The Neural Basis of the Dynamic Unconscious. *Neuropsychoanalysis*, 13 (1).

25 Edelman, G. (1987). Neural Darwinism: *The theory of neuronal group selection*. New York: Basic Books.

26 Vohs, K.D., Baumeister, R.F., Schmeichel, B.J., Twenge, J.M., Nelson, N.M. & Tice, T.M. (2008). Making choices impairs subsequent self-control. *Journal of Personality and Social Psychology*, 94, 883-98.

27 Beehr, T. & Newman, J. (1978). Job stress, employee health and organisational effectiveness: A facet analysis, model and literature review. *Personnel Psychology*, 31 (4), 665-699.

28 Sparrow, T. & Knight, A. (2006). *Applied emotional intelligence: The importance of attitudes in developing emotional intelligence*. Chichester: Wiley.

29 Buckingham, M. (2003). *Building the strength-based organisation*. The Gallup Organisation (Online: www.gallup.com).

Chapter Eight

1 Gallup Inc. (2010). *Employee engagement. What's your engagement ratio?* Gallup Inc. Performance Optimisation.

2 Zenger, J. & Folkman, J. (2009). *The extraordinary leader: turning good managers into great leaders*. New York: McGraw-Hill.

3 Freedman, J. (2008). *Workplace issues report*. Six seconds.

4 Goleman, D. (1996). *Emotional intelligence: why it can matter more than IQ*. New York: Bantam Books.

5 Research by Forum Corporation on Manufacturing and Service Companies, (1989-1995), cited in; Orioli, E. (2000). *Leader know thyself: Measuring and developing leadership using the EQ Map*. Workshop presentation at Linkage Emotional Intelligence Conference, Chicago, IL.

6 Denning, S. (2004). *The seven highest values of organisation storytelling*. Braintrust Presentation.

7 Dulewicz, V., Dulewicz, C. & Young, M. (2005). The relevance of emotional intelligence for leadership performance. *Journal of General Management*. Braybrooke Press Ltd.

8 Hunter, J., Schmidt, F. & Judiesch, M. (1990). Individual Differences in Output Variability as a Function of Job Complexity. *Journal of Applied Psychology*, 75, 28-42.

9 Cavallo, K. (2002). *Emotional competence and leadership excellence at Johnson & Johnson: The emotional intelligence and leadership study,* CREIO.

10 Cooper, R. & Sawaf, A. (1996). *Executive E.Q. Emotional Intelligence in Leadership and Organisations*. New York: The Berkley Publishing Group.

11 Bradberry, T. (2002). *Emotional intelligence and leader job performance*. Unpublished manuscript.

12 Egon Zehnder study on failed executives. In D.Goleman (1998). *Working with emotional intelligence*. New York: Bantam Books.

13 Boyatzis, R. (1999). Self Directed Change and Learning as a Necessary Meta-Competency for Success and Effectiveness in the twenty-first century. In Sims, R. and Veres, J. (Eds.). *Keys to Employee Success in Coming Decades.* London: Quorum books.

14 Spencer, L., McClelland, D. & Kelner, S. (1997). *Competency assessment methods: History and state of the art*. Boston: Hay/McBer.

15 Seligman, M. (1990). *Learned optimism: how to change your mind and change your life*. New York: Knopf.

16 Hay/McBer Research and Innovation Group (1997). This research was provided to Daniel Goleman and is reported in his book (Goleman, 1998).

17 Cannon, K. (1999). Conference Proceedings, NexusEQ 2000.

18 McClelland, D. (1999). Identifying competencies with behavioral-event interviews. *Psychological Science*, 9 (5), 331-339.

19 McCraty, R., Atkinson, M. & Tomasino, D. (2003). Impact of a Workplace Stress Reduction Program on Blood Pressure and Emotional Health in Hypertensive Employees. *Journal of Alternative and Complementary Medicine*, 9 (3), 355-369.

20 O'Boyle, E., Humphrey, R., Pollack, J., Hawyer, T. & Story, P. (2011). The relations between emotional intelligence and job performance: A meta-analysis. *Journal of Organisation Behaviour*, 32, 788-818.

21 Handley, R. (1999). Conference Proceedings, NexusEQ 2003.

22 Pesuric, A. & Byham, W. (1996). The new look in behavior modeling. *Training and Development*, 25-33.

23 Maddocks, J. (2011). *A decade of emotional intelligence*. JCA Occupational Psychologists.

24 Sibson, R.E. (1976). *Increasing employee productivity*. New York: AMACOM, 12.

25 Goleman, D. (1996). *Emotional intelligence: why it can matter more than IQ*. New York: Bantam Books.

26 Goleman, D. (1998). *Working with emotional intelligence*. New York: Bantam Books.

27 Goleman, D. (2006). *Social Intelligence: The new science of human relationships*. New York: Random House.

28 Maddocks, J. (2013). *The Emotional Intelligence Profile (EIP) technical manual*. JCA Occupational Psychologists.

29 Goleman, D. (1998). What makes a leader? *Harvard Business review,* November–December, 95, 99.

30 Goleman, D. (2000). Leadership that gets results. *Harvard Business review*, March-April, 81, 79-90.

31 Bar-On, R. (1997). *The Emotional Quotient Inventory (EQ-i): A test of emotional intelligence*. Toronto, Canada: Multi-Health Systems, Inc.

32 Mayer, J.D., Salovey, P. & Caruso, D.R. (2002). *Mayer-Salovey-Caruso Emotional Intelligence Test (MSCEIT™)*. Toronto, Canada: Multi-Health Systems, Inc.

33 Petrie, N. (2011). *Future Trends in Leadership Development, White Paper*, Centre for Creative Leadership, www.ccl.org/leadership/pdf/research/futuretrends.pdf.

34 Boury, D. & Sinclair, A. (2012). *The Management Agenda 2012*, Horsham: Roffey Park Institute.

35 PriceWaterhouseCoopers (2009). *Twelfth annual global CEO survey*.

36 McKinsey & Company (2001). *The War for Talent*. The McKinsey Quarterly, 3 (37).

37 Bennis, W. (1999). *On Becoming a Leader*. New York: Basic Books.

38 Fidgeon, R. (2010). *Strategic Leadership*. PhD thesis, City University London.

39 Goleman, D., Boyatzis, R. & McKee, A. (2002). *The New Leaders. Transforming the art of leadership into the science of results*. London: Time Warner.

40 Higgs, M. & Dulewicz, V. (2002). *Making Sense of Emotional Intelligence* (2nd edn.), Windsor: NFER-Nelson.

41 Kurz, R. & Bartram, D. (2002). Competency and individual performance: Modelling the world of work. In I. Robertson, M. Callinan & D. Bartram (Eds.), *Organsational effectiveness: The role of psychology*. Chichester: Wiley.

42 Elfenbein, H.A., Polzer, J.T. & Ambady, N. (2007). Can teams have emotional skills? The case of recognizing others' emotions. In C.E.J. Härtel, N.M. Ashkanasy & W.J. Zerbe (Eds.), *Research on emotion in organizations: Functionality, Intentionality and Morality*. Oxford: Elsevier/JAI Press.

43 Ilarda, E. & Findlay, B. (2006). Emotional intelligence and propensity to be a team player. *E-Journal of Applied Psychology: Emotional Intelligence*, 2 (2), 19-29.

44 Maddocks, J. & Seex, S. (2013). Team EIP 2013 update. In J. Maddocks, (2013). *The Team Emotional Intelligence Profile (Team EIP) technical manual*. JCA Occupational Psychologists.

45 Prati, L., Douglas, C., Ferris, G., Ammeter, A. & Buckley, M. (2003). Emotional intelligence, leadership effectiveness, and team outcomes. *International Journal of Organizational Analysis*, 11 (1), 21-40.

46 Lewis, K.M. (2000). When leaders display emotion: How followers respond to negative emotional expression of male and female leaders. *Journal of Organisational behaviour*, 21, 221-234.

47 Druskat, V.U. & Wolff, S.B. (2001). Group emotional competence and its influence on group effectiveness. In C. Cherniss & D. Goleman (Eds.), *Emotional competence in organisations*: San Francisco: Jossey-Bass.

48 Lewin, K. (1951). *Field Theory in Social Science*. New York, NY: Harper.

49 Landy, C. (1983). *Understanding organisation*. London: Penguin.

50 Buckingham, M. (2003). *Building the strength-based organisation*. The Gallup Organisation (Online: www.gallup.com).

51 Wong, C. & Law, K. (2002). The effect of a leader and follower emotional intelligence on performance and attitude: An exploratory study. *Leadership Quarterly*, 13, 243-274.

52 Cartwright, S. & Pappas, C. (2008). Emotional intelligence, its measurement and implications for the workplace. *International Journal of Management Reviews*, 10, 149-171.

53 Parkyns, R. & Walden, R. (2004). *The human element at work. A fieldbook of projects transforming people and organisations around the globe*. San Francisco: BCon WSA International.

54 Foo, M.D., Elfenbein, H., Tan, H. & Aik, V. (2004). Emotional intelligence and negotiation: The tension between creating and claiming value. *International Journal of Conflict Management*, 15 (4), 411-429.

55 Bachman, W. (1988). *Nice Guys finish first*. New York: Praeger.

56 George, J.M. & Bettenhausen, K. (1990). Understanding psychosocial behaviour. *Journal of Applied Psychology*, 75, 698-709.

57 Maddocks, J. (2009). Creating an emotionally intelligent organisation. *The Coaching Psychologist*, 5, (1).

58 Schutz, W. (1994, 2005, 2008). *The human element, productivity, self-esteem and the bottom line*. Business Consultants, Inc. The Schutz Company, San Francisco: Jossey-Bass.

59 Buckingham, M. (2003). *Building the Strength-Based Organisation*. The Gallup Organisation. (Online: www.gallup.com).

60 Kelner, S. Rivers, C. & O'Connell, K. (1994*). Managerial style as a behavioural predictor or organisational climate*. Boston: McBer.

61 Kozlowski, S.W. & Doherty, M.L. (1989). Integration of climate and leadership: Examination of a neglected issue. *Journal of Applied Psychology*, 74, 546-553.

62 Litwin, G. & Stringer, R.A.J. (1968). *Motivation and organisational climate*. Boston: Harvard University, Graduate School of Business Administration, Division of Research.

63 Schwartz, T. (2010). *The way we're working isn't working*. New York: Free Press.

64 William, D. (1994). *Leadership for the 21st century*. Boston, MA: Hay Group.

Appendix One

1 Stewart, I. & Joines, V. (1987). *TA today: A new introduction to transactional analysis*. Nottingham: Lifespace Publishing.

2 Rogers, C.R. (1959). *A theory of therapy, personality and interpersonal relationships, as developed in the client-centered framework*. In S. Koch (Ed.), Psychology: A study of science, New York, NY: McGraw Hill.

3 Gallwey, W.T. (1986). *The inner game of tennis*. London: Pan.

4 Lane, R.D. & Schwartz, G.E. (1987). Levels of emotional awareness: A cognitive developmental theory and its application to psychopathology. *American Journal of Psychiatry*, 144, 133-143.

5 Ekman, P. (1973). *Darwin and facial expression: A century of research in review*. New York: Academic Press.

6 Iacoboni, M., Woods, R.P., Brass, M., Bekkering, H., Mazziotta, J.C. & Rizzolatti, G. (1990). Cortical mechanisms of human imitation. *Science* 286 (5449), 2526-2528.

7 Saddiq, S. (2006). *Librarians 'suffer most stress'* (2006 January 12), http://news.bbc.co.uk/1/hi/4605476.stm.

8 Frankl, V. (1959). *Man's search for meaning*: the classic tribute to hope from the holocaust. London: Random House/Rider.

9 Mischel, W., Shoda, Y. & Rodriguez, M.L. (1992). *Delay of gratification in children*. In G. Lowenstein & J. Elster (Eds.), Choice over time, New York, NY, US: Russell Sage Foundation.

10 Aristotle, transl. Chase, D.P. (2008). *Nicomachean Ethics*. Book 2, Chapter 6.

11 Hochschild, A.R. (1979). Emotion Work, Feeling Rules, and Social Structure. *American Journal of Sociology*, 85, 551-575.

12 Naisberg-Fennig, S., Fennig, S., Kienan, G. & Elizur, A. (1991). Personality characteristics and proneness to burnout: A study among psychiatrists. *Stress Medicine*, 7 (4), 201-205.

13 Kosfeld, M., Heinrichs, M., Zak, P.J., Fischbacher, U. & Fehr, E. (2005). Oxytocin increases trust in humans. *Nature*, 453, 673-76.

14 Gallup Inc. (2010). *Employee engagement. What's your engagement ratio?* Gallup Inc., Performance Optimisation.

Appendix 2

1 Hippocrates (ca. 460 BC–ca. 370 BC), in *Hippocratic Corpus, On The Sacred Disease*. Also see, Noga, A. (2007). *Passions and Tempers: A History of the Humours*. New York: HarperCollins.

2 Aristotle, transl. Chase, D.P. (2008). *Nicomachean Ethics*. Book 2, Chapter 6.

3 Descartes, R. (1637). *Discours de la méthode* (*Discourse on the Method*). An introduction to the *Essais*, which include the *Dioptrique*, the *Météores* and the *Géométrie*. Translated by John Veitch (1924).

4 James, W. (1884). What is an emotion? *Mind*, 9, 188-205.

5 Herman, E. (1992). Being and doing: Humanistic psychology and the spirit of the 1960s. In B.L. Tischler (Ed.), *Sights on the sixties*, 87-101. New Brunswick, NJ: Rutgers University Press.

6 Darwin, C. (1872/1965). *The expression of the emotions in man and animals*. Chicago: University of Chicago Press.

7 Ekman, P. (1977). Biological and cultural contributions to body and facial movement. In J. Blacking (Ed.). *The anthropology of the body*. London: Academic Press.

8 Plutchik, R. (1980). *Emotion, a psychoevolutionary synthesis*. New York: Harper & Row.

9 Nesse, R. (1990). Evolutionary explanations of emotions. In *Human Nature*, 1, 261-289.

10 Watt, D.F. (2004). Consciousness, Emotional Self-Regulation and the Brain Review Article. *Journal of Consciousness Studies*, 11 (9), 77-82.

11 MacLean, P. (1950). Psychosomatic disease and the 'visceral brain', recent developments bearing on the Papez theory of emotion. In *Psychosomatic Medicine*, 11, 338-353. Also in MacLean, P.D. (1973). *A triune concept of brain and behaviour*. Toronto: University of Toronto Press.

12 Schioldann, J. (2011). "On periodical depressions and their pathogenesis" by Carl Lange (1886). *History of psychiatry*, 22, 85, Pt. 1, 108–130. Also in Amdisen, A. (1985). "Carl Lange på fransk visit i psykiatrien [C. Lange's flying visit to psychiatry]". *Dansk Medicinhistorisk Aarbog*, 14, 9-40.

13 Cannon, W.B. (1927). The James-Lange theory of emotion: A critical examination and an alternative theory. *American Journal of Psychology*, 39, 10-124.

14 Bard, P. (1928). A diencephalic mechanism for the expression of rage with special reference to the sympathetic nervous system. *American Journal of Physiology*, 84, 490-516.

15 Green, E. & Green, A. (1977). *Beyond biofeedback*. San Francisco: Delacorte Press.

16 Pert. C. (1997). *Molecules of emotion. The science behind mind-body medicine*. New York: Touchstone.

17 Damasio, A.R. (1994). *Descartes' error: Emotion, reason, and the human brain*. New York: Grosset/Putnam.

18 Bechara, A., Damasio, A.R., Damasio, H. & Anderson, S.W. (1994). Insensitivity to future consequences following damage to human prefrontal cortex. *Cognition*, 50, 7-12.

19 Zeelenberg, M., Nelissen, R.M.A., Seger, M., Breugelmans, S. M. & Pieters, R. (2008). On emotion specificity in decision making: why feeling is for doing. *Judgment and Decision Making*, 3 (1), 18-27.

20 Tuan Pham, M., Lee, L. & Stephen, A.T. (2012). Feeling the Future: The Emotional Oracle Effect. *Journal of Consumer Research*, 39 (3), 461-477.

21 Ramachandran, V. S. & Blakeslee, S. (1998). *Phantoms in the Brain*. London: Fourth Estate.

22 Libet, B. (1985). Unconscious cerebral initiative and the role of conscious will in voluntary action. *Behavioural and Brain Sciences*, 8, 529-566.

23 LeDoux, J. (1996). *The emotional brain: The mysterious underpinnings of emotional life*. New York: Simon & Schuster.

24 Schachter, S. & Singer, J. (1962). Cognitive, Social, and Physiological Determinants of Emotional State. *Psychological Review*, 69, 379-399.

25 Tomkins, S. (1962), *Affect Imagery Consciousness: The Positive Affects*. New York: Springer.

26 Solomon, R.C. (1977). The logic of emotion. *Noûs*, 11, 41-49.

27 Mandler, G. (1984). *Mind and Body: Psychology of emotion and stress*. New York: Norton.

28 Roseman, I. J. (1984). Cognitive determinants of emotions: A structural theory. In P. Shaver (Ed.), *Review of Personality and Social Psychology: Vol. 5. Emotions, relationships, and health*, Beverly Hills, CA: Sage.

29 Lazarus, R.S. (1991). *Emotion and adaptation*. New York: Oxford University Press.

30 Goldie, P. (2004). Emotion, feeling, and knowledge of the world. In R.C. Solomon (Ed.), *Thinking About Feeling: Contemporary Philosophers on Emotions*. Oxford: Oxford University Press.

31 Averill, J.R. (1980). A constructivist view of emotion. In R. Plutchik & H. Kellerman (Eds.), *Emotion: Theory, research, and experience*, New York: Academic Press.

32 Parkinson, B. (1996). Emotions are social. *British Journal of Psychology*, 87, 663–683.

33 Harlow, J.M. (1868). Recovery from the Passage of an Iron Bar through the Head. *Massachusetts Med Society*, 2, 327-347.

34 Gardner, H. (1983). *Frames of mind. The Theories of Multiple Intelligences*. New York: Basic Books.

35 Saarni, C. (1990). Emotional competence: How emotions and relationships become integrated. In R.A. Thompson (Ed.), *Socioemotional development. Nebraska symposium on motivation*, 36, 115-182. Lincoln, NE: University of Nebraska Press.

36 Bar-On, R. (2000). Emotional and social intelligence: Insights from the Emotional Quotient Inventory (EQ-i). In R. Bar-On and J.D.A. Parker (Eds.), *Handbook of emotional intelligence*. San Francisco: Jossey-Bass.

37 Thorndike, E.L. (1920). Intelligence and its uses. *Harper's Magazine*, 140, 227-235.

38 Hunt, T. (1928). The measurement of social intelligence. *Journal of Applied Psychology*, 12, 317-334.

39 Wedeck, J. (1947). The relationship between personality and psychological ability. *British Journal of Psychology*, 36, 133-151.

40 Doll, E.A. (1935). A generic scale of social maturity. *American Journal of Orthopsychiatry*, 5, 180-188.

41 Kelly, G.A. (1955). *A theory of personality: The psychology of personal constructs*. New York: Norton.

42 Atikinson, J.W. (1981). Studying personality in the context of an advanced motivational psychology. *American Psychologist*, 32, 117-129.

43 McClelland, D.C. & Koestner, R. (1992). The achievement motive. In C.P. Smith, J.W. Atkinson, D.C. McClelland & J. Veroff (Eds.), *Motivation and personality: Handbook of thematic content analysis*. New York: Cambridge University Press.

44 Murray, H.A. (1938). *Explorations in personality*. New York: Oxford Press.

45 Lewin, K. (1951). *Field Theory in Social Science*. New York: Harper.

46 Schutz, W. (1958). *FIRO, a three-dimensional theory of interpersonal behaviour*. WSA, New York: Holt, Reinhart & Winston.

47 Combs, M.L. & Slaby, D.A. (1977). Social-skills training with children. In B.B. Lahey & A.E. Kazdin (Eds.), *Advances in Clinical Child Psychology*, 1, 161-201. New York: Plenum.

48 Bandura, A. (1977). *Social Learning Theory*. Englewood Cliffs, NJ: Prentice-Hall.

49 Topping, K. (2000). The Effectiveness of school based programs for the promotion of Social Competence. In R. Bar-On and J.D.A. Parker (Eds.), *The Handbook of Emotional Intelligence*. San Francisco: Jossey-Bass.

50 Sternberg, R.J. (1985). *Beyond IQ: A triarchic theory of human intelligence*. New York: Cambridge University Press.

51 Hedlund, J. & Sternberg, R.J. (2000). Too Many Intelligences. In R. Bar-On and J.D.A. Parker (Eds.), *Handbook of emotional intelligence*. San Francisco: Jossey-Bass.

52 Sifneos, P.E. (1973). The prevalence of alexithymic characteristics in psychosomatic patients. *Psychotherapy and Psychosomatics*, 22, 255-262.

53 Ruesch, J. (1948). The infantile personality. *Psychosomatic medicine*, 10, 134-144.

54 MacLean, P.D. (1949). Psychosomatic disease and the "visceral brain": Recent developments bearing on the Papez theory of emotion. *Psychosomatic Medicine*, 11, 338-353.

55 Schore, A.N. (1994). *Affect regulation and the origin of the self: The neurobiology of emotional development*. Hillsdale, NJ: Erlbaum.

56 Booth-Butterfield, M. & Booth-Butterfield, S. (1994). The affective orientation to communication: Conceptual and empirical distinctions. *Communications Quarterly*, 42, 331-344.

57 Appelbaum, S.A. (1973). Psychological mindedness: Word, concept, and essence. *International Journal of Psycho-Analysis*, 54, 35-46.

58 Lane, R.D. & Schwartz, G.E. (1987). Levels of emotional awareness: A cognitive-developmental theory and its application to psychopathology. *American Journal of Psychiatry*, 144, 133-143.

59 Conte, H.R. & Ratto, R. (1997). Self-report measures of psychological mindedness. In M. McCallum & W.E. Piper (Eds.), *Psychological mindedness: A contemporary understanding*, Mahwah, NJ: Erlbaum.

60 Piaget, J. (1950). *The psychology of intelligence.* London: Routledge & Kegan Paul.

61 Farber, B.A. (1989). Psychological-mindedness: Can there be too much of a good thing? *Psychotherapy*, 26, 210-217.

62 Fenigstein, A. (1984). Self-consciousness and the over perception of self as a target. *Journal of Personality and Social Psychology*, 47, 860-870.

63 Piper, W.E., Joyce, A.S., McCallum, M. & Azim, H.F.A. (1998). Interpretive and supportive forms of psychotherapy and patient personality variables. *Journal of Consulting and Clinical Psychology*, 66, 558-567.

64 Averill, J.R. & Nunley, E.P. (1992). *Voyages of the heart. Living an emotionally creative life*. New York: The Free Press.

65 Steiner. C. (1974). *Scripts People Live*. New York: Grove Press. Also in Steiner. C., (2003). *Emotional Literacy; intelligence with a heart*. Fawnskin, CA: Personhood Press.

66 Steiner, C. & Perry, P. (1997). *Achieving Emotional Literacy*. London: Bloomsbury.

67 Mayo, E., (1949). *Hawthorne and the Western Electric Company. The Social Problems of an Industrial Civilisation.* Abingdon: Routledge.

68 Leuner, B. (1966). Emotional intelligence and emancipation: A psychodynamic study of women. *Prax Kinderpsychol Kinderpsychiatr*. Aug-Sep, 15 (6), 196-203.

69 Payne, W.L. (1983/1986). A study of emotion: developing emotional intelligence; self integration; relating to fear, pain and desire. *Dissertation Abstracts International*, 47, 203A, (University microfilms No. AAC 8605928).

70 Salovey, P. & Mayer, J.D. (1990). Emotional intelligence. *Imagination, Cognition, and Personality*, 9, 185-211.

71 Goleman, D. (1995). *Emotional intelligence; why it can matter more than IQ*. New York: Bantam Books.

72 Herrnstein, R.J. & Murray, C. (1994). *The bell curve: Intelligence and class in American life*. New York: The Free Press.

73 Gibbs, N. (1995). Cover story. New brain research suggests that emotions, not IQ, may be the true measure of human intelligence. *Time Magazine*, 146 (14).

74 Spielberger, C. (Ed.) (2004). *Encyclopedia of Applied Psychology*. Boston: Elsevier Academic Press.

75 Bar-On, R. (1997). *The Emotional Quotient Inventory (EQ-i): A test of emotional intelligence*. Toronto, Canada: Multi-Health Systems, Inc.

76 Goleman, D. (1998). *Working with emotional intelligence*. New York: Bantam Books.

77 Petrides, K.V., & Furnham, A. (2000). On the dimensional structure of emotional intelligence. *Personality and Individual Differences*, 29, 313-320.

78 Maddocks, J. (2013). *The Emotional Intelligence Profile (EIP) technical manual*. JCA Occupational Psychologists.

79 Binet, A. (1905), transl. Paul, K. (1907). *L'Annee Psychologique*, 12,191-244. Trench, Trubner & Co Ltd., London.

80 Wechsler, D. (1939). *The Measurement of Adult Intelligence*. Baltimore, MD: Williams & Witkins.

81 Wechsler, D. (1943). Nonintellective factors in general intelligence. *Journal of Abnormal Social Psychology*, 38, 100-104.

82 Wechsler, D. (1958). *The measurement and appraisal of adult intelligence* (4th edn.). Baltimore, MD: Williams & Wilkins.

83 Zirkel, S. (2000). Social intelligence: The development and maintenance of purposive behavior. In R. Bar-On and J.D.A. Parker (Eds.), *Handbook of emotional intelligence*. San Francisco: Jossey-Bass.

84 Mayer, J.D., Salovey, P. & Caruso, D.R. (1997, 2002). *Mayer-Salovey-Caruso Emotional Intelligence Test (MSCEIT™)*. Toronto, Canada: Multi-Health Systems, Inc.

85 Bar-On, R. (1985). *The development of an operational concept of psychological well-being*. Unpublished doctoral dissertation (first draft), Rhodes University, South Africa.

86 Boyatzis, R.E., Goleman, D. & Hay/McBer. (1999). *Emotional competence inventory*. Boston: HayGroup.

87 Boyatzis, R.E. (2007). *The Creation of the Emotional and Social Competency Inventory (ESCI)*. Boston: HayGroup.

88 Boyatzis, R.E. (1994). Stimulating self-directed change: A required MBA course called Managerial Assessment and Development. *Journal of Management Education*, 18, 304-323.

89 Burruss, J.A. & Boyatzis, R.E. (1981). *Continued validation of a competency model of alcoholism counselors in the Navy* (Report to the U. S. Navy on contract number N002-44-80-C0521). Boston: McBer and Company.

90 McClelland, D.C. (1985). *Human motivation*. Glenview, IL: Scott, Foresman & Co.

91 Eysenck, H. (2000). *Intelligence: A New Look*. New Brunswick, NJ: Transaction Publishers.

92 Locke, E.A. (2005). Why emotional intelligence is an invalid concept. *Journal of Organizational Behavior*, 26 (4), 425-431.

93 Landy, F.J. (2005). Some historical and scientific issues related to research on emotional intelligence. Journal of Organizational Behavior, 26, 411-424.

94 Zeidner, M., Matthews, G. & Roberts, R.D. (2001). Slow down, you move too fast: Emotional intelligence remains an 'elusive' intelligence. *Emotion*, 1 (3), 265-275.

95 Matthews, G., Roberts, R.D. & Zeidner, M. (2003). Development of emotional intelligence: A skeptical – but not dismissive – perspective. *Human Development*, 46, 109-114.

96 Mayer, J. & Salovey, P. (1995). Emotional intelligence and the construction and regulation of feelings. *Applied and Preventive Psychology*, 4 (3) 197-208.

97 Gough, H.D. (1986). *The California Psychological Inventory*. Palo Alto, CA: Consulting Psychologists Press.

98 Kobasa, S.C. (1979). Stressful life events, personality and health: An inquiry into hardiness. *Journal of Personality and Social Psychology*, 37, 1-11.

99 Epstein, S. (1998). *Constructive thinking: The key to emotional intelligence*. Westport, CT: Praeger.

100 Block, J.H. & Block, J. (1980). The role of ego-control and ego-resiliency in the organization of behavior. In W. A. Collins (Ed.), *Development of cognition, affect, and social relations: The Minnesota symposia on child psychology*, 13. Hillsdale, NJ: Erlbaum.

101 Goldstein, K. (1934). *The organism: a holistic approach to biology derived from pathological data in man*. New York: Zone Books.

102 Schutte, N.W., Malouff, J.M., Hall, L.E., Haggerty, D.J., Cooper, J.T., Golden, C.J. &

Dornheim, L. (1998). Development and validation of a measure of emotional intelligence. *Personality and Individual Differences*, 25, 167-177.

103 McCrae, R.R. & Costa, Jr., P.T. (1991). Adding *Liebe und Arbeit*: The full five-factor model and well-being. *Personality and Social Psychology Bulletin*, 17, 227-232.

104 Salovey, P., Mayer, J.D., Goldman, S.L., Turvey, C. & Palfai, T.P. (1995). Emotional attention, clarity, and repair: Exploring emotional intelligence using the Trait Meta-Mood Scale. In J. W. Pennebaker (Ed.), *Emotion, disclosure, and health*, Washington, DC: American Psychological Association.

105 Trull, T.J. & Sher, K.J. (1994). Relationship between the five-factor model of personality and Axis I disorders in a nonclinical sample. *Journal of Abnormal Psychology*, 103, 350-360.

106 Schroeder, M.L., Wormsworth, J.A. & Livesley, W.J. (1992). Dimensions of personality disorder and their relationships to the big five dimensions of personality. *Psychological Assessment*, 4, 47-53.

107 Mayer, J.D., Salovey, P. & Caruso, D.R. (2000). Emotional intelligence. In R.J. Sternberg (Ed.), *Handbook of intelligence* (2nd edn.), 396-420. New York: Cambridge University Press.

108 Davis, M. & Kraus, L. (1997). Personality and accurate empathy. In W. Ickes (Ed.), *Empathic accuracy*. New York: Guilford Press.

109 Paulhus, D. (1998). Self-Report Measures of Intelligence: Are They Useful as Proxy IQ Tests? *Journal of Personality*, 66 (4), 525-554.

110 Mayer, J.D. & Gaschke, Y.N. (1988). The experience and meta-experience of mood. *Journal of Personality and Social Psychology*, 55, 102-111.

111 Morgeson, F.P. Campion, M. *et al.* (2007). Reconsidering the use of personality tests in personnel selection contexts. *Personnel Psychology*, 60 (3), 683-729.

112 De Kesel, M. (2010). The rational(e) of an emotional society: a Cartesian reflection. *Annual Review of Critical Psychology*, 8, 123-132.

113 Walker, R. (2012). *The Human Brain Project. A report to the European commission.* Lausanne: The HBP-PS Consortium.

114 Markoff, J. & Gorman, J. (2013). Obama to unveil initiative to map the human brain. *New York Times*, http://www.nytimes.com/2013/04/02/science/obama-to-unveil-initiative-to-map-the-human-brain.html.

115 Button, K. (2011). Power failure: why small sample size undermines the reliability of neuroscience. *Nature Reviews Neuroscience*, 14, 365-37.

116 Lancaster, M.A. *et al.* (2013). Cerebral organoids model human brain development and microcephaly. *Nature*, 501, 373-379.

117 Evans, D. (2012). *The Internet of Everything. How More Relevant and Valuable Connections Will Change the World.* Points of view. Cisco IBSG. San Jose, CA: Cisco IBSG.

Appendix Three

1   Jung, C.G. (1921). *Psychological Types*. Princeton, New Jersey: Princeton University Press.

2   Myers, I.B. (1962). *Manual: The Myers-Briggs Type Indicator*. Princeton, NJ: Educational Testing Service. (Distributed by Consulting Psychologists Press. Palo Alto, CA.).

Appendix Four

1   Schutz, W. (1958). *FIRO, a three-dimensional theory of interpersonal behaviour*. WSA, New York: Holt, Reinhart & Winston.

2   Schutz, W. (1994, 2005, 2008). *The human element, productivity, self-esteem and the bottom line.* Business Consultants, Inc., The Schutz Company. San Francisco: Jossey-Bass.

3   Maddocks, J. (2008). *FIRO theory; 50 years of Emotional Intelligence.* Published internally by Business Consultants, Inc.

Index